7/30/91

BOWIE

D0840470

The Research
Library Med

The Research of School Library Media Centers

Papers of the Treasure Mountain Research Retreat, Park City, Utah, October 17-18, 1989

Edited by Blanche Woolls

1990

Hi Willow Research and Publishing
Castle Rock, Colorado

Hi Willow Research and Publishing
P.O. Box 266
Castle Rock, CO 80104

Library of Congress Cataloging-in-Publication Data

The Research of school library media centers : papers of the Treasure
    Mountain research retreat, Park City, Utah, October 17-18, 1989 /
    edited by Blanche Woolls.
        p.   cm.
    Includes bibliographical references.
    ISBN 0-931510-30-9 : $35.00
    1. School libraries--Congresses. 2. Media programs (Education)-
-Congresses.   I. Woolls, Blanche.
Z675.S3R46 1990   90-5075
027.8'223--dc20   CIP

Contents

Introduction ix

Part 1: School Library Media Center and the Curriculum

The Consulting Role of the School Library
Media Specialist
  Philip M. Turner and Stephen W. Zsiray, Jr. 1

The Library Media Program and the Social Studies,
Mathematics, and Science Curricula
  Melvin M. Bowie 21

Reading Research and School Library Media Programs
  David V. Loertscher 49

Enriching the Standard Curriculum
  Patsy H. Perritt and Kathleen M. Heim 65

Part 2: Information Skills

Information Literacy
  *American Library Association Presidential
  Committee on Information Literacy* 83

Current Themes Regarding Library and Information
Skills Instruction
  Michael B. Eisenberg and Michael K. Brown 99

Information Search Process: A Summary of Research
and Implications for School Library Media Programs
  Carol C. Kuhlthau 111

Critical Thinking: Implications for Library Research
  Kathleen W. Craver 121

Part 3: Intellectual Freedom

Intellectual Freedom Relating to School
Library Media Centers
  Dianne McAfee Hopkins 135

Intellectual Freedom and Censorship Research:
School Library Media Resources
  Frances Beck McDonald 151

Part 4: Technology and the School Library Media Center

Access to Information: The Effect of Automation
    Catherine Murphy 163

Networking: Studies of Multitype Library Networking
with Implications for School Library Media Practice
    Barbara Froling Immroth 175

Educational Computing Research: Status and Prospectus
    Gary Marchionini 189

Part 5: Miscellaneous Topics

State, Regional and District-Level Media Programs
    Carole J. McCollough 203

Research Related to the Education of School
Library Media Specialists
    Daniel Barron 215

Collection Development in School Library Media Centers
    Daniel Callison 231

Facilities
    Blanche Woolls 259

PREFACE

What does the research say about how information skills should be taught? What are the best tactics for involving the library in the reading program? What implications does research draw for providing information access via automation? All these questions and many more are addressed in this collection of papers, which summarize the research about school libraries.

The current collection constitutes the most comprehensive review of research ever done in the school library field at any one time. Each paper reviews the research and then draws implications for practice and implications for research. Thus, the book is of interest to building and district level library media specialists and to anyone interested in reading research summaries or doing research in this field.

As the book was being prepared, the American Library Association Presidential Committee on Information Literacy issued its impressive final report. Because of its importance and relevance to the section on information skills, it is reprinted here.

The Treasure Mountain Research Retreat was the occasion for which all of these papers were created. Because the event was extremely successful in bringing researchers and practitioners together, additional retreats have been planned. The royalties from the sales of this volume will help fund such efforts.

Blanche Woolls, editor
David V. Loertscher, publisher

INTRODUCTION:
THE TREASURE MOUNTAIN RESEARCH RETREAT

At 12:00 noon on October 17, 1989, fifty people gathered together in Park City, Utah to begin an intensive discussion about research needs for the school library media profession. Twenty-four hours later, they emerged exhausted, but largely satisfied. What had come to be called the Treasure Mountain Research Retreat might not have provided the answers, but it had certainly helped clarify many questions.

This volume contains most of the reviews of the literature upon which the retreat's discussions were based. As a preliminary to these reviews, this introduction presents a brief background of the conference, a description of the procedures used in organizing the conference, and a look at a possible follow-up to these efforts.

Background of the Retreat

The Research Committee of the American Association of School Librarians has held a research forum during the summer conference each year for many years. These have been well attended and have received very positive evaluations. While the research forums have provided an outlet for the dissemination of research results and a platform for discussion of topics critical to the field, their length and format have hindered in-depth discussion. Three years ago, the Research Committee began considering an opportunity for an extended discussion of research needs for school library media professionals.

The process of creating Information Power served as a catalyst for the planning of a research retreat. A primary goal of the writing committee for this document was to establish a research base for as many of the recommendations as possible. However, it quickly became apparent that a research-based guideline was not possible because the research base lacked sufficient depth and breadth. In addition, there was a growing perception that research productivity was decreasing, and the probability that future guidelines would be significantly research-based was also decreasing. This concern was discussed in a column by the editors in the Spring 1989 issue of School Library Media Quarterly.[1]

To optimize productivity during the retreat, it was decided to provide the participants with a review of the literature on a wide range of research topics in the field. In an attempt to focus research on the creation of subsequent guidelines, Information Power was used as a basis for the generation of topics for the reviews. Forty persons, including practitioners as well as educators, were asked to respond to the following: "Which research questions should be answered by the time the next guidelines are written?"

From these responses, seventeen research questions emerged. Research reviews were invited on each of these seventeen topics. In selecting the reviewers, a research record in the topic was an important consideration, as well as a willingness to lead discussions at the retreat. Each reviewer was requested to do the following:

1. Analyze and synthesize the major research studies dealing with the topic.
2. Describe the implications of these studies for practitioners.
3. Identify research needs in the topic area for the next decade.
4. Discuss the best approaches to use in designing and carrying out this research.
5. Describe the infrastructure which must be present.

Organization and Implementation of the Retreat

The retreat was organized by three individuals. Phil Turner accepted the responsibility for organizing the entire conference. Blanche Woolls volunteered to collect and edit the papers, both for the retreat and for publication. David Loertscher set up local arrangements for the conference and agreed to publish the papers commercially.

Notices describing the retreat were sent to over 200 school library media preparation programs. In addition, information about the retreat appeared in various school library media publications. A track record of research was not a requirement for participation. Rather, prospective participants were told that they should have a goal of carrying out research in the field in the immediate future.

Thirty to fifty was established as the appropriate number of participants to attend in order to achieve a sufficiently large group for discussions while retaining the intimacy which can be achieved at retreats. Fifty participants actually attended, and they self-selected into four groups. Each group discussed four of the topics, concentrating on tasks 3 and 4 from the list.

During the final two hours of the retreat, individual groups reported the summary of their discussions to the entire group. In this way everyone shared, at least briefly, in the discussions of all of the topics.

The Next Step

It should be emphasized that this research retreat did not have as its purpose the establishment of the research agenda for the field. The main purpose was to provide an opportunity for an extended discussion, based on a review of the literature, of a number of research topics. Beyond this important benefit of personal growth of the participants, what was achieved, and what needs to be done?

The participants provided a great deal of feedback to those who had written the reviews, and this feedback was used in the revision of the reviews. This document is largely a compilation of these revised papers.

A recurring theme throughout the retreat was a call for networking and cooperation between researchers. This cooperation is even more vital since much of the research must be carried out on a small scale and, therefore, must be replicated in several locations. A small start was made toward this cooperation at the conclusion of the retreat when a network of participants was established to continue discussions and, perhaps, pursue research. One benefit in publishing these papers may be to expand this networking. Readers should contact the authors of the papers to inquire into cooperative activity.

Representatives from the United States Department of Education, the American Library Association, and the Association for Educational Communications and Technology attended the retreat. The stage is set to pursue and obtain funding for research projects that might emerge out of the retreat. At the least, the interest and expertise shown at the retreat should demonstrate to those outside the field that school library media research is a legitimate pursuit.

Phil Turner, Conference Chair

List of Participants

Roger Ashley	Leslie Edmonds	Paula Montgomery
Joan Atkinson	Michael Eisenberg	Betty J. Morris
Daniel Barron	Carolyn Folke	Catherine Murphy
Donna Baumbach	Kathleen Heim	Kenneth Pengelly
Melvin Bowie	Dianne Hopkins	Patsy Perritt
Pauletta Bracy	Barbara Immroth	Judy Pitts
Brenda Broadbent	Diane Kester	Pam Pritchett
Carolyn Brodie	Carol Kroll	Cecile Saretsky
Michael Brown	Carol Kuhlthau	Nathan Smith
Janis Bruwelheide	Elaine Leggett	Barbara Stein
Daniel Callison	David V. Loertscher	Barbara Stripling
C. Herbert Carson	Joy Lowe	Roger Tipling
Yvonne Carter	Mary Jo Lynch	Philip Turner
Kathleen Craver	Mike Marchant	Maureen White
Ruth Curtis	Gary Marchionini	Savan Wilson
Mary Dalbotten	Carole McCollough	Blanche Woolls
Jean Donham van	Fran McDonald	Tom Zane
Deusen	Adrian Mondfrans	Steve Zsiray

Notes

1. J. Pitts and B. Stripling, "Editors' Forum," School Library Media Quarterly 17 (Spring 1989), 117.

Part 1

School Library Media Center and the Curriculum

THE CONSULTING ROLE OF THE SCHOOL LIBRARY MEDIA SPECIALIST

Philip M. Turner
Dean, Graduate School of Library Service
The University of Alabama, Tuscaloosa

and

Stephen W. Zsiray, Jr.
Assistant Superintendent/Director of Middle Schools
Cache County School District
North Logan, Utah

Introduction

National guidelines have called for the merger of the school library media program with the curriculum through a systematic institution of a consultative role by the library media specialist. The consulting role must first be defined, both from an exclusive and an inclusive viewpoint. First, the consulting role, as used in this paper, does not include activities involving the direct instruction of students by the school library media specialist. Instructional consultation is a helping role in which the school library media specialist helps the teacher be more effective and efficient in the teaching process. A useful method of looking at the instructional consultation role is to consider the steps that a teacher follows in the teaching process. A successful teacher:

1. Determines the content of the subject matter to be taught.
2. Has clear expectations of the students.
3. Knows the conditions under which the students learn best.
4. Uses valid and reliable measurements of student performance.
5. Selects quality instructional materials.
6. Designs quality instructional activities.
7. Maintains a productive classroom environment.
8. Uses the results of teaching to modify subsequent instructional efforts.

The instructional consultation role includes any activities in which the school library media specialist attempts to help the teacher perform any of these eight functions. In instructional design consultation, the school library media specialist uses system theory as a model to help one or more teachers plan, implement, and evaluate instruction. Traditionally, the instructional design consultant assists through all eight of the steps above, from determination of content (needs assessment) through modification of subsequent instruction (evaluation). Instructional design consultation is a small subset of the much broader instructional consultation.

With the publishing of Information Power, the instructional consultation role of the school library media specialist was formalized, if not succinctly defined.[1] The development of this role has been accompanied by a great deal of emotion, both positive and negative. While the majority of literature dealing with instructional consultation has portrayed it as a very positive force, there have been those who have put their doubts in writing. An example of an extremely positive viewpoint is Chisholm and Ely's 1979 work.[2] Olson's 1984 article is an example of the vehemence with which the role can be assailed.[3] The vast majority of authors and practitioners fall between these extremes, seeing the worth in the role, but realizing that barriers exist to its implementation in the real world.

Over the past two decades, there have been a substantial number of studies conducted on the topic. With the publishing of Information Power, all but the most savage critic would agree that a reflection upon that research is appropriate. The benefits of such a reflection would be guidance for the practitioner as well as for the future researcher.

This review of the literature covers the following topics:

- The studies that attempted to determine the extent to which instructional consultation was being practiced by school library media specialists.
- The effects of various factors on the performance of instructional consultation.
- Effects of instructional consultation by the school library media specialist on student attitude and behavior.
- Effects of instructional consultation by the school library media specialist on teacher attitude and behavior.
- Implications for school library media practice.
- Research needs for the next ten years.

The Diffusion of Instructional Design Consultation

School Library Media Specialists as Instructional Consultants

To what extent, during the last thirty years, have school library media specialists worked to help their teachers through instructional consultation? As one attempts to answer this question by analyzing research reports, special care must be given to the methods used in describing and quantifying "instructional consultation." While activities that clearly fall into this category are represented in instruments developed for national implementation, an instrument designed solely for quantifying this topic has not been developed on a national level.

Mullen utilized an investigator-designed questionnaire and interviews, based on the quantitative standards of the 1960 ALA standards, to determine the practices of school libraries in Missouri. Information was gathered on the extent to which teachers shared their lesson plans with the librarian and the librarians produced simple instructional materials for the teachers. In general, teachers were not found to be doing the former, and only 20 percent of the librarians reported doing the latter.[4]

Lane, in the same year, used a questionnaire to determine the instructional role of 265 school librarians in Oregon.[5] The results were not as disheartening as Mullen's. Slightly over half of the respondents reported working with teachers in selecting materials. Forty-three percent provided professional materials and 23 percent helped their teachers plan units of instruction.

In the 1970s several studies attempted to determine the extent to which school library media specialists were helping their teachers. Typically, these studies investigated the frequency with which school library media specialists reported consulting in such activities as writing performance objectives, helping to match instructional materials to learner characteristics, and conducting inservices on evaluation procedures. Usually, the investigator also collected data on performance of more traditional library media activities such as providing reading guidance or organizing materials.

Kerr mailed questionnaires to 450 principals, teachers, and school library media specialists in the state of Washington to collect attitudinal data on these groups toward performance of technical service, information, and instructional design (ID) activities by the school library media specialist.[6] Information services were seen as most important by all three groups, followed by instructional design activities. Interestingly, both teachers and administrators rated the ID activities as more important than did the library media specialists.

Using a questionnaire, Loertscher studied forty senior high schools in Indiana during the 1972-73 school year.[7] Data were collected on the importance and frequency of sixty-four services in the categories of accessibility, utilization, awareness, instructional design, production, acquisition, evaluation, and professional. The more traditional activities were preferred and implemented to a significantly greater extent than instructional design, evaluation, and utilization activities.

Rosenberg used Loertscher's scale in a study to determine, among other things, the principal's attitude toward the performance of instructional design services by the library media specialist.[8] He concluded that the principals in his sample ranked this task as significantly less important than did the library media specialists whom he polled.

In 1978, Mohajerin and Smith used factor analysis to separate twenty-seven school library media specialist activity statements into six categories. They then polled teachers, principals, library media specialists, and media educators about attitudes toward the performance of these activities by the library media specialist. There was very little difference in attitudes between the four groups, with the major differences occurring because the media educators polled had a more negative attitude than the members of the other groups. The external validity of these findings is suspect because media educators from only one state were surveyed.[9]

In an attempt to create an instrument based on a recognized definition of instructional design and to determine the extent to which this role was practiced, Turner and Martin administered a questionnaire to 300 library media specialists during the 1977-78 school year.[10] The questionnaire consisted of twenty-eight activities drawn from the Task Analysis Survey Instrument[11], and the results were factor analyzed. Four factors were formed, including twenty-five of the twenty-eight activities. These factors represented four of the six functions delineated in Educational Technology: Definition and Glossary of Terms.[12] While a positive attitude was evidenced toward all of the activities, the logistics and evaluation factors were more highly regarded and practiced than the production and design factors.

Two dissertations investigating the extent to which school library media specialists were involved in the planning, implementing, and evaluating of instruction outside of the library media center were written in the early 1980s. Stanwich used interviews and a questionnaire with teachers, administrators, and library media specialists, and found that library media specialists were not involved in assisting teachers as the teachers planned and carried out their instruction.[13] However, he also found that all three groups had majorities who believed that the library media specialist should render such assistance.

Using a questionnaire based on the School Library Manpower Checklist, Leung polled library media and curriculum coordinators in New York.[14] She concluded that library media specialists had no involvement in building level or district level curriculum committees. Results also indicated that, for all instructional endeavors outside the classroom, library media specialists played only a passive role.

Turner and Dalton studied the process by which elementary school teachers identify the instructional materials that they use in their teaching.[15] They concluded that the library media specialist played a major consultative role in selecting materials housed within the library media center. However, for their sample at least, the library media specialist had only a marginal consultative role in locating instructional materials housed anywhere else. In a study designed to elicit written responses from elementary school library media specialists regarding the eight program components of the 1975 standards, Zsiray determined that the consultative role of the library media specialist focused on instructional materials selection and utilization.[16]

An investigator-designed questionnaire was distributed to three levels of library media specialists in Nevada.[17] The fifteen items on the questionnaire collected information on curriculum involvement and role perceptions. The authors concluded that, while the library media specialists were heavily involved in the reading program and provided "auxiliary" support, they were not involved in curriculum planning.

Certainly, these studies do not represent the entirety of those done on the topic of instructional assistance to teachers by school library media specialists. They are, however, representative and provide a clear picture. School library media specialists, in general, are not and never have been involved in instructional design consultation, i.e, working with teachers through all the steps in the instructional design process. As for the more broadly defined instructional consultation role, the library media specialist has had an impact on what takes place in the classroom. Based on available research, the extent of this impact remains unclear, but it is known that those library media specialists who provide extensive support are very special professionals.

Others as Instructional Consultant

Interestingly, the school psychologist/counselor profession has witnessed a similar upsurge in the literature calling for a role as instructional consultant. This is a much more recent phenomenon than in the library media profession (see especially Instructional Consultation.)[18] A study by Miele of the implementation of this role concluded that school psychologists did not act as instructional consultants, and that teachers did not expect them to.[19]

Idol-Maestas and Ritter followed the activities of twenty-seven instructional consultants who had been trained specifically to work with teachers and whose entire job was dedicated to this task.[20] Despite the educational preparation and the single purpose position, the consultants reported spending only a small amount of their time actually working with teachers.

Preparation for Instructional Consultation

Since the roles of instructional consultant and instructional design consultant are relatively recent phenomena, the question of whether library education programs prepare persons for these roles is a valid one. Royal questioned 503 library media specialists about the degree to which they possessed twenty-one instructional design competencies.[21] Respondents indicated that they possessed almost all of the competencies. Interestingly, they overwhelmingly indicated that the source of the competencies was their undergraduate program, rather than their library education.

Two studies polled library education programs to determine the extent to which these programs reported providing preparation in instructional design competencies. The first study targeted all programs in the southeast.[22] The second study polled all ALA programs in the United States.[23] While the competencies were available in most of the preparation programs, not one competency was required at all programs. Essentially, both studies concluded that instructional design had penetrated the curricula of the preparation programs as a unity. Programs either required all of the competencies or very few of them.

In summary, persons entering the school library media profession have received an uneven preparation for instructional design consultation. Few practitioners actually work with faculty through the instructional design process. While more school library media specialists work informally with teachers, this assistance is usually confined to helping them locate instructional materials. Furthermore, there is evidence that formidable barriers exist within the K-12 establishment that make it difficult for persons who have been trained solely to carry out this task to do so.

Factors Related to the Performance of Instructional Design Consultation

As was concluded in the previous section, instructional design consultation is not widely practiced in the school library media profession. There are school library media specialists who are involved in instructional consultation and work with teachers to help in planning, implementing, and evaluating instruction. This activity has been labeled with a variety of names such as "innovative practices," "public services," "integrated programming," or "instructional design." There has been a continuing effort to relate various factors to the performance of this activity, whatever the label assigned.

Each of the studies reviewed in this section attempted to relate one or more independent variables to the performance of a "helping" activity on the part of the school library media specialist. These independent variables fall into the following three categories:

- Personal characteristics of the school library media specialist.
- Environmental factors, which involve the sociology of the school, including the attitudes and expectations of the teachers and the administration.
- Logistical factors, which include those related to scheduling, budgeting, and the academic structure of the school.

Personality

The personality of the school library media specialist has been repeatedly studied to determine the characteristics that can be linked to successful work with teachers. Intuition would lead to the prediction that school library media specialists who are outgoing and who like to build relationships with others would tend to enter into instructional relationships more than those who do not have these characteristics. This relationship was observed in studies by Schulzetenberge[24] and Adams.[25] While the former linked extroversion with work with teachers in the curriculum area, Adams used a more ambiguous dependent variable. Her study linked the desire to enter into personal relationships with the performance of "public service" activities. While "public service" included activities that can be labeled instructional consultation, it was meant to have a much broader meaning.

Evelyn Daniel employed as a dependent variable the amount of responsibility assigned to the library staff for overall school functions and arrived at what seem to be counter-intuitive findings.[26] She found that the programs of librarians who were more humble and accommodating had a greater amount of responsibility assigned to them. In view of other studies, how can Daniel's results be explained? First, "overall school functions" might include instructional consultation as a subset, but certainly include many other functions. Second, Daniel also found that the personality characteristics of conscientiousness, responsibility, and perseverance were also related to the dependent variable. There is considerable opportunity for co-linearity in these variables. Even so, her results might provide a warning that the environment of the school does not always reward the outgoing change agent. Certainly there are principals who prefer the quiet, hard-working type who will take on yet another task without complaint.

In their pioneering work on the diffusion of innovation, Rogers and Shoemaker stated that the most important personality characteristic of a change agent is empathy.[27] Kerr found that role-taking ability, a subset of empathy, was related to attitude toward instructional design work with teachers.[28] Turner utilized an empathy scale developed by Hogan to study the relationship between empathy and reported performance of instructional design consultation,and found a significant relationship.[29] In a study of teacher/consultant relationships, empathic understanding on the part of the library media specialist was linked to teacher satisfaction with the consultation and with the resolution of any problems that arose during the consultation.[30]

Competence

The purpose of an instructional consultation is to solve an instructional problem. As the previously cited studies concluded, the personality of the library media specialist must provide the basis on which a relationship can be developed so that the problem can be addressed. This relationship allows the library media specialist to bring the appropriate competencies to bear on the problem.

If this is the case, then the amount and kinds of competencies possessed by the library media specialist would relate strongly to the success and ultimately to the amount of instructional consultation performed. The competency of the library media specialist in instructional design has been linked to the perception of the importance and performance of instructional consultation.[31,32]

Three studies linked other independent variables relating competence to instructional consultation activities.[33,34,35] The findings of these studies, in aggregate, conclude that a library media specialist who keeps up with the professional literature, has taken several curriculum courses, and is familiar with the subject topic of the lesson being constructed is most likely to be successful in the instructional consultation effort.

Gutkin's study also demonstrated that efficiency, in addition to competence, can be related to the success of an instructional consultation.[36] He found that the number of interactions that occurred in the course of a consultative effort was not related to the success of the effort.

Experience

Presumably, relationships are created and strengthened and competencies gained with the passage of time. Therefore, experience would seem to be a useful independent variable to explore in relationship to instructional consultation. Bowie found that the length of time that the school library media specialist had been in service in the school was related to the perception of the importance of instructional consultation.[37] The same independent variable was studied by Adams and linked to the number of public service activities performed.[38] Finally, Schulzetenberge linked the amount of time in service by the library media specialist within the district to instructional consultation activities.[39]

The second variable category is environmental factors. The school is a complex web of subsystems, of which the library media program is but one. Each subsystem has its own formal and informal goals, and its own gatekeepers, innovators, and late adopters. Any attempt by the library media specialist to move beyond the boundaries of the library media center to link with teachers must take into account a wide variety of variables within these other subsystems. There have, however, been only a limited number of studies that have attempted to link environmental factors with instructional consultation activity.

Mullin and Musella conducted a study that attempted to determine the factors related to successful instructional consultation.[40] The study utilized a questionnaire distributed to superintendents, principals, teachers, and consultants in fifteen randomly selected schools in four school districts. Although the "consultants" studied in their research were not library media specialists, their results have clear implications for this field and provide a strong foundation for future research. Based on the findings of this study, a description emerges of a school where the probability of successful instructional consultation is greatest. In this school:

- There is an absence of the "self-contained classroom mentality." The relationships between the members in the school are clearly understood and viewed as important.
- There exists a clear, non-ambiguous role for the instructional consultant.
- There is a high degree of knowledge among the teachers about the consultative services available.
- Teachers are involved in formulating their own consultative needs.
- There is a high priority given to consultative services for new teachers.

No doubt the principal is an important player in establishing the environment just described. Turner linked the principal's attitude with instructional consultation activities of the school library media specialist.[41] Hellene's findings went beyond attitude to include a wide range of activities by the principal.[42] She concluded that in schools where the principal clearly demonstrated a perceived value for the library media program, there was significantly more interaction between the library media program and teachers.

In a study of textbooks used in school principal preparation programs, it was determined that the eight currently used textbooks contain little information describing effective library media programming and virtually no information describing the consulting role of the school library media specialist.[43]

Finally, teachers with six or more credit hours in library science or audiovisual media utilization were found to be more "sophisticated" users of the library.[44] Another variable category was logistical factors. A school library media specialist may have the requisite personal characteristics and work within a supportive environment. Common sense tells us that there are still logistical constraints to successful instructional consultative activities. The following studies included one or more logistical variables as part of the investigation.

Number of Library Media Specialists

Several studies concluded that the number of faculty that each library media specialist must serve would influence the quality of service rendered. In a study of services rendered to faculty in nine "typical" schools, Loertscher found that there was a significant correlation between the size of staff and the number of services rendered.[45] Since the number of teachers is usually directly proportional to the number of students, Turner and Martin's findings corroborate Loertscher's. They concluded that there was a significant correlation between the ratio of professionals to students and the amount of instructional consultation that took place in the school.[46] Mullin and Musella, who studied the activities of in-school consultants in general, also concluded that a low number of teachers per consultant increased the probability of success.[47]

Open Time

If the library media program operates under a rigid schedule where virtually all of the library media specialist's time is taken up teaching classes, then there will be little opportunity for work with teachers. This was the conclusion of Turner and Martin[48] and Hellene.[49]

Clerical Assistance

Turner and Martin found a significant correlation between the amount of paid clerical assistance available in the library media center and the amount of instructional consultation performed by the library media specialist. On the other hand, they also found a significant negative correlation between the number of student helpers available per hour and the amount of instructional consultation performed. The same inverse relationship was observed for parent volunteers. They hypothesized that the effort entailed in supervising a large number of volunteers more than offset any open time that might result from their assistance.[50] Perhaps this negative correlation involving volunteers could be attributable to the amount of initial training given that student by the library media specialist.

Budget/Equipment

The total budget of the library media program was significantly correlated to the amount of instructional consultation performed in Turner and Martin's study. There were even stronger correlations between the dependent variable and the budget for nonprint materials and the budget for production supplies. They also found that the amount of audiovisual production equipment and the presence of a production area was related to instructional consultation activity.[51]

Summary

There were few surprises in the conclusions of the research reviewed. School library media specialists who want to work with teachers, who are knowledgeable, and who can make their teacher-clients feel valued, will be more likely to work with teachers than those who do not exhibit these characteristics.

A supportive environment is very important to the performance of instructional consultation. Such an environment includes a principal who encourages the library media specialist to work with teachers and also rewards the teachers for improving instruction. The teachers recognize the role of instructional consultant and work, in cooperation with others in the school, to improve teaching. Finally, the library media specialist has solid clerical support and an adequate budget. There is time available to build relationships with teachers and to carry out consultative activities.

Effects of Instructional Consultation by the School Library Media Specialist on Behavior and Attitudes of Students

For the past twenty years there has been a continuing effort to determine the extent to which school library media specialists undertake instructional consultative activities with their teachers. A reasonably clear picture has emerged from these studies. There is also a body of research dedicated to determining the factors that lead to such consultative activities.

The consultative role for the library media specialist has been discussed in the literature for over twenty years. The rationale for this role is the assumption that, if a library media specialist works with a teacher in the design and/or the implementation of instruction, the outcome of that instruction will be positively affected. The behavior and attitudes of the students will be different than in a similar case in which the consultation did not occur.

This assumption has not been tested within the research arena. A number of studies have attempted to relate gross indicators of library media services with gross measures of student achievement. These include Yarling's, which was a part of the evaluation phase of the Knapp School Libraries Project.[52] He tested and compared library skills of students in schools with and without a centralized library. Students in the schools with a centralized library demonstrated a significant improvement in the skills tested over a two year period, and the students without centralized libraries did not. Similar conclusions were stated by Becker[53] and Greve.[54]

During this decade, one of the most quoted of this type of study is that done by Didier in 1982.[55] She attempted to match school systems on expenditures for instruction and then compare schools with and without full-time library media specialists. The study concluded that student achievement in reading, study skills, and use of newspapers was significantly greater in the schools with full-time library media specialists.

A study by Smith utilized a more precise independent variable and investigated the relationship of consultative activities to student achievement.[56] This study, compared processes in which teachers worked with a library media specialist to design units of instruction that integrated library skills into regular classroom units, where the library media specialist prepared and taught the skills independently, and where a control group received no instruction. The control group performed significantly worse than the students taught by the library media specialist. No statistical significance was attributed to the instruction by the classroom teacher.

It seems to be an article of faith that if instruction is carefully designed and implemented, learning will be enhanced. Furthermore, if the library media specialist consults with a teacher to improve instruction, learning will be enhanced. There is little, if any, evidence on which to base such suppositions. In fact, major studies that have attempted to relate a wide range of factors within schools to student outcomes often do not even consider the library media program as a potential factor.[57,58] Apparently, for now, this must remain a conclusion whose basis lies outside of the empirical realm.

The Effects of Instructional Consultation by the School Library Media Specialist on Behavior and Attitudes of Teachers

Clearly, very little research-based evidence links consulting activity by school library media specialists with teachers to enhanced learning on the part of the students. A logical next point of inquiry would be to determine if there is research evidence links instructional consultation activities by the library media specialist with a change in the behavior and/or attitudes of the teacher-client.

Unfortunately, very little evidence in the form of research results exists. Jay's study cast some light on the question by investigating barriers to the use of the library as a teaching tool by teachers.[59] She concluded that teachers who did not use the library in their teaching believed that they did not have enough time, were not familiar with the materials, and/or did not believe that the materials housed in the library were needed to teach their subjects.

George attempted to determine whether the existence of school media centers could be related to teachers' use of non-print materials in teaching.[60] She concluded that the presence of the media center did encourage the use of these materials.

Implications for Practitioners

Should a school library media specialist consider increasing instructional consultation activities? There are compelling reasons to answer in the affirmative, although a discussion of these reasons is outside the scope of this paper. For now, let it suffice to say that this is a role identified in the latest set of guidelines for the profession.

If a school library media specialist is interested in increasing efforts to help teachers, does the research in this area provide any guidance? The answer is a very qualified yes. This library media specialist should expect a certain amount of frustration in implementing the role. Research projects have repeatedly concluded that school library media specialists are not involved in a formal instructional design consultation role, i.e., working with one or more teachers through all of the steps in designing, implementing, and evaluating instruction. Several studies have concluded that many library media specialists believe that instructional design consultation is too time consuming and difficult to undertake. If library media specialists are involved in instructional consultation at all, it is usually in the selection of instructional materials. Furthermore, there is evidence that principals clearly value this assistance over helping teachers in the other steps in the teaching process. Clearly the first attribute that a library media specialist who wants to increase participation in this role must possess is a strong desire to help teachers improve instruction. Research results echo this self-evident assertion.

Library media specialists should take some time to reflect on their ability to see the instructional world through the eyes of their teacher-clients. While there are those who assert that empathy cannot be taught, there is strong evidence that communication and facilitating skills can be imparted quite easily.[61]

Library media specialists also need to reflect on the competencies which they possess in the areas of the design, implementation, and evaluation of instruction. Studies have demonstrated that the possession of these competencies is not the automatic result of the completion of a library media preparation program. Fortunately, there are methods such as additional coursework, peer interactions, and reading through which competencies can be acquired. There is also some evidence that effort and experience will increase the probability for success.

There are clearly certain logistical minima for increasing one's role in helping teachers. Studies have identified a manageable number of clients, a sufficient amount of flexible time, access to consistent and competent clerical support, and an adequate budget as key requirements.

Finally, based on the studies reviewed, the library media specialist should carefully examine the environment within which the instructional consultation will take place. Is the principal supportive of this role? Has the role been clearly delineated in terms of expectations of all parties involved? Is there an atmosphere in the school in which good teaching is expected and rewarded? Do teachers work and share with each other?

Perhaps a school library media specialist will want to increase the amount of assistance that is provided to teachers, and have the competencies to do so. If the environmental and logistical factors are not present, what can be done? In this case, the library media specialist must be very committed to the role and undertake a program to obtain the requisite support. The principal is the key target in this program, with more visible teachers as logical secondary targets.

Ideally there would exist a solid body of research linking instructional consultation activities by the library media specialist with enhanced learning on the part of students. Also beneficial would be quality research which demonstrating that such consultation resulted in a change in the way in which the teacher-client proceeds through the instructional sequence. The library media specialist could use these results in an effort to build support for these activities. Unfortunately, virtually no such evidence exists. The library media specialist must rely on personal persuasive powers, prowess in the political arena of the school, and the results of projects carried out with cooperative teachers to build such support. Perhaps by the time the next guidelines are written, such a body of research will exist.

Implications for Researchers

Given the research that has been carried out in the past twenty years, and given that the role of helping teachers is an appropriate and valuable one, research needs are clear. First, terms must be clearly defined and the discernible difference that the school library media specialist makes when acting as an instructional consultant with one or more teachers must be substantiated.

Defining Instructional Consultation

Instructional consultation should not be viewed as synonymous with instructional design consultation. This is far too narrow a focus and one which, for the foreseeable future, will exclude the vast majority of the field. Conversely, excluding the rich research base and problem solving techniques that are the basis for the instructional design methodology would be overlooking a powerful tool.

The best approach seems to be to direct initial efforts toward defining instructional consultation based on one or more of the models that have emerged in the past few years. Using such an approach, any activity in which a library media specialist was involved that was intended to help teachers design, implement, or evaluate instruction would come under the aegis of instructional consultation. In such a system, the highest level of activity would be that which most resembles formal instructional design consultation, such as using the principles of instructional design to assist teams of teachers in the development of entire units of instruction.

From this viewpoint, an activity such as purchasing a book for the professional collection would be considered instructional consultation, even though no interaction might have taken place between the school library media specialist and a teacher. Likewise, an informal exchange in the teachers' lounge in which the library media specialist suggests a title of instructional material to a teacher would be considered instructional consultation at a higher level. This way of defining instructional consultation provides a continuum along which the activities of virtually every school library media specialist fall. Based on this definition, reliable and valid instruments should be designed so that the variable of instructional design consultation can be studied systematically.

This definition and instrument design should take place before any other research. Unless agreement can be reached on what is being investigated and a reliable method developed of determining whether, and to what degree, this phenomenon is present, attempts to answer other questions will be futile.

Implementation Studies

There should be a limited number of descriptive studies to determine and document the amount and level of instructional consultation that is taking place. This is especially important in view of the mention of this role in Information Power. However, care must be taken not to concentrate too many resources in this effort. This is also true for studies that attempt to determine the attitude of various populations toward instructional consultation activities by the school library media specialist. It is reasonably certain that instructional design consultation activities are few and that, currently, there is not strongly positive attitude by any group regarding its performance.

The School as a System

The design of any study, beyond one purely descriptive in nature, should be done from the viewpoint of the school as a system. The library media program, administration, teacher, and student subsystems all interact, and the instructional consultation variable must be studied in the light of this interaction. Figure 1 is a model of the instructional system and demonstrates the interactions of the subsystems that would be of research interest.

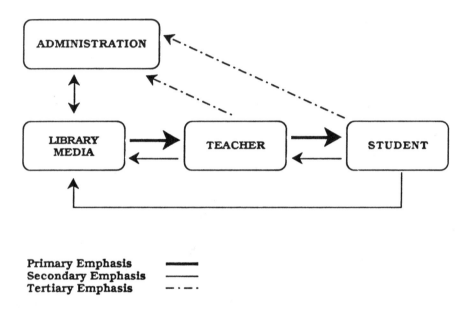

Figure 1. Instructional Consultation Research Emphases

The Student. The primary and most important area of interest is the effect of varying levels of instructional design activity on student learning. The designers of these studies need to refrain from using macro-level dependent variables such as yearly standardized test scores. Unless the instructional consultation activity was of the highest level and of a very long duration, significant differences will be rare. Instead, unit or even single lesson results should be targeted. If a library media specialist helps a teacher design a lesson on the solar system, will the results of the tests be different from the previous year's? Are the bibliographies of term papers different if the library media specialist assists in the design of the unit on biographies?

The Teacher. Do varying levels of instructional consultation result in a variety of teacher behavior and attitudes? Do teachers teach differently if the library media program provides a service of producing and mounting overhead transparencies, of obtaining computer software for preview, or of maintaining a bank of computer-generated test items? Do teachers teach differently after quality materials on learning styles have been added to the professional collection and publicized?

In general, as a library media program enhances support to its teachers, is instruction designed, delivered, and evaluated differently? Once the method has been established by which the level of instructional consultation can be determined, a wide variety of studies linking this variable with teacher behavior and attitude can and should be implemented.

The Library Media Specialist. Researchers need to be wary of studies that investigate the relationship of various personality traits and the performance of instructional consultation activities. This ground has been thoroughly worked in the past and solid generalizations are possible now. Research in the area of personality needs to concentrate on enhancing empathy on the part of the library media specialist and on ways in which communication skills can be improved in an efficient manner.

Logistical Factors. If instructional consultation is defined and quantified based on a levels approach, a significant amount of research into logistical factors is necessary. From past research, it is known that a great deal of logistical support is needed to carry out large-scale instructional design projects. Is there a linear relationship between the level of instructional consultation undertaken and the resources required? Is the relationship curvilinear, falling within the paradigm of diminishing returns? Does the relationship change over time and as a function of other classes of variables, especially those within the environmental area?

Environmental Factors. A number of studies have investigated the influence of environmental factors on the teacher assistance provided by the library media specialist. There are at least two reasons why this remains a fertile area of research. First, few of these studies were based on a model that considered the school as a dynamic system, where each component influenced and was influenced by the others. Second, instructional consultation viewed as a continuum of sophistication adds a dynamism to studies that was missing in the past.

Conoley called for studies of the triadic nature of school consultation.[62] She urged that research be carried out to establish the interrelationship between consultant, teacher, and student. A "quadrate" approach adds the administration to the equation. How the administrator's attitude and, more important, actions affect the instructional consultation activities of the library media specialist? As the library media specialist increases the level of instructional consultation, do the attitudes and actions of the administrator change? How does preservice training of principals affect their attitudes and actions regarding instructional consultation activities of the library media specialist?

Studies of the Instructional Consultation Process

A topic that might prove to be fecund is the consultative process itself. The multitude of social factors and expectations within a school need to be explored for their implications for the rendering of assistance to teachers. There exists a solid theoretical basis in sociology and psychology for these studies. How can a library media specialist encourage teachers to ask for assistance within certain parameters? How are consultative interactions best carried out to maximize concentration on instructional problems, and minimize time spent discussing personal problems and other non-instructional matters? Does there exist an optimum time window, such as a fifty minute session within which the output of the consultation is maximized? While research in the instructional design and development areas might provide some guidance, the unique characteristics of the school environment call for additional study.

Research in the field of expert systems should be studied to determine the advisability of an effort to create an automated consultation process. In such a process, the more repetitive and predictive steps in the consultation process could be performed at a terminal, thus maximizing the efficiency of the library media specialist.

Research Design

Whatever the topics studied, the effort within the field should be of a programmatic nature and should be sustained. Since many of the studies will be quasi-experimental in design, there need to be a great deal of replication and extension of studies. To do this, there will need to be cooperation and sharing of methods and results. A variety of methodologies should be considered. These should include those based on the naturalistic approach as well as those of a positive nature. Research leaders should cooperate to organize and facilitate field-based studies, carried out by practitioners.

In the school library media profession, the importance of what is done is often based on an untested belief that what media specialists do makes a difference. Oliver Wendell Holmes once pointed out that "Certainty is not the test for certitude." Now is the time to determine exactly what is meant by "instructional consultation" and decide how to measure this phenomenon. Furthermore, the impact of a school library media specialist taking on this role should be documented and methods to enhance the role should be determined.

Education will undergo a substantial change in the last decade of this century, there are too many forces calling for change for it to remain static. School library media specialists can either be prominent players in this change or they can be onlookers with a steadily diminishing impact. If they want to guide instructional change, their actions need to be based, at least partially, on research.

Concluding Summary

A review of the literature in this area led to the following conclusions:

1. Very little instructional design consultation has been practiced by school library media specialists, and the attitude toward such practice is mixed.

2. School library media specialists with well-developed interpersonal skills, competence in instructional design, the backing of the principal, and logistical support are more likely to work with their teachers.

3. Little is known about the impact of instructional consultation by the library media specialist on student or teacher behavior.

Practitioners who wish to increase their instructional consultation activities should study the school environment, clearly define their goals, use their political skills, enlist school administration support, and work initially with teachers with whom the probability of success is high. Future research efforts should begin with a concerted effort to define and measure instructional consultation, most likely using a levels approach. Research in instructional consultation should be done in the context of system theory. The interaction of instructional consultation and teachers, students, administrators, and the school library media specialist should be studied to determine the impact of instructional consultation by the school library media specialist on each subsystem.

Notes

1. American Library Association and Association for Educational Communications and Technology, Information Power: Guidelines for School Library Media Programs (Chicago: ALA, 1988).

2. M. E. Chisholm and D. P. Ely, Instructional Design and the Library Media Specialist (Chicago: American Library Association, 1979).

3. L. E. Olson, "Unassailable Truth," School Library Media Quarterly 12:44 (1983).

4. B. C. Mullen, "A Survey of Problems, Practices, and Conditions Affecting the Use of the Library in Instruction in North Central Association Schools in Missouri" (Ed.D. dissertation, University of Missouri, 1966).

5. M. B. Lane, "A Study of School Library Resources in Oregon as Compared to State and National Standards" (Ph.D. dissertation, University of Washington, 1966).

6. S. T. Kerr, "Are There Instructional Developers in the Schools?" AV Communication Review 25:243-267 (1977).

7. D. V. Loertscher, "Media Services to Teachers in Indiana Senior High Schools, 1972-73" (Ph.D. dissertation, Indiana University, 1973).

8. M. J. Rosenberg, "A Study of the Belief System Structure of Principals and Media Specialists as Related to Their Role Expectations for the Media Specialist" (Ph.D dissertation, Kent State University, 1977).

9. K. S. Mohajerin and E. P. Smith, "Perceptions of the Role of the School Media Specialists," School Media Quarterly 9:152-163 (1978).

10. P. M. Turner and N. N. Martin, Environmental and Personal Factors Affecting Instructional Development by the Media Professional at the K-12 Level (Bethesda, Md.: ERIC Document Reproduction Service, ED 172796, 1979).

11. American Library Association, Task Analysis Survey Instrument (Chicago: American Library Association, 1969).

12. Association for Educational Communications and Technology, Educational Technology: Definition and Glossary of Terms (Washington, D. C.: Association for Educational Communications and Technology, 1977).

13. E. E. Stanwich, "School Library Media Specialist's Involvement in Curriculum Planning" (Ed.D. dissertation, State University of New York at Buffalo, 1982).

14. M. C. Leung, "The Role of the School Library Media Specialist in Curriculum Planning" (Ed.D. dissertation, State University of New York at Buffalo, 1983).

15. P. M. Turner and J. Dalton, "Identifying Instructional Materials: A Study of a Selected Group of Elementary School Teachers," International Journal of Instructional Media 14:326-331 (1987).

16. S. W. Zsiray, "A Study of the Impact of Staffing Patterns in Elementary School Library Media Centers on Program Development" (Ed.D. dissertation, Utah State University, 1986).

17. N. L. Masters and L. S. Masters, Perceptions of School Librarians as Curriculum Leaders (Bethesda, Md.: ERIC Document Reproduction Service, 1986) ED 271120.

18. S. A. Rosenfield, Instructional Consultation (Hillsdale, N.J.: Erlbaum, 1987).

19. M. F. Miele, "The Role of the School Psychologist in Curriculum Planning: A Descriptive Study of Prevailing and Preferred Practices" (Ed.D. dissertation, State University of New York at Buffalo, 1983).

20. L. Idol-Maestas and S. Ritter, "A Follow-up Study of Resource/Consulting Teachers: Factors that Facilitate and Inhibit Teacher Consultation," Teacher Education and Special Education 8:121-131 (Summer 1985).

21. S. W. Royal, "An Investigation of Relationships Between the Educational Level of School Library Media Personnel and Perceived Competencies Needed to Develop Instructional Activities" (Ph.D. dissertation, Florida State University, 1981).

22. S. K. Stone and P. M. Turner, Factors Related to the Requiring and Availability of Instructional Design Competencies and the Programs of Library Schools in the Southeast (Bethesda, Md.: ERIC Document Reproduction Service, ED 191485, 1980).

23. P. M. Turner, "Instructional Design Competencies Taught at Library Schools," Journal of Education for Librarianship 22: 275-282 (1982).

24. A. C. Schulzetenberge, "Interests and Background Variables Characterizing Secondary School Librarians Who Work with Teachers in Curriculum Development and Improvement of Instruction" (Ed.D. dissertation, University of North Dakota, 1970).

25. E. P. Adams, "An Analysis of the Relationship of Certain Personality Factors to the Amount of Time Allotted to Specified Public Service Tasks by Selected School Librarians" (Ph.D. dissertation, University of Southern California, 1973).

26. E. H. Daniel, "The Organizational Position of School Media Centers: An Analysis of the Role of the School Library and the School Librarian" (Ph.D. dissertation, University of Maryland, 1974).

27. E. Rogers and F. Shoemaker, Communication of Innovations (New York: The Free Press, 1971).

28. Kerr, "Are There Instructional Developers."

29. P. M. Turner, "Empathy and the K-12 Instructional Developer," International Journal of Instructional Media 7:199-206 (1979-80).

30. J. W. Weissenburger, M. J. Fine, and J. P. Poggio, "The Relationship of Selected Consultant/Teacher Characteristics to Consultation Outcomes," Journal of School Psychology 20: 263-270 (1982).

31. M. M. Bowie, "The Relationship of Demographic Variables to the Perceived Performance and Importance of Selected Functions of School Media Specialists" (Ph.D. dissertation, Iowa State University, 1981).

32. Turner and Martin, Environmental and Personal Factors.

33. Ibid. p. 13.

34. Schulzetenberge, "Interest and Background Variables."

35. T. B. Gutkin, "Consultees' Perception of Variables Relating to the Outcomes of School-Based Consultation Interactions," School Psychology Review 15: 375-382 (1986).

36. Ibid. p. 379.

37. Bowie, "The Relationship of Demographic Variables."

38. Adams, "An Analysis of the Relationship."

39. Schulzetenberge, "Interest and Background Variables."

40. D. D. Mullin and D. F. Musella, Educational Consultancy: Perceptions and Reality (Bethesda, M.D.: ERIC Document Reproduction Service) ED 245333).

41. P. M. Turner, "The Relationship Between the Principal's Attitude and the Amount and Type of Instructional Development Performed by the Media Professional," International Journal of Instructional Media 7:127-138 (1979-80).

42. D. L. Hellene, "The Relationship of the Behaviors of Principals in the State of Washington to the Development of School Library/Media Programs" (Ed.D. dissertation, University of Washington, 1973).

43. S. W. Zsiray, "A Content Analysis of Textbooks on the School Principalship as Related to School Library Media Programs" (Unpublished manuscript, 1989).

44. E. M. Griffin, "Library Instructional Support Services in Elementary School in the District of Columbia Public School System" (Ed.D. dissertation, American University, 1980).

45. Loertscher, "Media Services to Teachers."

46. Turner and Martin, Environmental and Personal Factors.

47. Mullin and Musella, Educational Consultancy.

48. Turner and Martin, Environmental and Personal Factors.

49. Hellene, "The Relationship of the Behaviors."

50. Turner and Martin, Environmental and Personal Factors.

51. Ibid.

52. J. R. Yarling, "Children's Understanding and Use of Selected Library-Related Skills in Two Elementary Schools, One With and One Without a Centralized Library" (Ed.D. dissertation, Ball State University, 1968).

53. D. E. Becker, "Social Studies Achievement of Pupils in Schools with Libraries and Schools Without Libraries" (Ed.D. dissertation, University of Pennsylvania, 1970).

54. C. L. Greve, "The Relationship of the Availability of Libraries to the Academic Achievement of Iowa School Seniors" (Ph.D. dissertation, University of Denver, 1974).

55. E. K. Didier, "Relationships Between Student Achievement in Reading and Library Media Programs and Personnel" (Ph.D. dissertation, University of Michigan, 1982).

56. J. B. Smith, "An Exploratory Study of the Effectiveness of an Innovative Process Designed to Integrate Library Skills into the Curriculum" (Ph.D. dissertation, George Peabody College for Teachers, 1978).

57. J. Azumi and S. Madhere, Characteristics of High Achieving Elementary Schools in Newark (Bethesda, Md.: ERIC Document Reproduction Service, 1982) ED 217099.

58. D. U. Levine and J. Stark, Instructional and Organizational Arrangements and Processes for Improving Academic Achievement at Inner City Elementary Schools: Extended Summary and Conclusions (Bethesda, Md.: ERIC Document Reproduction Service, 1981) ED 213814.

59. H. L. Jay, "Increasing the Use of Secondary School Libraries as a Teaching Tool" (Ed.D. dissertation, New York University, 1970).

60. D. D. George, "A Descriptive Study of Some of the Variations in School Media Center Organization and Operation in Selected School Districts in California" (Ed.D. dissertation, University of Southern California, 1974).

61. A. Ivey, Microcounseling: Innovations in Interviewing, Counseling, Psychotherpy, and Psychoeducation (Springfield, Ill: Thomas, 1978).

62. J. C. Conoley, Research Methodology in the Study of Consultation (Bethesda, MD.: ERIC Document Reproduction Service, 1986) ED 274696.

THE LIBRARY MEDIA PROGRAM AND THE SOCIAL STUDIES, MATHEMATICS, AND SCIENCE CURRICULA: INTERVENTION STRATEGIES FOR THE LIBRARY MEDIA SPECIALIST

Melvin M. Bowie
Associate Professor
Department of Instructional Technology
The University of Georgia, Athens

Social Studies and the Library Media Program

The Goals of the Social Studies Curriculum

The classic goal of the social studies curriculum has been to educate citizens to live in a democratic society. Upon completion of secondary training, students are expected to demonstrate the skills, knowledge and values needed for social participation. Good solid citizens in our society should be able to:

- View the world as a global community.
- Understand that peoples of the world have different languages, history, cultures and customs that make them unique as groups, but that each group contributes to the progress of mankind.
- Understand and articulate the relationship between history, geography and economics.
- Understand and articulate the significance of major historical movements and events.
- Understand that individuals do make a difference in our lives.
- View historical events as they really happened.
- Understand that change has consequences.[1]

Such goals require that students be taught to:

- conduct reflective inquiry by asking higher order questions.[2]
- make sound and useful decisions.[3]
- engage in basic problem solving.[4]
- read critically to identify propaganda techniques.[5]
- read to distinguish fact from opinion.[6]
- recognize cause and effect relationships.[7]
- construct images and meanings of the social world.[8]
- relate prior knowledge to new data.[9]

The Response of Research

Much of the research in social studies has centered around reaching a consensus on how teachers can help students develop the deeper insights needed to function effectively in a socially changing environment. The move has been away from presenting "knowledge as predetermined sets of rules, standards, and ideas."[10] Instead, theory building around how to teach social studies should focus on decision making as a social process.[11] Researchers are finding that most young adults are severely deficient in the skills, knowledge and values that should have been developed from a study of the social sciences. For example, Alan Bloom, a professor of social thought at the University of Chicago, has found that the young people he has encountered in the mid-1980's cannot "distinguish between the sublime and trash, insight and propaganda."[12] Too many students, he feels, believe that "the here and now" is all there is. There appears to be a complete disdain for anything remotely connected with the past or the future.

A 1983 study in Dallas revealed that more than 20 percent of the twelve-year-olds taking a geography test could not locate the United States or Brazil on a world map. The Joint Committee on Geographic Education stated:

> It is a serious problem when our students fail to achieve a minimum standard of competency in global understanding. It is more serious when we overlook these deficiencies in our educational system. It is critical when we formulate national policies that rely on imprecise information and unclear interpretations about our own geography and that of other nations.[13,14]

A 1980 survey of elementary school children reported that only 3 percent of the nine-year-olds taking part in the study said that social studies was their favorite subject, while 24 percent said language arts was their favorite and 48 percent reported mathematics as being the preferred subject.[15] The Bradley Commission on History recently found "a shameful lack of knowledge" about history among high school students and recommended increased quantity and quality in history instruction.[16]

Many curriculum specialists and researchers suggest that the complexity of the social sciences themselves makes teaching and learning in the area difficult. Woodbury referred to the social sciences as "at best, an uncertain eclectic hodgepodge incorporating, among other fields, geography, economics, history, political science, anthropology, and psychology -- all presumably reflecting some common principles and scholarly discipline."[17] William Bennett recently wrote: "Many of today's children pick up bits of these lessons from an odd, amorphous grab-bag called 'social studies' derived from such disciplines as anthropology, sociology, law, psychology, history, science, economics and geography."[18]

There is even further evidence that the complex nature of the social studies continuum contributes to the difficulties inherent in social studies research:

> While problem solving in mathematics and physics has been rather extensively studied, little work has been conducted on social science problems or on social problems. What research has been conducted has examined the processes students employ as they solve well-defined and well-structured problems. But problems in the social sciences are not always as clearly defined as they are in mathematics or physics. Specific, agreed-upon solutions are not always readily available, if available at all.[19]

Armento goes on to suggest that teaching students the process of decision-making in the social sciences is quite different and more complex than in other fields.

Major Findings

•   Students learn democratic processes through experience. If we are to cultivate future citizens for our democratic society, then we must allow students to experience constitutional and democratic concepts in and out of the classroom.[20]

•   Reading historical literature and fiction helps students understand the past. Young people are able to personally react to people and events in history through reading biographies and historical fiction.[21]

•   Students learn decision-making and problem solving through role-playing and "think-out-loud" techniques. Such techniques have been found to aid learners in organizing large bodies of factual knowledge. [22]

•   Student learning in the social sciences is best facilitated when learners are required to construct images and meanings by relating new information to past experiences.[23]

•   The social studies classroom is a minisociety in which each learner has cooperative, competitive and individualistic goals.[24]

How Should It Be Taught?

Critical Reading. Learners should be taught to search for emotionally charged words and phrases in written text. Recognition of such words and phrases helps learners to develop skills in distinguishing opinions from facts. Learners should also be taught to detect half-truths and quotes of words and sentences out of context. Early in their schooling, students should begin to understand that much of what is written about social problems and issues must be regarded as propaganda in which a writer attempts to sway readers to a particular position on the issue at hand.

Developing the power to sense biases in written accounts of current or historical events is essential to learning to read critically. Students who are able to distinguish fact from opinion and/ or propaganda will be able to develop a better view of the "real world" and a better understanding of why such a view is the real world. If critical reading involves "analytic thinking for the purpose of evaluating what is read," then it is essential that young people learn that writers, like others in our society, speak and write from a set of personal and political values.[25]

Critical Viewing and Listening. Equally important to a useful study of the social sciences is acquiring the ability to critically evaluate what is seen and what is heard. So much of the information to which young people are exposed today comes via audiovisual media: television/video, film/movies, and live speeches/oration. John Splaine of the University of Maryland reports that almost 70 percent of the American public uses television as its primary source for information about political campaigns and issues, while 50 percent of the people said it was their only source. Less than a fourth of the American public uses two or more sources to inform them of political issues. So we can see the importance of television as an information medium on social problems. Splaine maintains that students need to understand that politicians who usually win elections are those who have learned to take advantage of the medium at hand, not those whose messages are more vital than their opponents'. [26]

Map Study. It is impossible to teach a record of human interaction and behavior devoid of the influences of climate and location. Therefore, effective instruction in history and other social science subjects should be consistently integrated with geographical concepts. Events occur in particular places at a particular time and influence human behavior. "Students need to understand how the presence of isolating geographic factors, like a mountain range or a desert, affects cultural development, and how physical characteristics of the land affect migration patterns, trade routes, invasions, wars, and economic development." [27]

It follows, then, that instruction in the social studies cannot be effective lacking an integration of map study. Is it possible to fully grasp a discussion of the twentieth-century history of sub-Saharan Africa without a very close study of the changing political geography of the region? Can one begin to understand and comprehend the full impact of "The Trail of Tears" on Native Americans without tracing the Trail on a map? Can one study the the Vietnam War and its significance with little or no understanding of the political and physical geography of Southeast Asia?

Broad Concepts and Themes. Much of the research on effective pedagogical methods in the social studies has centered around the dichotomy of facts versus concepts or themes. While the "back to basics" and standardized test proponents argue the need to teach the facts, those who have insisted that broad understandings should be the cornerstone of the social science curriculum have gained much support. The Bradley Commission on History in Schools [28] stressed that the study of history should go well beyond simply acquiring useful information. The Commission specifically stated:

> To develop judgment and perspective, historical study must often focus upon broad, significant themes and questions, rather than short-lived memorization of facts without context. In doing so, historical study should provide context for facts and training in critical judgment based upon evidence, including original sources, and should cultivate the perspective arising from a chronological view of the past down to the present day. [29]

Without a context, the facts and interpretations of social studies are hard to remember and apply. Unlike, say, grammar or addition, social studies as a curriculum area does not lend itself to drill and repetition.[30] Further, "social science concepts are mental filing systems and sets of associations which should, hopefully, enable us to process and organize new experiences and information in a changing world." [31]

In keeping with the goals of the social studies curriculum at all levels-- kindergarten through senior high school -- teachers should guide students away from simply memorizing isolated social studies vocabulary and help them to "grasp ideas and develop generalizations," keeping in mind that facts provide examples with which to illustrate or test concepts.[32] Therefore, good teaching in the social studies lessens fragmentation and develops big pictures. It blends facts with major concepts so that broad understandings emerge -- understandings so needed in a culturally literate and informed society.

Problem Solving. A recent thrust of social studies instruction has been to involve students in actual social problem solving activities: learning by doing. Woodbury reports findings of the National Council for the Social Studies that suggest "students learn best when they are actively considering problems."[33] The National Council for Geographic Education and the Association of American Geographers recently issued joint guidelines for geographic instruction. The guidelines state that instruction should help students conduct sound geographic inquiry that helps them answer two major questions: "Why are such things located in those particular places and how do those particular places influence our lives?" Asking these higher order questions leads the learner to data sources and interpretations of the data that help unravel the answers. Problems under study, cautions Woodbury, should be truly significant to students. Unless teachers work to make concepts and activities relevant, students will withdraw and continue to complain that social studies courses are meaningless and have nothing to do with them or their lives.[34]

Implications for Practitioners

What can school media specialists do to help teachers implement the findings from research in the social studies? How can they make their media programs more responsive to the needs of social studies teachers who are trying to heighten student interest and achievement in the social studies curriculum?

1. Critical Reading. Library media specialists can do a number of things to help students read written materials critically. Among these are:

A. Design (with teachers) library media center visits in which students are encouraged to find, sort, evaluate and analyze materials containing opposing viewpoints on social issues. Students should be required to use both primary and secondary sources whenever possible. Vertical file materials, C-Span broadcasts, the Congressional Record and other government publications should be made available for study and evaluation.

B. Help sponsor clubs and classroom experiences that debate social issues and encourage leadership development. Students must read critically to make decisions about their own positions on issues. Positions should be carefully documented from both original and secondary sources.

C. Students should be encouraged to read fictional accounts of historical events and persons to make them "seem more real." Encourage students to compare fictional accounts with non-fictional ones to separate fact from conjecture.

D. Design activities in the library media center that use original and secondary sources as the basis for storytelling, writing biographies and traditional research papers. It is also a good idea to let students read and compare various versions of legends, myths and folktales.

2. Critical Viewing/Listening. Media specialists can help teachers in a number of ways to strengthen children's abilities to evaluate and judge the significance of what they see and hear:

A. Keep a file of popular advertisements from newspapers and magazine. Have students make a list of terms and phrases frequently used by advertisers to sell products and services. Have children listen for these and similar terms while watching television.

B. Schedule a viewing session of a major cultural or historical television program with a class. Create with the teacher an after-viewing analytical discussion/debate of the major ideas presented.

C. Promote the use of filmstrip sets that invite discussion and critical thinking rather than those that simply cover facts in a news-type format.

3. Broad Themes/Concepts. Helping students see "big pictures" in social studies is sometimes not easy to do, but there are steps that media specialists can take to help:

A. Help students create infinite bibliographies that correspond with units of instruction. An infinite bibliography is not a simple author/title list of books, but brings together key words, subject headings from the card catalog and periodical index, names of relevant personalities, place names, literary works and other helpful suggestions for gathering information on a given theme or concept. Students should be encouraged to evaluate the success of such bibliographies after they are used in completing an assignment.

These bibliographies can be created at the beginning of a unit and can be examined by a class as an evaluation activity at the end of the unit.

B. Require students to produce an audiovisual product where analysis of a number of different information sources is necessary in order to create scenery, costuming, script and setting. Student projects can include overhead transparencies, display boards, video and audio tapes and laminated or mounted materials.

C. Promote special events such as Constitution Day/Week/Month.

D. Promote multicultural programs that enhance and broaden concepts encountered in the classroom and that broaden students' perspectives. For example, for inner city children, create a farm life project, or for farm children, an inner city project.

4. Map Study. The media specialist can be responsible for helping teachers integrate map skills throughout the social studies curriculum:

A. Create activities that require students to use a variety of maps to produce a paper or project. For example, students can produce a map-line of the Louisiana Purchase as it was gradually carved into the various states.

B. Create games, contests and other activities that utilize prominently displayed maps, globes and gazetteers in the media center.

C. Help students in the study of geographical settings of picture books by attaching notes to maps indicating settings of students' favorite stories. Have students create their own pictures of the universe based on accounts from the science fiction collection.

D. Plan with teachers for acquisitions of better maps and more extensive utilization of maps and globes.

5. Problem Solving. Problem solving in the social studies emphasizes learning by doing. It is an activities-oriented curriculum in which students create many of their own learning materials and draw inferences and conclusions from data they have collected. The library media specialist can help in this process by doing some of the following:

A. Encourage student productions of videos on investigations of community problems to present to the class. Collect data on the responses of classmates to the presentations.

B. Use the library media center for small group discussions of topics under investigation.

C. Teach students to use computerized word processing, databases and spreadsheets to store data and report findings of investigations.

D. Collect free and inexpensive materials from social and community agencies and inform teachers of their availability.

Summary

The social studies curriculum should be a rich and rewarding experience for children and young adults throughout their schooling. Research findings suggest better ways for achieving this in the classroom by teaching learners to read, listen and view critically. Problem solving activities should replace passive work so that students become involved in their own learning and begin to understand and see the world as it really is. Map skills should be integrated throughout the curriculum so that youngsters can understand the influences of location and climate on human endeavors, both past and present.

Library media specialists can aid in these processes with intervention programs that work with classroom teachers to achieve the goals of social studies instruction. Working with teachers to design activities that encourage student use of a variety of primary and secondary sources in creating their own projects is important to helping students understand social studies concepts. Including rich offerings of biographies and autobiographies as well as historical fiction and narratives for storytelling, research and analytical study will help students with critical reading and broad understandings of social and historical events.

Working together, the library media specialist and social studies teachers can improve student enjoyment and achievement in social studies. Their combined efforts should help ensure that in the future, fewer high school students will choose Abraham Lincoln as the author of Uncle Tom's Cabin on a test, as some 600 eleventh graders recently did.[35]

Mathematics and the Library Media Program

The Goals of the Mathematics Curriculum

The aims of the mathematics curriculum in K-12 classrooms have been regularly articulated in many quarters over a good many years. Clark, Klein and Burks believed the ultimate goal of the study of mathematics was to help citizens control the time and space in which they live. [36] Seventeen years later, the National Council of Teachers of Mathematics stated the overall aim of the mathematics curriculum as being mathematical literacy.[37] Emphases on curriculum reform stress new goals needed to prepare students for citizenship in a highly technological and information-oriented society. Among these are:

- Present students with the strategies needed for solving complicated problems in real life and in the work place.[38]
- Develop in students a sense for and understanding of numbers.[39]
- Eliminate mathematics anxiety, particularly among female and minority students.[40]
- Help students understand that mathematics is a dynamic and changing body of knowledge.[41]
- Help students understand that mathematics is useful and powerful.[42]
- Develop in students a spirit of inquiry.[43]

The National Council of Teachers of Mathematics recommended goals to accommodate the needs of businesses and industries in the twenty-first century. Attributed to Henry Pollak, a noted mathematician, the goals suggest that workers of the next century must be able to:[44]

- set up problems with the appropriate operations.
- use a variety of techniques and approaches to work on problems.
- understand the underlying mathematical features of a problem.
- see the applicability of mathematical ideas to common and complex problems.
- deal with open problem situations, since most real problems are not well formulated.
- believe in the utility and value of mathematics.

The council set forth its own goals for the curriculum:

- help students value and appreciate the role of mathematics in our contemporary society.
- help students become confident in their own abilities.
- develop in students the ability to solve problems using mathematics.
- teach students to communicate mathematically.
- help students learn to reason mathematically.

Such goals require that students be taught to:

- understand the number system.
- select and use a variety of ways to compute.
- make estimations.
- build connections between concepts and procedural operations.
- think and reason rather than simply find answers to problems.
- use calculators and computers with ease and proficiency.

The Response of Research

Mathematics is both abstract (inferential) and concrete (specific). The structure of the discipline thus precipitated a dyad in approaches to its study. The first, known as the traditional or "back-to-basic" approach, is rich in computation, exercises, drill, repetition and rote memorization of formulas. It is largely textbook and teacher driven. It is oriented toward acquiring survival skills for jobs and daily living. The "new math" can be placed in this category because it, too, relied heavily on computation and rote drill. [45]

On the other hand, the discovery method places emphases on investigations, measurements and manipulations. Supposedly, it is based on the logical structure of mathematics, and students are challenged to use powers of reasoning. According to Kaplan, Yamamoto and Ginsburg, this approach emphasizes "developing children's problem-solving and critical-thinking skills. The new orientation usually stresses teaching children how to identify key aspects of problem situations and to use particular strategies to arrive at solutions."[46] It is problem/student driven. "The emphasis is on the cognitive skills that will allow students to handle real-life and workplace problems that seldom are laid out the way traditional math books present them." [47]

Recent studies on student achievement in mathematics reveal that many of today's students are not achieving well with the old, new or discovery methods.

Instead, researchers are finding that, when compared to students from other industrialized nations, American junior high and high school students lag far behind in mathematics test scores. "In school mathematics, ... the United States is an underachieving nation, and our curriculum is helping to create a nation of underachievers."[48] Researchers are finding, however, that American students do achieve at comparable levels on tests of low-level skills, but do not do well with higher-level items, such as geometry and problem-solving.

Quite a few young people, however, are not performing well even with lower-level mathematics. This author, who often teaches college students, has found that many of them cannot construct pie or bar graphs when given sets of data because they lack a workable knowledge of percentages, decimals, proportions, ratios or fractions. Consistent with the research, many report that they have never used a compass, protractor, slide rule or graph paper. Some even find it difficult to use a simple standard/metric ruler. Further, it is not unusual to encounter high school graduates today who cannot determine a 15 percent tip in a restaurant or a 40 percent discount in a department store.

Current research on learning and teaching mathematics is finding that young people find computations and exercises dull and tedious.[49] Complaints such as these have lead researchers to suggest that we need to look at how students think and solve problems, as this might hold the key to better classroom instruction. Researchers argue that analyzing scores on standardized tests does not tell us how students think, which is more important than simply looking at the number of correct or incorrect answers on the tests.

Romberg and Carpenter feel that the notion of teaching for the test or traditional teaching has given rise to an almost meaningless fragmentation of mathematics instruction in the curriculum.[50]

> For schools, the consequences of this traditional view of mathematics are that mathematics is divorced from science and other disciplines and then separated into subjects such as arithmetic, algebra, geometry, trigonometry, and so on. ... This is followed by subdividing each subject into topics, each topic into studies, each study into lessons, and each lesson into specific facts and skills. This fragmentation of mathematics has divorced the subject from reality and from inquiry.[51]

If students are to value the beauty and power of mathematics, teaching must guide them to that beauty and power.

Major Findings

• Children bring a great deal of informal knowledge about mathematics to school.[52]

• Learners often "invent" procedures and methods of their own for solving problems and computing based on their own observations and interactions with the environment.[53]

• The formal mathematical procedures taught in school are perceived by students to be more powerful than their own personal and informal knowledge.[54]

• Most students feel that the textbook and the teacher are the "authorities" in the mathematics classroom.[55]

- Teachers can teach students to think about their own thinking/reasoning strategies (metacognition).[56]
- Analyzing student errors or bugs will shed insight on how students choose mathematical procedures.[57]
- Use of calculators and computers can reduce the tedium associated with rote paper-pencil computations and exercises.[58]
- Use of computers and other interactive technologies can help concept attainment when the concept under study is suited to such media.[59]
- More females and minority students suffer from "mathophobia" than majority males.[60]

How Should It Be Taught?

Teach Meanings of Operations. Much poor student performance in testing situations involving mathematics has been attributed to students' lack of understanding of just what they are really doing when they perform an operation. "Children's difficulty should remind us that genuine understanding of mathematics is more than memorizing number facts or using algorithmic procedures to get correct answers." [61]

Too often, students have been led to "believe that mathematics consists of doing a computation to get the answer in the book."[62] Teachers must focus on helping learners understand the fundamental operations of addition, subtraction, multiplication and division. What this means is that students, with understanding, can recognize conditions in real world situations where a given operation(s) would be applicable.

Put another way, "to understand means to know that a number fact makes sense in terms of counting, or that an algorithm is based on a principle, or that a principle relates to common sense. "[63] With such understanding students can apply these operations meaningfully and with flexibility. Teachers must also work to help students see the interrelationships among the operations and algorithms and connect them to symbols and mathematical language. Unless such understanding is achieved, transfer of knowledge to unique situations will remain difficult for many students.

Build on Students' Existing Mathematical Knowledge. Children enter school with some kind of knowledge about mathematics. They often understand concepts like "more" and "less" and most have some understanding of numbers. A good teacher builds upon this base and helps youngsters validate this "informal knowledge," connecting it with new concepts before introducing the more "formal knowledge."[64] Once the base has been established and children have gained confidence in their "invented" operations, instruction can then begin to introduce students to the highly organized, codified written system of formal mathematics. Kaplan, Yamamoto and Ginsburg believe this method is important because children assimilate school-taught mathematics into their existing mental framework and often develop nonstandard procedures for performing operations. "Teaching proceeds more effectively when an adult mentor takes into account the child's framework and encourages and guides the child's inquiry and experimentation."[65]

Focus on Problem Solving and Reasoning. Problem solving is both intellectual and physical. It involves ideas and reasoning power, but at the same time, it can involve hands-on manipulation of objects. It is not a topic in and of itself, but a process. It should provide the context in which skills and concepts are taught. According to Romberg and Carpenter, "the daily lessons of the traditional classroom are obviously geared to absorption and not inquiry."[66] Simple absorption of factual information does not lead learners to higher reasoning and problem solving activities. Absorption is static and not a process that results in long-term memory and understanding.

Problems should be meaningful to learners and should arise from their environments.[67] Learners should be encouraged to share their thinking and ideas and should be allowed to select and use several strategies in their problem solving activities. Students should be free to explore, investigate, experiment, ask questions, conjecture and make mistakes. They should be exposed to a number of tools to help them in the process. These include making inferences, using statistics, and estimating.

Problems should arise from real life situations. Teachers can pose such problems or allow students to determine their own. Schoenfeld has stated:

> For any student, a mathematical problem is a task (a) in which the student is interested and engaged and for which he wishes to obtain a resolution, and (b) for which the student does not have a readily accessible mathematical means by which to achieve that resolution. ...a task isn't a problem for you until you've made it your problem."[68]

"All mathematics should be studied in contexts that give the ideas and concepts meaning."[69]

Problem solving, because it usually entails a combination of intellectual and hands-on activities, aids students in transferring knowledge and skills already learned to new and unique situations. This is one of the main goals of the mathematics curriculum.

Reduce Time Devoted to Computation and Drill. Much of the research has shown that students do not like the tedious repetition of drill and computing meaningless columns of numbers. Too much drill makes them withdraw from the learning situation and they ultimately learn to hate mathematics.

While some immediate recall of number facts and operations is necessary for problem solving, rote memorization and a steady diet of exercises in computing are not recommended.[70] Coburn feels that, while computation should not be considered the most important part of the mathematics curriculum, some skill in computation is needed in measurement, statistics and problem solving. Here, calculators can help reduce the amount of time spent on routine arithmetic, subtraction and the like. Teachers should also help students use mental computing, estimation and other shortcuts to reduce the boredom and drudgery associated with computation drill. A balance between skills and concepts is needed, but the bulk of class time should be spent on concept development.

Use Interactive Technology Where Applicable. While much of the research on the overall value of interactive technologies in the classroom is still inconclusive, there is evidence that some concepts are better taught through such channels and that students appear more motivated when these channels are used.[71] Graphing is one such concept. "National test results show that students do poorly at graphing, despite the fact that graphing receives considerable attention in both algebra and geometry classes. ... Graphs are a powerful way to see functional relationships, for example, relationships between temperature change and time, or pulse rate and exercise."[72] The U.S. Congress report suggests that, based on the research, computers are ideal in teaching graphing skills because the computer frees the student from having to perform lower-level tasks such as manually plotting points on a graph. Instead, the computer can provide "an instant representation of the relationships between variables and allows students to see graphs in real time as an experiment unfolds."[73]

Explore, Investigate and Experiment with Everyday Materials. Children acquire spatial sense through experiments with models, blocks, geoboards, graph paper, straws, tiles, paper cutouts, yarn, string and other objects that suggest patterns and dimensions. The National Council of Teachers of Mathematics defines spatial sense as a feeling for one's surroundings and the objects in it. To develop this sense, children must have experiences that focus on shapes, sizes, orientations and geometric relationships. Teachers can ask students to visualize, draw, or compare dimensions of various objects in the environment. Such exercises prepare learners for more abstract concepts to be encountered later in the curriculum.

Encourage Girls and Minorities to Excel. Too often teacher expectations of females and minorities in mathematics classrooms differ from those they have for majority males. According to the Standards of the National Council of Teachers of Mathematics: "Whenever possible, students' cultural backgrounds should be integrated into the learning experience. Black or Hispanic students, for example, may find the development of mathematical ideas in their cultures of great interest."[74] The standards go on to suggest that different students bring different everyday experiences to the study of mathematics. Students from rural areas may differ in their ideas from students in urban or suburban environments. Teachers must be sensitive to these differences and create a caring learning situation in which all are free to explore mathematical ideas. There was even a time when mathematics was thought to be the exclusive prerogative of the gifted.[75] If the schools are to produce citizens who value and understand mathematics, all mathematics teachers must equally challenge all students in the classroom.

Implications for Practitioners

Traditionally, library media specialists have had little interaction with the mathematics classroom. It has generally been felt that mathematics teachers only use the blackboard and the textbook. So why bother? New emphases on increased problem solving activities for students offer media specialists unique opportunities to work with mathematics teachers. A number of useful strategies might be employed.

1.   Teach Meanings of Operations.   Work closely with teachers in selecting microcomputer tutorial and simulation packages that effectively integrate algorithms and operations with meaningful examples from the everyday environment.   Such programs as   "Green Globs" and "Algebra Tutor" are good examples for helping learners understand operations and logarithms.   Keep teachers informed of the availability of such software along with evaluations of the software.   Too often, however, such programs are designed for middle grades and higher so that teachers in the lower elementary grades might find it difficult to locate programs appropriate for their students.   For younger children, the media center should acquire as many electronic learning devices, objects, toys and other educational devices as possible.

2. Problem Solving and Reasoning. The media center program can support student investigations and inquiry into mathematical problems in a number of ways:
   A. Evaluate the mathematics collection, making sure it contains books and other materials with mind teasers, mind extenders, puzzles, games of logic and the like.   Such materials help students think and rationally select problem solving strategies.
   B. See that microcomputer software packages containing thinking games are used properly, not abused.
   C. Teach students to use microcomputer databases and spreadsheets as tools for data storage and retrieval. Create library based problems, perhaps with other disciplines that would use the computer to solve major data analysis problems.
   D. Make sure the media center collection contains a wide variety of mathematics trade books across all reading levels to aid in concept development. Books on measurement, statistics, estimation, geometric relationships, etc., will often provide exposure to broad concepts in a more interesting manner than the textbook.   Work with teachers to create interesting math projects based on these materials.
   E. Have students create their own mathematics reference materials such as glossaries, dictionaries and handbooks. Include materials for ready reference in the collection.
   F. Encourage students to use the media center for small group discussions and problem strategy meetings.
   G. Require students to produce models and other projects using mathematical principles.
   H. Promote "show and tell"   sessions in the media center where students present and explain their projects and findings to other students and teachers.
   I.   Prominently display student-produced math projects in the media center on a regular basis.
   J.   Sponsor contests and games of logic in the media center.

3.   Use Materials from the Everyday Environment.   Many of the instructional materials appropriate for the mathematics classroom should come from students' immediate surroundings so that mathematics connects with the real world.   The media specialist and the teacher can work together to identify and select a variety of useful items for this purpose:
   A. Keep on hand in the media center such objects as blocks, yarn, string, tiles, cubes and other manipulatives. Help students create their own manipulatives that demonstrate mathematical operations.

B. Subscribe to newspapers that carry stock market reports so that students can use them to compute dividends, profits and losses. Help students set up their own "companies" where they keep track of assets, profits and losses.

C. Gather materials from insurance agencies that students can use to compute ideal weights, caloric intake, life spans, etc.

D. Include in the collection books and other materials that stress the value of mathematics to everyday survival and then see that they are the basis of creative resource based math projects.

4. Use Interactive Technology Where Applicable. Media specialists can be of great assistance to teachers and students in using computers and other interactive media in the mathematics classroom:

A. Provide teachers with inservice training when they need help in mastering a new computer system or other technology. Talk with teachers and find out what type of help would be most useful. Help train students also, or help reinforce what has been learned in the classroom.

B. Work with teachers to identify mathematics concepts and units of instruction where computers could be most useful.

C. Help teachers select and evaluate software packages designed for the mathematics curriculum.

5. Encourage Girls and Minorities to Excel. The media specialist can support the mathematics teacher who is trying to encourage students to overcome their anxiety about mathematics. Because they are often girls and/or minority students, the media specialist must see to it that the media program is responsive to these students and their needs in mathematics:

A. Have students collect information on personalities from different cultures who excelled in mathematics. For example, African-American students should know that Ronald McNair and Charles Drew were good students of mathematics before they became noted scientists.

B. Evaluate the mathematics collection for biased or stereotypical material, both print and non-print. Purchase additional materials to provide balance in the collection.

C. Provide materials in the media center that encourage mathematics as a career choice. Pamphlets, books, videos, etc., on careers in mathematics should be made available to students who have traditionally felt that such careers were beyond their reach.

Summary

The goals of the mathematics curriculum challenge teachers to prepare students to function competently in the next century. Current test scores indicate that American youth lag far behind students in other industrialized nations. If this deficiency is to be overcome, new strategies for teaching mathematics must be implemented. These include teaching children to understand fundamental operations of addition, subtraction, multiplication and division. They must understand what they are doing when they perform a mathematical operation. Children must also be taught to use the power of estimation in many problem situations to reduce the time and attention given to rote computations of sums, totals, etc.

Teachers must engage students in problem solving activities where they use their brains, eyes, ears, hands and sources of relevant data. Problems must be relevant to students and made more meaningful through the use of ordinary everyday materials. Without such an approach to mathematics, children and young people will find it difficult to connect the ideas and concepts taught in the classroom to the real world.

Calculators, computers and other interactive technologies are now available to assist teachers in designing and implementing more meaningful lessons in mathematics. These devices can dramatically reduce the time learners spend on lower-level task mastery and allow them more time to spend on reasoning, concept formation and problem solving.

Research has shown that many female and minority students suffer from mathematics anxiety largely because teachers and society in general tend to expect less of them than majority male students. New standards for the K-12 mathematics curriculum challenge teachers to help <u>all</u> students realize the power of mathematics in their lives and to encourage them to become proficient in manipulating mathematical ideas.

The library media specialist can choose among a number of intervention strategies and ideas to help teachers of mathematics carry out the goals of the curriculum. Working together with teachers selecting materials, teaching the use of instructional delivery systems, sponsoring contests, sponsoring special games of logic and reasoning, providing facilities and space for mathematics problem solving activities and encouraging mathematically "shy" youngsters to excel are among the many contributions that library media specialists can make to the mathematics curriculum.

Science and the Library Media Program

The Goals of the Science Curriculum

A great deal of money, time, energy and effort are currently being directed to improving science education in the schools. Science educators who are concerned about the kind of scientific knowledge young people will need as citizens in the next century are recommending new goals for the curriculum. The American Association for the Advancement of Science (AAAS) believes that the schools should help students to:[76]

- become aware of the social value of science.
- become aware of science as an intimate part of everyday life.
- become curious about the world around them.
- develop positive attitudes toward the study of science.
- develop a spirit of inquiry.

In its <u>Project 2061 Report on Literacy Goals in Science, Mathematics and Technology</u>, the American Association for the Advancement of Science further stresses that science literacy means that all citizens, by the time they finish high school, should know that:[77]

- The world can be understood.
- Scientific ideas are subject to change.
- Scientific knowledge is durable.
- Science cannot provide all answers to all questions.
- Science demands evidence.

- Science is a blend of logic and imagination.
- Science attempts to explain and predict.

The National Center for Improving Science Education has advanced similar goals. It recommends that the curriculum in school science should:[78]
- develop in students a broad base of scientific vocabulary and knowledge.
- help students to broaden their investigative and problem solving skills.
- develop in students a reliance on data.
- help students accept ambiguity.
- help students to work cooperatively with others.

Such goals require that students be taught to:
- understand that there is orderliness and organization in the world.
- understand the relationship between cause and effect.
- apply the concept of system in unique situations.
- apply the concept of scale in a variety of situations
- develop models of phenomena.
- understand change and its consequences.
- understand the concept of structure or function.
- identify variations of properties
- understand the concept of diversity.

The study of science consists of exposure to processes and experiences that are essential to an understanding of the nature of science. Woodbury and the Center for Improving Science Education identified thirteen such processes:[79]
- Observing: Noting change, identifying properties, etc.
- Classifying: Classification of systems, coding, etc.
- Using Numbers: Finding averages, using decimals, etc.
- Measuring: Working with lengths, volumes, areas, etc.
- Using Space/Time Relationships: Identifying shapes, directions, changes in position, etc.
- Communicating: Graphing, diagraming, describing
- Predicting: Using interpolation and extrapolation, formulating
- Inferring: Making inferences from observations
- Defining Operationally: Distinguishing operational and non-operational definitions
- Formulating Hypotheses: Constructing and testing hypotheses
- Interpreting Data: Relating data to hypotheses, generalizing
- Controlling Variables: Identifying variables and describing how they are controlled
- Experimenting: Carrying out experimental procedures, interpreting accounts of scientific experiments, etc.

The Response of Research

Recent activities to improve science education have been based largely on the nation's need to maintain and "sustain its economic vitality, and to remain secure in a world torn by hostilities."[80] The AAAS iterates a number of immediate problems that are global in nature. Among these are unchecked growth in population, disease, acid rain, shrinking of the world's rain forests and other vital natural resources, and the huge investments of brain power and scarce resources in preparing for and fighting wars. The association believes that solutions to these and other major problems lie in better human use of scientific ideas and technology. "By emphasizing and explaining the dependency of living things on each other and the physical environment, science fosters the kind of intelligent respect for nature that should inform decisions on the uses of technology; without that knowledge, progress toward a safe world will be unnecessarily handicapped."[81]

Research on student achievement in science paints a grim picture. A recent report from the National Science Foundation found that American adults failed miserably on a science literacy test.[82] Termed "science illiterates," many of these people had finished high school, but most had not. Bennett suggested that courses in elementary school science had failed to provide even the most basic of understandings of scientific concepts.

Much of the research has traced poor student performance on science tests to poor preparation of science teachers. "Few elementary school teachers have even a rudimentary education in science and mathematics, and many junior and senior high school teachers of science and mathematics do not meet reasonable standards for preparation in those fields."[83] Consequently, "science gets shortchanged in the typical elementary school."[84] There is further evidence that teachers tend to spend more class time on the subjects they like, usually reading and language arts.

The Association for Supervision and Curriculum Development (ASCD) found in another study, that fourth graders received an average of only 28 minutes a day of science instruction.[85] The National Center for Improving Science Education reports 1985-1986 research findings that show grades K-3 spend 19 minutes per day on science, while students in grades 4-6 spend 38 minutes per day studying science subjects. Teachers in these grades indicated the order in which the amount of time was allocated to teaching the various subjects: (1) reading, (2) mathematics, (3) social studies, and (4) science.[86] When one considers the goals and objective of the science curriculum listed earlier in this paper and the amount of time being devoted to science instruction, it is not surprising that students are performing poorly on science tests.

Poor textbooks and other materials should also share in the blame for student failures in science understanding.[87] "Textbooks focus on learning about science rather than encouraging active involvement by students. Subjects are fragmented in most textbooks. Textbooks emphasize descriptions, explanations, and identification, and generally neglect higher order processes, such as interpretation, evaluation, analysis, and synthesis."[88] Woodbury accused most science textbooks of being:[89]

- stereotyped,
- inadequate for interdisciplinary concerns,
- inadequate for research or concepts,
- out of date when adopted,
- inadequate for students interested in or gifted in science,
- inadequate for teachers who wish to teach for excellence.

Science teachers, nonetheless, rely heavily on textbooks.[90] Data show that 69 percent of K-3 classes in science use published textbooks, and 89 percent of 4-6 grade classes use textbooks. A 1982 study found that 93 percent of science classes at the secondary school level used textbooks.[91] The center feels that such reliance poses a significant obstacle to reforming elementary school science programs. If textbooks are to contribute appreciably to the science program, they must be designed to do the following:[92]

- Get students ready to learn new information.
- Help students to integrate old and new information.
- Accommodate diversity in learning styles and interests.

Major Findings

- Prior knowledge influences science learning.[93]
- The use of advance organizers tends to help students who lack prior knowledge in science.[94]
- Use of constructive or active learning theory offers the most productive means for learning science concepts.[95]
- Children come to school with their own views and beliefs about the world.[96]
- Many children come to school with misconceptions about science that are difficult to correct.[97]
- Cooperative learning often promotes motivation and concept attainment.[98]
- There is inconclusive evidence as to the value of the laboratory experience.[99]
- Poor skills in reading comprehension hamper science learning.[100]
- Effective teaching in science requires considerable amounts of classroom time.[101]
- Motivation is a key ingredient in the learning and enjoyment of science.[102]
- Science simulations via the microcomputer offer more efficient ways of teaching some science concepts.[103]

How Should It Be Taught?

Actively Involve Students in Learning. New research shows that students learn better when they are allowed to explore and try out their own ideas. Passive learning --sitting and listening to the teacher or simply reading the textbook-- denies learners opportunities to compare and contrast new information against their own conceptions. "In science classrooms, many teachers attempt to transmit to passive students scientific knowledge that consists largely of definitions, terminology, and facts." [104]

The new view of teaching encourages students to construct their own conceptual frameworks in which the learner makes connections between the existing framework and new knowledge. These connections are best made when the learner is actively trying out ideas and links to see what fits and what does not.

Help Learners Restructure Their Own Knowledge. Teachers must deal effectively with students' preconceived notions about phenomena and help them restructure their existing knowledge. "If instruction does not deal with many of these conceptions, students leave class without having appreciably changed their ideas."[105] Many of the scientific notions that learners initially have are not necessarily incorrect, but they often lack the organization and structure to make them useful. The teacher's job is to help students organize and structure their thoughts and ideas so that they can become integrated with new knowledge:

The learner-centered approach looks at the learner's prior level of understanding, how preconceptions or misconceptions from earlier formal or informal experience may affect understanding, and where conceptual stumbling blocks exist. Recent research has focused on diagnosing the understanding, preconceptions, and interests a learner brings to formal instruction, so that additional instruction can build upon this base and deal with specific areas of difficulty.[106]

Helping students restructure their own knowledge involves using advance organizers and structured overviews of new information.[107] Advance organizers provide students with generalized concepts that can later serve as hooks for grasping new knowledge. In this way the new information can be readily incorporated into a student's existing framework. The structured overview implies that the teacher selects key concepts prior to the development of a lesson to provide the student with a sense of direction. The techniques are particularly important when students lack sufficient prior knowledge to help them learn the new material.

Use Cooperative Learning as a Motivation Strategy. Cooperative learning, as defined by the National Center for Improving Science Education "is not the same as the small-group learning that many teachers use."[108] Here, students are assigned to teams and each team member is assigned a role with responsibilities. While interdependence among team members develops, each learner is responsible for his or her own learning, as well as that of teammates. Such structure uses competitive, individualistic and cooperative strategies. Cooperative learning also helps students become skilled at verbalizing and gives them opportunities to consider the viewpoints of others.[109]

Cooperative learning heightens the motivation to learn. Because each team member is assigned a task or responsibility, the challenge to reach the team's goal becomes both intrinsic and extrinsic motivation. "Challenge promotes the desire for achievement, a sense of personal competence, or self-efficacy."[110] Teachers must be careful to consider the difficulty level and nature of tasks before assigning students to them. Tasks that are too easy may undermine motivation by removing the challenge, while tasks that are too difficult decrease motivation by causing frustration.

Stress Problem Solving and Major Concepts. This strategy is closely tied to the three above. Actively engaging learners in science, working cooperatively, and helping learners restructure their thinking are all best done within the context of problem solving and reaching broad understandings. Problem solving leads students to ask questions, seek relevant data, interpret data, pose hypotheses and test them, make observations, communicate findings and draw conclusions. It helps youngsters dispel the notion that all scientists are men in white coats who have all the answers. It also helps them gain confidence and feel that science really is a part of their personal lives.[111] "Seen only as a laundry list of theorems in a workbook, science can be a bore. But as a 'hands-on' adventure guided by a knowledgeable teacher, it can sweep children up in the excitement of discovery. Taught by the regular classroom teacher, it can illustrate the point that science is for everyone -- not just scientists."[112]

A number of sources in the literature suggest lists of broad themes and concepts for the science curriculum. However, the National Center for Improving Science Education recommends the following criteria for selecting themes and concepts for study:

- They build upon student's prior experiences and knowledge.
- They are interdisciplinary so learners can see their relationship to other subjects.
- They should integrate well with other science disciplines.
- They help in organizing concepts, attitudes and skills.
- They capture students' interests.
- They allow a balance of science and technological activities.

Reduce Time Spent on Meaningless Vocabulary Drill. One of the frequent criticisms of current science teaching is that it gives too much attention to memorizing terms and definitions.[113] Part of the problem stems from the fact that textbooks commonly found in the schools abound with new vocabulary words for mastery. "Unfortunately, students have responded by rotely learning the new information, by focusing only on the appropriate keyword in a question, by searching for the word in the text, and by copying the sentences that contain the word."[114] Learning keywords and their definitions does not necessarily imply understanding.[115]

Supplement the Textbook with a Variety of Resources. Earlier discussions in this paper imply that textbooks alone are inadequate in providing students with all of the learning experiences needed for higher levels of achievement in science. Teachers must, therefore, turn to a variety of other materials to expose students to different approaches to the breadth and depth of various concepts and themes.

Teach Reading Comprehension Skills in Science. Much of the information and understanding needed for science literacy comes from reading. Students who lack good reading comprehension skills are thus handicapped when trying to reach this goal. "Much science content knowledge must be gained through reading. As with most academic subjects, reading is a vital tool for the successful science student."[116]

While some science teachers simply argue they do not know how to teach reading,[117] others are finding that working cooperatively with reading teachers is paying off. One science teacher reported:

> Although presentation of reading, studying, and learning techniques initially takes some class time, I have found that in the long run, I save time. As students learn to apply reading strategies to scientific text, they are better able to read and understand assignments outside of class, and I have more time to focus on the problem solving and laboratory aspects of my courses.[118]

Use Computer Simulations. While research on the value of laboratory experiences in science learning is inconclusive,[119] there is a body of evidence that suggests simulations via the computer aid learning of some science concepts.[120] Programs such as Graphs and Tracks and Geometry Supposer are good examples. The computer allows the learner to see relationships between variables through illustrations, animations and graphs based on simulated data. Many science teachers in biology, chemistry and physics are finding these programs effective, particularly when laboratory experiences are not feasible.

Encourage Girls and Minorities to Excel. Science teachers, the same as mathematics teachers, must support and encourage female and minority students in the classroom. If the nation is to strive for science literacy for all, no segment of the school population can be neglected. Teachers can draw examples from the work of female scientists and scientists of other cultures during class discussions and presentations whenever appropriate. They can provide feedback to these students on their progress and invite their questions and curiosity. Give them lots of experiences using tools from their cultures and highlight their achievements in class. Select non-biased materials for classroom use.

Implications for Practitioners

The science curriculum offers rich opportunities for the library media specialist to get involved with the instructional program. Broad understandings in science require more than just textbook and teacher presentations. The media program can provide other needed resources and support to help learners explore the vast world of science and become efficient users of scientific knowledge.

1. Stress Problem Solving and Broad Concepts. The media specialist can help learners explore scientific concepts and engage in problem solving activities by providing a supportive environment in the media center:
   A. Evaluate the science collection with teachers to see that it contains print and non-print materials containing puzzles, games, science project examples, etc.
   B. Teach students to use microcomputer databases, spreadsheets and word processing software to help in storing, manipulating and communicating data.
   C. Use a wide variety of trade books across all reading levels to expose learners to unique approaches to science concepts.
   D. Use ready reference materials in science to create data banks, data analysis problems, and data comparison problems as a part of resource based teaching units.
   E. Use the facilities of the center for collaborative group projects in science.
   F. Display student science projects in the media center.
   G. Provide an area in the center where students can produce their own materials for projects and class presentations.

2. Teach Reading Comprehension in Science. The media specialist can support the science teacher who is working to improve students' reading skills:
   A. Gather the best trade books available to support the science curriculum. Booklist's annual list of notable books in science is a good place to start. Inform teachers and students of their availability. Take them to classes for booktalks and short discussions. Encourage students to read science biographies and science fiction for book reports.
   B. Sponsor science fiction storytelling in the media center. Alternate storytellers from students, teachers and media specialist.
   C. Subscribe to a variety of science magazines for young people. Work articles into student science units and as a source for recreational reading.

D. Sponsor science reading contests in the media center. Award winners with science books for their personal libraries.

3. Supplement the Textbook with a Variety of Resources. A natural extension of the science classroom is a media center rich in resources to support units of instruction:

A. Have students design and produce multimedia kits of science materials. Kits should contain games, slides, videotapes, transparencies, worksheets, etc. Kits can be kept and used in the media center or circulated to classrooms.

B. Help teachers develop "Kids Kits." Kids Kits (Kids Interest Discovery Studies Kits) guidelines are available through the National Diffusion Network. Each kit contains a variety of commercially produced print and non-print materials -- books, filmstrips, tapes, models, study prints, etc. Student-produced materials can be added to the kits. Kits have been designed around astronomy, birds, colors, dinosaurs, earth, ecology and many other subjects in elementary science.

C. Keep teachers informed about such hands-on programs as Kidsnet from the National Geographic Society. Kidsnet is an elementary school project that integrates concepts from science, mathematics and geography. It is student driven and uses a communications network, maps, lab notes and specimens from the natural environment.

4. Encourage Girls and Minority Students to Excel. The media specialist has an obligation to help science teachers encourage all students to learn and enjoy science. The challenge is often with girls and students from minority groups:

A. Include in the collection biographies and autobiographies of females and personalities from other cultures who succeeded as scientists. Booktalk titles in the classroom and in the media center.

B. Sponsor programs in which women and scientists from other cultures discuss their careers.

C. Improve the collection so that it includes information on a variety of careers in science. See that it gets used.

Summary

Recent goals of the science curriculum stress science literacy for the twenty-first century. Global problems that threaten the future of all forms of life on the planet make the goals imperative. Research is finding that American students are not performing well on science achievement tests, and many students report a dislike for the subject. Much of this negative response is a a function of poor textbooks, lack of class time devoted to science instruction and inadequate preparation of science teachers. Science anxiety among female and minority students accounts for some of the poor performance.

Recommendations from various quarters in the science community suggest increased class time for science instruction, less time on technical vocabulary with definitions and more time devoted to science problem solving using the scientific method, teaching reading comprehension across the science curriculum and using computer simulations to replace the often meaningless laboratory experience. Guidelines suggest that teachers expect excellence from all students, not just majority males.

School library media specialists can intervene in the science curriculum to help teachers carry out its goals in a number of imaginative ways. Together, science teachers and media specialists can assist with problem solving activities, help students increase their reading skills, sponsor supportive media program activities, and provide an environment that nurtures investigation and curiosity.

Implications for Researchers

The focus of this paper has been recent research findings in social studies, mathematics and science curricula and how library media specialists can intervene to aid teachers in carrying through with recommendations for effective instruction. Much has been said about the findings and how teachers and media specialists can work together to help students optimize their learning opportunities in these areas. The goal is to help students achieve on a level that prepares them for life in a changing global society.

While current research in the school library media field speaks to the need for media specialists to become increasingly involved in the school's curriculum, there is much we don't know about how or when this should be done. The suggestions at the end of each section of this paper are ideas from the author's work, the library media literature, curriculum researchers and scholars and practitioners in the school library media field. But are these the best intervention strategies? If there are better methods, how do we determine what they are? Which strategies work best for a given curriculum area? How does flexible scheduling at the elementary level relate to integration of information skills in the subject areas? These are questions that need to be answered so that media programs can become more responsive to the curriculum.

If real life problem solving allows students better avenues for transferring knowledge and skills to other contexts, the school library media field needs to investigate how teachers and media specialists can work to create meaningful ways in which this can be accomplished. What media program elements must be in place to allow student problem solving activities to flourish? What kinds of programs promote student curiosity and inquiry? What kinds of programs help poorer students with problem solving? Is there a special approach needed for gifted or talented students? Is there a way in which female and minority students can make the best use of media center resources in mathematics and science problem solving? How can the media specialist guide this process? Is there a relationship between content and quality of media center collections and student learning in the subject areas of the curriculum?

Interactive technologies are beginning to offer exciting opportunities for student control of, and participation in, their own learning. What can school media specialists do to enhance these opportunities? How can teachers and students interact with the media program to ensure that these technologies are used efficiently and effectively? What is the media specialist's ultimate responsibility in this process? What model or models should be followed? What kinds of empirical data are needed to design such models?

Comparative research in the field of instructional technology convinced us long ago of the value of media in helping students view the real world. We already know that when compared with the teacher lecture method, media-driven lessons in many cases are just as effective, if not more so. We are left, however, with a hodgepodge of findings that do not focus on a given scope and sequence in a single discipline. As school media specialists, we need to know how to help teachers design lessons of increasing difficulty using appropriate types of media. In this same vein, we also don't know the best sequence in which to expose students to types of print materials to help them form broader understandings in social studies, for example. Should we proceed from primary sources to secondary sources to tertiary sources? Or is another sequence more effective in reaching a particular instructional objective? Or should the sequence vary with the student's learning style? What part should the media specialist play in determining this sequence?

Finally, we need to design and test models to help teachers integrate concepts from one curriculum area into those of related areas -- history and geography, geography and economics, art and history, history and science, science and mathematics, etc. We know entirely too little about designing cooperative programs that help students acquire "big pictures" and authentic images of the world. If we are to prepare today's youngsters for life in the twenty-first century, we must begin to seek answers to some of these questions through empirical research so that future school media specialists can better spend their time implementing and refining effective programs.

<u>Notes</u>

1. Woodbury, M. (1980). Selecting Materials for Instruction: Subject Areas and Implementation. Littleton, CO: Libraries Unlimited; Bennett, W. (1986). First Lessons; a Report on Elementary Education in America. Washington, DC: U.S. Department of Education.

2. Armento, B. (1986). "Research on Teaching Social Studies." In Wittrock, M. (ed.). Handbook of Research on Teaching. 3rd ed. New York Macmillan, pp. 942-951.

3. Ibid.

4. Remy, R. (1978). "Social Studies and Citizenship Education: Elements of a Changing Relationship." Theory and Research in Social Education, 6(4), pp. 40-59.

5. Armento.

6. Hickey, G. (1988). "Creative Activities for Fostering Critical Reading in Elementary Social Studies." Georgia Social Science Journal, 19(2), pp. 20-21.

7. Ibid.

8. Ibid.

9. Cherryholmes, C. (1982). "Discourse and Criticism in the Social Studies Classroom." Theory and Research in Social Education, 9(4), pp. 57-73.

10. Tobias, S. (1982). "When Do Instructional Methods Make a Difference?" Educational Researcher, 11(4), pp. 4-9.

11. Armento.

12. Bloom, A. (1987). The Closing of the American Mind. New York: Simon and Schuster, p. 64.

13. Association of American Geographers and National Council for Geographic Education (1984). Guidelines for Geographic Education: Elementary and Secondary Schools. Washington, DC: The Authors.

14. Ibid.

15. Ravitch, D., and C. Finn (1987). What Do Our 17-Year-Olds Know? New York: Harper & Row.

16. Rothman, R. (1989, May 17). "What to Teach: Reform Turns Finally to the

Essential Question." Education Week, 8(34), pp. 1+.

17. Woodbury, p. 149.

18. Bennett, p. 29.

19. Armento, p. 947.

20. Wolf, A. (1988). "Teaching Democracy by Practicing Constitutional Concepts in the Classroom." Georgia Social Science Journal, 19(2), pp. 22-24.

21. McCann, R. (1988). "Making Social Studies Meaningful by Using Children's Literature." Georgia Social Science Journal, 19(2), pp. 13-16.

22. Voss, J., T. Greene, T. Post, and B. Penner (1984). "Problem Solving Skills in the Social Sciences." In Bower, G. (ed.). The Psychology of Learning and Motivation: Advances in Research Theory. New York: Academic Press.

23. Wittrock, M. (ed.). (1977). The Human Brain. Englewood Cliffs, NJ: Prentice-Hall

24. O'Neill, J. (1981). "The Effects of a Team-Games-Tournaments Reward Structure on the Self-Esteem and Academic Achievement of Ninth Grade Social Studies Students." Dissertation Abstracts International, 41(12), 5053A.

25. Hickey, G. (1988). "Creative Activities for Fostering Critical Reading in Elementary Social Studies." Georgia Social Science Journal, 19(2), pp. 20-21.

26. Splaine, J. (1988). Televised Politics and the 1988 Presidential Election: A Critical View." Georgia Social Science Journal, 19(2), pp. 1-7.

27. Ravitch and Finn, p. 27.

28. Bradley Commission on History in Schools (1988). Building a History Curriculum: Guidelines for Teaching History in Schools. New York: Macmillan.

29. Ibid, p. 7.

30. Woodbury, p. 150.

31. Ibid., p. 151.

32. Ravitch and Finn, p. 16.

33. Woodbury, p.155.

34. Association of American Geographers and National Council for Geographic Education.

35. Ravitch and Finn.

36. Clark, L., R. Klein, and J. Burks (1972). The American Secondary School Curriculum. 2nd ed. New York: Macmillan.

37. National Council of Teachers of Mathematics (1989). Curriculum and Evaluation Standards for School Mathematics. Reston, VA: The Author.

38. Bennett; Education Commission of the States (1989, June 14). "Tomorrow's Math and Science." Education Week, 8(38), p. 30.

39. Leutzinger, L., and M. Bertheau (1989). "Making Sense of Numbers." In National Council of Teachers of Mathematics. New Directions for Elementary School Mathematics; 1989 Yearbook, pp. 111-122.

40. Woodbury; National Council of Teachers of Mathematics.

41. Lindquist, M. (1989). "It's Time to Change." In National Council of Teachers of Mathematics, New Directions for Elementary School Mathematics; 1989 Yearbook, pp. 1-13.

42. Ibid.

43. Lappan, G., and P. Schram (1989). "Communication and Reasoning: Critical Dimensions of Sense Making in Mathematics." In National Council of Teachers of Mathematics, New Directions for Elementary School Mathematics; 1989 Yearbook, pp. 14-30.

44. National Council of Teachers of Mathematics.

45. Woodbury, p. 41.

46. Kaplan, R., T. Yamamoto, and H. Ginsburg (1989). "Teaching Mathematics Concepts." In Resnick, L., and L. Klpofer (eds.). Toward the Thinking Curriculum: Current Cognitive Research. Reston, VA: Association for Supervision and Curriculum Development, pp. 59-82.

47. Education Commission of the States, p. 30.

48. Rothman, p. 8.

49. Woodbury.

50. Romberg, T., and T. Carpenter (1986). "Research on Teaching and Learning Mathematics: Two Disciplines of Scientific Inquiry." In Wittrock, M. (ed.). Handbook of Research on Teaching. 3rd ed. New York: Macmillan, pp. 874-905.

51. Ibid, p. 851.

52. Ibid; Kaplan, Yamamoto, and Ginsburg.

53. Kaplan, Yamamoto, and Ginsburg.

54. Ibid.

55. Lappan and Schram.

56. Romberg and Carpenter; Schoenfeld, A. (1989). "Teaching Mathematical Thinking and Problem Solving." In Resnick, L., and L. Klopfer (eds.). Toward the Thinking Curriculum: Current Cognitive Research. Reston, VA: Association for Supervision and Curriculum Development, pp. 83-103.

57. Romberg and Carpenter.

58. National Council of Teachers of Mathematics.

59. U.S. Congress, Office of Technology Assessment (1988). Power On! New Tools for Teaching and Learning. OTA-SET-379. Washington, DC: U.S. Government Printing Office.

60. Woodbury; National Council of Teachers of Mathematics.

61. Kaplan, Yamamoto, and Ginsburg.

62. Lappan and Schram.

63. Ibid., p. 63.

64. Kaplan, Yamamoto, and Ginsburg.

65. Ibid., p. 64.

66. Romberg and Carpenter, p. 851.

67. National Council of Teachers of Mathematics.

68. Schoenfeld, pp. 87-88.

69. op. cit., p. 67.

70. Coburn, T. (1989). "The Role of Computation in the Changing Mathematics Curriculum." In National Council of Teachers of Mathematics. New Directions for Elementary School Mathematics; 1989 Yearbook, pp.43-56.

71. U.S. Congress, Office of Technology Assessment.

72. Ibid., p. 54.

73. Ibid.

74. National Council of Teachers of Mathematics, p. 68.

75. Clark, Klein, and Burks.

76. American Association for the Advancement of Science (1989). Science for All Americans; A Project 2061 Report on Literacy Goals in Science, Mathematics, and Technology. Washington, DC: The Author.

77. Ibid.

78. National Center for Improving Science Education (1989). Science and

Technology Education for the Elementary Years: Frameworks for Curriculum and Instruction. Andover, MA: The Network, Inc., and Colorado Springs, CO: The Biological Sciences Curriculum Study.

79. Woodbury, p. 15.; National Center for Improving Science Education, p. 56.

80. American Association for the Advancement of Science, p. 12.

81. Ibid.

82. Bennett.

83. American Association for the Advancement of Science, p. 13.

84. Ibid., p. 28.

85. Ibid.

86. National Center for Improving Science Education.

87. Woodbury; Bennett; American Association for the Advancement of Science; National Center for Improving Science Education.

88. National Center for Improving Science Education, p. 101.

89. Woodbury, p. 21.

90. op. cit.

91. Thelen, J. (1984). Improving Reading in Science. 2nd ed. Newark, DE: International Reading Association.

92. National Center for Improving Science Education, p. 78.

93. Thelen; U.S. Congress, Office of Technology Assessment; Minstrell, J. (1989). "Teaching Science for Understanding." In Resnick, L., and L. Klopfer (eds.). Toward the Thinking Curriculum: Current Cognitive Research. Reston, VA: Association for Supervision and Curriculum Development, pp. 129-149.

94. White, R., and R. Tisher (1986). "Research on Natural Sciences." In Wittrock, M. (ed.). Handbook of Research on Teaching. 3rd ed. New York: Macmillan, pp. 874-905.

95. Ibid.; National Center for Improving Science Education.

96. Ibid.

97. U.S. Congress, Office of Technology Assessment; Larkin, J., and R. Chabay (1989). "Research on Teaching Scientific Thinking: Implications for Computer-Based Instruction." In Resnick, L., and L. Klopfer (eds.). Toward the Thinking Curriculum: Current Cognitive Research. Reston, VA: Association for Supervision and Curriculum Development, pp. 150-172.

98. National Center for Improving Science Education; Larkin and Chabay.

99. White and Tisher; Atwater, M. (1989, July 14). Status of Research in Science Education. Athens, GA: Department of Science Education, University of Georgia (personal interview).

100. Thelen.

101. Bennett; National Center for Improving Science Education.

102. Larkin and Chabay.

103. U.S. Congress, Office of Technology Assessment.

104. National Center for Improving Science Education, p. 67.

105. Minstrell, p. 142.

106. U.S. Congress, Office of Technology Assessment, p. 172.

107. Thelen.

108. National Center for Improving Science Education, p. 74.

109. Ibid.

110. Larkin and Chabay, p. 159.

111. National Center for Improving Science Education.

112. Bennett, p. 27.

113. Atwater.
114. National Center for Improving Science Education, p. 78.
115. Thelen, p. 27.
116. Ibid., p. 1.
117. Atwater.
118. Thelen, p. 49.
119. White and Tisher;   Atwater.
120. U.S. Congress, Office of Technology Assessment;   Larkin and Chabay.

READING RESEARCH AND SCHOOL LIBRARY MEDIA PROGRAMS

David V. Loertscher
Head, Editorial Department
Libraries Unlimited
Englewood, Colorado

Introduction

Historically, school libraries and reading have been synonymous. In the early years of school libraries, recreational reading was the major reason to have a school library. Early professional literature emphasized the role of the librarian as reader's advisor rather than the curricular role discussed today. School librarians prided themselves that they taught the love of reading and good literature to young people. They left the teaching of reading skills to the classroom teacher and the remedial reading teacher. Today, the traditional emphasis on reading in the elementary library media program is alive and well. and so it should be. But times have changed. Teachers of reading, textbook publishers, reading researchers, and state departments of education are shifting the emphasis of reading instruction from a skills-based curriculum to a literature-based one. The nation has realized that we have a generation of young people who can read but don't and who would usually choose most other recreational activities over reading (Wittrock, 1986).

Library media specialists should be extremely pleased when they realize that literature and reading programs are merging in many parts of the country. Opportunities for collaboration are plentiful. But do library media specialists know how to collaborate in a field once considered "their territory?" What do library media specialists know about the teaching of reading? What do teachers know about literature and how to motivate readers? The assumption of this paper is that whatever distance now exists needs to be bridged if we are to raise a generation of readers, who can and like to read.

This literature review first considers what the experts say should be taught to produce a generation of readers, and how reading should be taught. Implications for library media center programs are then discussed, and the paper ends with a discussion of some major research questions that might be addressed.

What Should Be Taught

The Goals

The English Coalition Conference, a remarkable group of professionals, has suggested that the type of students they would like to see emerging from the elementary classroom would include the following (Lloyd-Jones & Lunsford, 1989, pp. 3-5):

- That they be readers and writers, individuals who find pleasure and satisfaction in reading and writing and who make those activities an important part of their everyday lives, voluntarily engaging in reading and writing for their intrinsic social and personal values.

- That they use language to understand themselves and others and to make sense of their world, and as a means of reflecting on their lives; that they engage in such activities as telling and hearing stories, reading novels and poetry, and keeping journals.

- That they use oral and written language in all its varieties as a tool to perform tasks done, to take charge of their lives, to express their opinions, and to function as productive citizens. Reading, writing, speaking, and listening will, for example, help them succeed in the workplace and conduct other everyday activities such as shopping and paying bills. They will, among other things, write letters to editors, read newspapers, fill out forms, and speak persuasively.

- That they leave the classrooms as individuals who know how to read, write, speak, and listen effectively. As competent language users they will:

  — use prior knowledge to comprehend new oral or written texts;
  — possess a variety of strategies for dealing with unfamiliar words and meanings in texts;
  — respond personally to texts;
  — comprehend the literal messages in texts;
  — read and listen interpretively;
  — read and listen critically;
  — be able to write in a wide variety of forms for a wide variety of purposes and audiences;
  — be able to read varied types of texts, including poems, essays, stories, and expository texts in both print and electronic media;
  — make connections within texts and among texts;
  — use other readers' experiences with, responses to, and interpretations of texts;
  — be able to hear literature, appreciating its sounds and cadences.

- That they recognize when language is being used to manipulate, coerce, or control them, and that they and others around them use oral and written language, and learning how to describe these uses in terms of grammar, syntax, and rhetoric. In writing, they understand how to develop different pieces and what those pieces do. In reading, they notice and monitor their own reading processes and their purposes for reading. Self-evaluation is a key component of their oral and written language activities, one that leads to a sense of ownership of their language.

- That they will have an appreciation and respect for their own language and for the language and culture of others. They will understand enough about the dynamic nature of language, language change, and language variety to be open to and understanding of communications from people of linguistic and cultural groups different from their own. They will have had many opportunities, through reading literature from various cultural groups and interacting orally with a variety of people, to be able and willing to see the world from the perspectives of others. They will not only have a sense of the richness and distinctiveness of the life of particular cultural groups, but also a sense of common humanity.

Secondary school students should:

- use language effectively to create knowledge, meaning, and community in their lives;

- reflect on and evaluate their own language use;

- recognize and evaluate the ways in which others use language to affect them (Lloyd-Jones & Lunsford, 1989, p. 19).

The Response of Research

A number of studies have been published regarding how well the children and young adults of the United States read (Anderson, 1985; Reading Report, 1985; Alvermann et al., 1987; Thimmesch, 1984; Two Reactions, 1989; Kirsch & Jungeblut, 1986) Researchers tend to agree that the nation's children are not any better readers than their parents in spite of movements such as "back to basics." They can read routine and uncomplicated reading materials, but beyond this, the failure rate is much higher than our society would be thought to have. One study stated: "Our analyses of these findings lead us to conclude that we are not a nation of careful readers nor are we highly competent information processors. In an information age, these deficiencies of young adults should be viewed as particularly troublesome. Another major finding--that there are wide gaps between racial and ethnic groups in basic and middle-level literacy skills--also has political implications." (Venezky et al., 1987, pp. 29, 52).

Thousands of research studies have been conducted in the past 20 years searching for answers to questions such as: "How do children learn to read? What is the best method to teach reading?" Little research has been done on how young people learn to enjoy reading. (Spiegel, 1988, pp. 18-24).

Researchers have divided the process of reading into skills and subskills. For example, Calfee and Drum's model of reading suggests that readers develop in five stages:

1. learning to decode (letter sounds and pronunciation skills),
2. building vocabulary,

3.   sentence comprehension,
4.   paragraph comprehension,
5.   text comprehension (Wittrock, 1986, p. 810).

Following these models, publishers have created basal reading series that concentrate on teaching skills and subskills. While the method has been somewhat successful, many have felt that a generation of readers exists who can read, but don't, because the process of learning to read is both painful and dull. Rigid basal instruction ignores the fact that "skilled readers are flexible and that how they read depends upon the complexity of the text, their familiarity with the topic, and their purpose for reading." (Anderson, 1985, p. 13).

In the late 1980s, attention focused on rejecting a skills-based reading program. (Two Reactions, 1989). Another popular method is one that embraces a whole language philosophy. Thus, we read such statements as: "It is probably a mistake to design an instructional program in which one component (e.g., decoding) becomes an unnecessary barrier to the acquisition of other components." (Wittrock, 1986, p. 813).

The California reading initiative is currently the most influential of the ideas of what and how reading should be taught. Its essential components include:

- Reading is attainable and pleasurable.
- The emphasis is on readers (students) not on reading (books).
- Learning to read is a means toward the goal of becoming a lifelong reader.
- Teachers model and inspire as well as teach.
- Parents are teachers, also. When they read aloud, listen to children read, and encourage reading, they enhance the learning process.
- Literature should be the core of the language arts curriculum.
- Books are treasures that should be accessible to all. (Cullinan, 1987, p. 151).

No matter the method, the advice from research tends to favor a phonics-based program in the early grades moving toward comprehension strategies as soon as possible (Anderson, 1985).

Major Findings

1. In a well-designed reading program, mastering the parts does not become an end in itself, but a means to an end, and there is a proper balance between practice of the parts and practice of the whole. (Anderson, 1985, p. 17).

2. Reading must be seen as a part of a child's general language development and not as a discrete skill isolated from listening, speaking, and writing (Anderson, 1985, p. 20).

3. As proficiency develops, reading should be thought of not so much as a separate subject in school but as integral to learning literature, social studies, and science (Anderson, 1985, p. 61).

4. Teachers from all content areas should be reading teachers; not just elementary teachers and reading specialists (Dupuis, 1984).

How Reading Should Be Taught

Decoding.

Decoding is most often taught through a drill and practice method of learning individual letter sounds and applying those sounds to words that follow the rules and then to words that are exceptions. A simple test of the effectiveness of decoding skills is to have a person read orally, measuring fluency as well as accuracy. Paper and pencil tests are less accurate (Wittrock, 1986, p. 825). Research has questioned the value of round-robin reading groups in which the teacher corrects the reader's pronunciation of words. On the one hand, the reader might be helped, but on the other, equally likely is that the student's concentration on the meaning of the text is broken, and loss of attention can often be embarrassing (Wittrock, 1986, p. 824).

Vocabulary.

Much attention has been focused on building vocabulary. Children come to school with a large oral vocabulary. Early vocabulary building methods try to convert this oral vocabulary into a print one and at the same time develop a sense of word meaning. Basal textbooks start with a narrow range, presenting lists of vocabulary words to learn and then providing reading passages to practice those words, both to develop decoding skills and vocabulary skills; thus the concentration on books and stories containing controlled vocabularies, and reading material "on your reading level" (Wittrock, 1986, p. 828). As students progress, vocabulary is most often taught as a function of context, i.e., the student is assumed to infer word meaning from clues given in the context, although readers can often get by without figuring out a word's meaning (Wittrock, 1986, p. 829).

The most common strategy to build vocabulary is to provide a list of vocabulary words to memorize and then require the student to be able to write sentences using the words properly. Such practices improve performance on vocabulary tests but are thought to have little effect on reading comprehension (Wittrock, 1986, p. 831; Marzano & Marzano, 1988).

Another method of developing vocabulary concentrates on grouping words into clusters that are associated in some way (Marzano & Marzano, 1988). Three popular types of clustering include webbing, weaving, and hierarchical classification, as illustrated in the following diagrams:

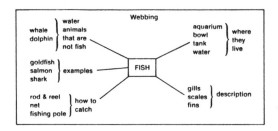

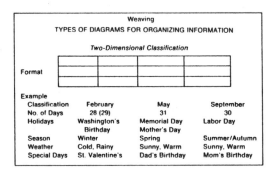

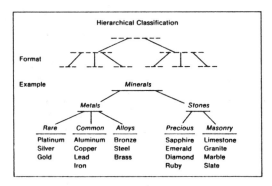

(Wittrock, 1986, p. 827; Heimlich & Pittelman, 1986)

A third method of developing vocabulary is to study the structure of the English language, building knowledge of prefixes and suffixes, roots, and word origins. Students can then deduce word meaning by recognizing the subparts of words.

Comprehension.

Students are often asked the question "What happened?" as they first read sentences, then paragraphs, then chapters, then books. Another question is: "Who did what to whom and why?" (Wittrock, 1986, p. 836). To increase the amount of thinking, students are asked to summarize and draw conclusions, to question what they read, to clarify in their own minds what they have read, and to interpret and draw inferences from what they read (Wittrock, 1986, p. 839).

A Longitudinal View

G. Robert Carlsen, a scholar who spent his career studying readers and writing one of the most used textbooks on young adult literature, summarized the conditions that discourage reading, from hundreds of interviews and written responses about reading. Below are some of his points (Carlsen & Sherrill, 1988, pp. 151-155):

Growing Up with Nonreaders. Some young people grow up in families that don't read and don't value reading. Reading motivation comes from schools and libraries.

Traumatic Learning Experiences. Young people report negative and embarrassing experiences with teachers during reading skill instruction that negatively affect their attitude toward reading. The same negative experiences happen with librarians who restrict access to materials and make libraries less than appealing.

Obstacles during the Teenage Years. Extracurricular activities limit reading time as young people get older. At the same time, pressure to read the classics, an ofttimes unpleasant experience, increases.

Educational Methodology. Book reports are cited as the number one deterrent to reading by young people. The literary notebook or reading journal fared no better. Neither did extended literary analysis of a single work. Likewise, pressure to agree with critics' interpretation on literary meaning discourages young adult readers.

> Here then are the conclusions that we have drawn from the more than one thousand reading autobiographies collected over nearly thirty years. The autobiographies preserve a record of how people remember their experiences with reading and books from their earliest years up through maturity. At times, the process may have a strange forward and backward movement. There are surprising accidents that make people readers; for others, there are just as many occurrences that keep them from becoming so. Efforts in the classroom that are designed to make young people readers were sometimes profitable and at other times detrimental. Perhaps the old farmer's comment, "I know how to farm twice as good as I do" might be applied to our teaching of reading: we know how to make readers out of people "twice as good as we do." The voices are clear and strong in articulating the direction that reading instructions should follow. The advertiser's injunction "Give me a person who reads" is but a modern echo of Bacon's statement, "Reading maketh a full man."

Other Major Findings

1. The single most important activity for building the knowledge required for eventual success in reading is reading aloud to children (Anderson, 1985, p. 23; Carlsen & Sherrill, 1988, p. 7). There is no substitute for a teacher who reads children good stories. It whets the appetite of children for reading, and provides a model of skillful oral reading. It is a practice that should continue throughout the grades (Anderson, 1985, p. 51).

2. Children of every age and ability should be doing more extended silent reading (Anderson, 1985, p. 54; Spiegel, 1988, p. 8).

3. Children improve their reading ability by reading a lot (*What Works*, 1987, p. 8; Cullinan, 1987, p. 13; Spiegel, 1988, p. 7).

4. Telling young children stories can motivate them to read. Storytelling also introduces them to cultural values and literary traditions before they can read, write, and talk about stories by themselves (*What Works*, 1987, p. 23; Aiex, 1988).

5. Hearing good readers read and encouraging students repeatedly to read a passage aloud helps them become good readers (*What Works*, 1987, p. 36; Cullinan, 1987, p. 8).

6. Analyses of schools that have been successful in promoting independent reading suggest that one of the keys is ready access to books (Anderson, 1985, p. 78; Spiegel, 1988).

7. Summer reading programs contribute not only to enjoyment of reading but to retention of knowledge over vacation periods (Carlsen & Sherrill, 1988, p. 16; Harmer, 1959).

8. The use of libraries enhances reading skills and encourages independent learning (*What Works*, 1987, p. 60).

9. The classroom environment should be filled with literature and opportunities to interact with it. Avid readers report access to a wide variety of reading materials as part of their development (Cullinan, 1987, p. 30; Carlsen & Sherrill, 1988, p. 149).

10. Gifts of books and book ownership seem to be important techniques in creating a pleasurable feeling connected with reading (Carlsen & Sherrill, 1988, p. 13; Spiegel, 1988).

11. Parents play roles of inestimable importance in laying the foundation for learning to read (Anderson, 1985, p. 27; Carlsen & Sherrill, 1988, p. 146).

12.   Reading motivation strategies complete with prizes often attract readers (Carlsen & Sherrill, 1988, p. 11; Spiegel, 1988).

13.   Efforts to make reading a pleasurable experience and an accepted practice among youth are major payoffs in encouraging reading (Carlsen & Sherrill, 1988, pp. 13, 149; Spiegel, 1988).

14.   Librarians who are competent reader's advisors are remembered fondly by avid readers (Carlsen & Sherrill, 1988, pp. 148-149).

15.   Teachers and librarians should be aware that books may produce intense personal experiences and reactions on the part of the reader (Carlsen & Sherrill, 1988, p. 150).

16.   The issue is no longer, as it was several decades ago, whether children should be taught phonics. The issues now are specific ones of just how it should be done (Anderson, 1985, p. 36; *What Works*, 1987, p. 19; Goodman, 1986).

17.   Well-written materials will not do the job alone. Teachers must instruct students in strategies for extracting and organizing critical information from text (Anderson, 1985, p. 71).

18.   Students experiencing stress in learning to read need to be able to set goals for themselves, learn how to apply the necessary skills to complete reading assignments successfully, and develop self-confidence as they master more and more reading skills (Gentile & McMillan, 1987, p. 26; Melton, 1988; Cook, 1988).

19.   A good foundation in speaking and listening helps children become better readers (*What Works*, 1987, p. 12)

20.   Comprehension is built when the teacher precedes the lesson with background information and follows it with discussion (*What Works*, 1987, p. 20; Carlsen & Sherrill, pp. 147-148; Goodman, 1986).

21.   Students read more fluently and with greater understanding if they have knowledge of the world and their culture, past and present. Such knowledge and understanding is called cultural literacy (*What Works*, 1987, p. 71).

22.   Computers can assist in learning to read, but only if the programs employed follow certain well-known guidelines common to other techniques of teaching reading (Strickland et al., 1987; Rasmussen, 1989; Reinking, 1987).

23. Linking reading and writing experiences builds both reading and writing competency (Cullinan, 1987, p. 45).

24. Techniques such as inferring character traits, recognizing story structure, inferring comparisons, distinguishing between fact and opinion/verifying authenticity, and recognizing the characteristics of a genre are useful in building comprehension (Cullinan, 1987, pp. 89-95; Beyer, 1987; Ruggiero, 1988).

25. Young people should be encouraged to develop their own interpretation of an author's meaning rather than search for the "right" interpretation (Spiegel, 1988, p. 8; Goodman, 1986).

26. Readers of all ages should be encouraged to develop the ability to understand words through context clues (Spiegel, 1988, pp. 14-15; Marzano & Marzano, 1988; Goodman, 1986).

27. A good story is an essential element in building comprehension skills (Cullinan, 1987, p. 2).

28. There is a fine line between using children's literature to teach reading skills and destroying the literature we use (Cullinan, 1987, p. 7; Pugh, 1988).

29. Books that have sequential plots and use repetitive sequences (are read repeatedly) help build reading skill (Cullinan, 1987, pp. 47-50).

Implications for Practitioners

Based upon the research findings, library media specialists can build powerful programs that mesh with the reading curriculum. A beginning list includes:

1. The amount read is critical.
   a. Flood young people with reading materials.
   b. Provide time to read, i.e., SSR, making reading something desirable when there is spare time.
   c. Promote the amount read through contests, special events, individual goal setting, etc.

2. Listening to well-read stories promotes reading.
   a. Learn to read out-loud effectively to young people, and do it often.
   b. Use storytelling whenever possible.
   c. Use tape recorded stories if they seem to help.
   d. Create programs that encourage oral reading by teachers to students on a daily basis.

3. Parental involvement in reading helps.
    a. Encourage parents to be role models: reading themselves, having reading materials easily available at home, talking about reading, etc.
    b. Involve parents in reading motivational activities.

4. Read significant works.
    a. Encourage reading the best of all genres, rather than the classics alone.
    b. Encourage reading for pleasure.
    c. Build analysis of literature.
    d. Don't destroy interest in literature with over-analysis.

5. Explore values in literature.
    a. Encourage the reading of good literature that explores values.
    b. Discuss literature in various group sizes and settings.

6. Integrate reading with listening, speaking, and writing.
    a. Create dramatic experiences with literature: choral speaking, reader's theater, dramatic productions.
    b. Use literature as a springboard to writing in any curricular area.
    c. Provide opportunities for young people to share literature orally with others.

7. Cause the reader to think as the reading takes place.
    a. Discuss literature in various group configurations. Use both content oriented questions and questions that require interpretation and synthesis of what has been read.
    b. Design one-on-one reading experiences with plenty of discussion both for analysis and enjoyment.

8. Start with phonics (decoding skills).
    a. Assist early grade teachers in the phonics program effort by helping to create enjoyable activities involving word sounds through literature (alphabet books, books featuring word sounds).
    b. Provide a plentiful supply of materials that stress sounds in a creative way.

9. All teachers should participate in a reading motivational program.
    a. Organize, plot, encourage, build, push, and create motivational strategies that involve everyone in the school.
    b. Analyze non-participation by some teachers and create strategies to encourage support.

10. Build comprehension.
    a. Engage in discussion of literature.
    b. Encourage choral reading.
    c. Promote reader's theater.

      d.   Experiment with debates.

      e.   Create any activity which has as its antecedent the understanding of written material.

11.   Promote a diversity of genres.

      a.   Build a variety of literary genres into storytelling sessions, oral reading programs, motivational reading strategies, and curricular units.

12.   Over-the-summer (holiday or break) reading helps retain learning.

      a.   Sponsor a reading motivational program for summers or breaks.

      b.   Cooperate with public libraries in summer reading programs.

13.   Book ownership seems to encourage interest and value in reading.

      a.   Develop strategies to encourage book ownership such as RIF program, book sales, etc.

      b.   Encourage young people to write and "publish" their own writing.

14.   Provide alternatives to the ubiquitous book report.

Implications for Researchers

Much effort has been made in the past probing how children learn to read, but little on the factors needed to create lifelong readers: persons who use reading both as an information tool and as a tool for enjoyment. A major review of the literature, more thorough than the one presented here, needs to be done, looking for studies in the area of reading motivation, reading enjoyment, and longitudinal studies of adult readers looking for antecedents of success. Are there good techniques of measuring how much and what children and young adults read? Could these measures be used to look at the effects of reading motivation, storytelling, and reading aloud strategies? What is the impact of whole language and literature-based reading on reading skills, reading habits, and reading enjoyment? Documentation of successful strategies for library media specialist/teacher involvement in literature-based reading and whole language programs would be of value.

Someone should follow up on the work of G. Robert Carlsen with longitudinal studies that probe the various factors responsible for creating lifelong readers, particularly the role that libraries play, since Carlsen found a number of negative influences that libraries and librarians have on reading. For example, a study of programs in which students equate good reading with libraries and programs in which students don't perceive the library as a place to get good books would be enlightening. Researchers doing studies in the area of children's literature should make a link, where possible, between what is done in reading research and their own methodologies.

References

Aiex, Nola Kortner. "Storytelling: Its Wide-Ranging Impact in the Classroom" ERIC Digest (Clearinghouse on Reading and Communication Skills), no. 9, 1988.

Alvermann, Donna E., David W. Moore and Mark W. Conbley, eds. Research Within Reach: Secondary School Reading: A Research Guides Response to Concerns of Reading Educators. Newark, Del.: International Reading Association, 1987.

Anderson, Richard C., et. al. Becoming a Nation of Readers: The Report of the Commission on Reading. Washington, D.C.: The National Institute of Education, 1985.

Beyer, Barry K. Practical Strategies for the Teaching of Thinking. Boston: Allyn and Bacon, 1987.

Carlsen, G. Robert, and Anne Sherrill. Voices of Readers: How We Come to Love Books. Urbana, Ill.: National Council of Teachers of English, 1988.

Cook, Christine W. "Self-Concept and the Disabled Reader: An Annotated Bibliography." April 1988. ED 298 440.

Cullinan, Bernice E., ed. Children's Literature in the Reading Program. Newark, Del.: International Reading Association, 1987.

Dupuis, Mary M. Reading in the Content Areas: Research for Teachers. Newark, Del.: International Reading Association, 1984.

Gentile, Lance M., and Merna M. McMillan. Stress and Reading Difficulties: Research, Assessment, Intervention. Newark, Del.: International Reading Association, 1987.

Goodman, Ken. What's Whole in Whole Language? Richmond Hill, Ont., Canada: Scholastic, 1986.

Harmer, William R. "The Effect of a Library Training Program on Summer Loss or Gain in Reading Abilities." Ph.D. dissertation, University of Minnesota, 1959.

Heimlich, Joan E., and Susan D. Pittelman. Semantic Mapping: Classroom Applications. Newark, Del.: International Reading Association, 1986.

Kirsch, Irwin S., and Ann Jungeblut. Literacy: Profiles of America's Young Adults. Princeton, N.J.: National Assessment of Educational Progress, Educational Testing Service, 1986.

Lloyd-Jones, Richard, and Andrea A. Lunsford, eds. The English Coalition Conference: Democracy through Language. Urbana, Ill.: National Council on Teachers of English, 1989.

Marzano, Robert J., and Jana S. Marzano. A Cluster Approach to Elementary Vocabulary Instruction. Newark, Del.: International Reading Association, 1988.

Melton, Ann D. "Reading Self-Concept: The Key for Success." The Delta Kappa Gamma Bulletin, vol. 54, no. 3 (Spring 1988): 21-24.

Pugh, Sharon L. "Teaching Children to Appreciate Literature: Two Complementary Approaches." ERIC Digest (Clearinghouse on Reading and Communication Skills), no. 1, 1988.

Rasmussen, Sonya. "Computers in Elementary Reading Instruction." ERIC (Focused Access to Selected Topics; a bibliography prepared by Clearinghouse on Reading and Communication Skills) (Fast Bib, no. 28, RCS), 1989.

The Reading Report Card: Progress Toward Excellence in Our Schools: Trends in Reading Over Four National Assessments, 1971-1984. Princeton, N.J.: Educational Testing Service, 1985.

Reinking, David, ed. Reading and Computers: Issues for Theory and Practice. New York: Teachers College Press, 1987.

Ruggiero, Vincent Ryan. Teaching Thinking Across the Curriculum. New York: Harper, 1988.

Spiegel, Dixie Lee. Reading for Pleasure: Guidelines. Newark, Del.: International Reading Association, 1988.

Strickland, Dorothy S., Joan T. Feeley, and Shelley B. Wepner. Using Computers in the Teaching of Reading. New York: Teachers College Press, 1987.

Thimmesch, Nick. Aliteracy: People Who Can Read But Won't. Washington, D.C.: American Enterprise Institute for Public Policy Research, 1984.

Two Reactions to the Report Card on Basal Readers: Constance Weaver: The Basalization of America: A Cause for Concern; Patrick Groff: An Attack on Basal Readers for the Wrong Reasons. ERIC Clearinghouse on Reading and Communication Skills, 1989.

Venezky, Richard L., Carl F. Kaestle, and Andrew M. Sum. The Subtle Danger: Reflections on the Literacy Abilities of America's Young Adults. Princeton, N.J.: Center for the Assessment of Educational Progress, Educational Testing Service, 1987.

What Works: Research About Teaching and Learning. 2nd ed. Washington, D.C.: United States Department of Education, 1987.

Wittrock, Merlin C. Handbook of Research on Teaching: A Project of the American Educational Research Association. 3rd ed. New York: Macmillan Publishing Company, 1986.

Other Publications of Interest

Anderson, Valerie, and Suzanne Hidi. "Teaching Students to Summarize." Educational Leadership, vol. 46, no. 4 (December 1988/January 1989): 26-28.

Children Who Can Read, But Don't: How to Help Reluctant Readers Aged 9-13 Discover the Fun of Reading. Washington, D.C.: Reading Is Fundamental, 198- .

Cullinan, Bernice E. Children's Literature in the Reading Program. Newark, Del.: International Reading Association, 1987.

English-Language Arts Framework for California Public Schools: Kindergarten through Grade Twelve. Sacramento, Calif.: California State Department of Education, 1987.

Eppele, Ruth. "Gifted Students and Reading." ERIC (Focused Access to Selected Topics; a bibliography prepared by Clearinghouse on Reading and Communication Skills) (Fast Bib, no. 25, RCS), April 1989.

Frankenbach, Charlie. "Teaching Poetry: Generating Genuine, Meaningful Responses." ERIC Digest (Clearinghouse on Reading and Communication Skills), April 1989.

Handbook for Planning an Effective Literature Program: Kindergarten through Grade Twelve. Sacramento, Calif.: California State Department of Education, 1987.

Harker, W. John, ed. Classroom Strategies for Secondary Reading. 2nd ed. Newark, Del.: International Reading Association, 1985.

Husen, Torsten, and T. Neville Postlethwaite. The International Encyclopedia of Education: Research and Studies. Oxford: Pergamon Press, 1984.

Johnson, Marjorie Seddon, Roy A. Kress, and John J. Pikulski. Informal Reading Inventories. 2nd ed. Newark, Del.: International Reading Association, 1987.

Kress, Roy. "Remedial Reading: Some Caveats When Applying Two Trends in Diagnosis." ERIC Digest (Clearinghouse on Reading and Communication Skills), no. 6, 1988.

Krippendorff, Klaus. Content Analysis: An Introduction to Its Methodology. Beverly Hills, Calif.: Sage Publications, 1980.

Lamme, Linda Leonard, ed. Learning to Love Literature: Preschool through Grade 3. Urbana, Ill.: National Council of Teachers of English, 1981.

Morgan, Mary. "Ability Grouping in Reading Instruction: Research and Alternatives." ERIC (Focused Access to Selected Topics; a bibliography prepared by Clearinghouse on Reading and Communication Skills) (Fast Bib, no. 21, RCS), March 1989.

---------. "Content Area Reading in Elementary Education." ERIC (Focused Access to Selected Topics; a bibliography prepared by Clearinghouse on Reading and Communication Skills) (Fast Bib, no. 24, RCS), 1989.

---------. "Content Area Reading in Secondary School." ERIC (Focused Access to Selected Topics; a bibliography prepared by Clearinghouse on Reading and Communication Skills) (Fast Bib, no. 26, RCS), 1989.

Pearson, P. David. Handbook of Reading Research. New York: Longman, 1989.

Resnick, Lauren B., and Leopold E. Klopfer, eds. Toward the Thinking Curriculum: Current Cognitive Research: 1989 Yearbook of the Association for Supervision and Curriculum Development. Alexandria, Va.: ASCD, 1989.

Rosenblum-Cale, Karen. Teaching Thinking Skills: Social Studies. Washington, D.C.: National Education Association, produced in cooperation with the NEA Mastery in Learning Project, 1987.

Santeusanio, Richard P. A Practical Approach to Content Area Reading. Reading, Mass.: Addison-Wesley, 1983.

Summary of Investigations Relating to Reading. Newark, Del.: International Reading Association, Annual.

Teenagers & Reading. Washington, D.C.: Reading Is Fundamental, Inc., 198- .

Thelen, Judith N. Improving Reading in Science. 2nd ed. Newark, Del.: International Reading Association, 1984.

"Understanding the Stages of a Child's Reading Development." ERIC (Focused Access to Selected Topics; a bibliography prepared by Clearinghouse on Reading and Communication Skills) (Fast Bib, no.3, RCS), 1988.

Venezky, Richard L., Carl F. Kaestle and Andrew M. Sum. The Subtle Danger: Reflections on the Literacy Abilities of America's Young Adults. Princeton, N.J.: Center for the Assessment of Educational Progres, Educational Testing Service, 1987.

Wolf, Dennie Palmer. Reading Reconsidered: Literature and Literacy in High School. New York: College Entrance Examination Board, 1988.

ENRICHING THE STANDARD CURRICULUM

Patsy H. Perritt
Associate Professor
School of Library and Information Science

and

Kathleen M. Heim
Dean of Graduate Studies
Louisiana State University, Baton Rouge

Introduction

This review focuses on research generated primarily in the library field since 1970 that suggests methods by which the school library media program can enrich the standard curriculum. Information Power (1988) addresses these efforts in the chapter, "The School Library Media Program." This chapter identifies the centrality of the school library media program to the learning process (p.15), urges library media staff members to introduce new materials (p.17), and emphasizes the need for library media specialists to engage in "intermediary" activities that ensure intellectual access to information (p.18). These activities are aimed at improving individual and group instruction and should provide motivation and excitement about learning and enjoying literature. These prescriptions incorporate ideas presented in a 1986 AASL position paper (Vandergrift and Hannigan, 1986), in which it was asserted that

> the school library media program not only enriches the curricular and intellectual offering of the school, it takes the lead in helping young people develop the kind of educated imagination that empowers them to consider alternatives and to construct possible models of a better and more humane world.

Activation of these idealistic pronouncements is difficult indeed. This review provides a synthesis of research findings to assist school library media specialists in isolating discrete variables that have been tested and found effective or ineffective in curriculum enrichment. To provide a clear understanding of this research the review is divided into five parts: (1) studies that examine overall factors associated with use of the school library media center, (2) studies that investigate the reading/information interests of students, (3) studies that assess the influence of literature, (4) studies of motivation, and (5) studies that demonstrate academic success.

Use of the Library Media Center

In most of the studies examined for this topic, school library media personnel were found to affect library use. Their interaction with teachers and selection of innovative materials were aspects of service style contributing to overall use.

A twenty-week study of seventh and eighth grade gifted students in mathematics classes was intended to determine the motivational factors for use of non-required library materials. The hypothesis that increased utilization of media center resources by a teacher will increase the use of materials by students was confirmed, but it was concluded that the teacher must be perceived as personable and knowledgeable before students will respect a recommendation (Blazek, 1975).

Policies and practices that had the greatest influence on teacher use of libraries in secondary schools of Tucson, Arizona, were informal conversations with the librarians, bibliographies prepared by the library staff, and involvement in selection of library materials (Johnson, 1975). An analysis of the use of the libraries in New York's inner-city elementary schools concluded that (1) utilization of library resources by teachers was positively related to the teachers' previous training in the use of the library, (2) teachers who made use of a variety of teaching resources made extensive use of the library, (3) there was a strong relationship between a positive attitude of the administrator toward the librarian and that librarian's qualifications for the position, (4) 82 percent of the librarians interviewed perceived the principal's attitude toward the library as critically important in the extent of library use, and (5) those administrators who rated the library "high" on a school resources scale tended to involve themselves more in school library policies and programs (Hinds, 1976). Hartley studied outstanding schools in three different sections of the United States and concluded that the teacher's attitude toward the school library and the librarian influences the predisposition to use the library (Hartley, 1980). Factors identified by teachers that act as deterrents to the utilization of media centers in secondary schools of the San Diego school district included personal and professional factors, instructional constraints, and deficiencies in the media centers (Ogman, 1977).

The introduction of comic books into a public junior high school library in Missouri resulted in an 82 percent increase in adjusted traffic counts and a 30 percent increase in circulation counts (Dorrell, 1980). Students valuing and extensively using the library program in selected senior high schools in Calgary, Canada, were positively correlated with the existence of an audiovisual component, as cataloged by the Liesener Inventory, in the school library program (Hodges, 1982).

Reading Interests of Students

Reading interest studies are complex. There are so many ways to isolate variables (by age, by gender, by ethnicity) that the overall picture tends to blur. Studies highlighted here are those that demonstrate the effect of some of these variables. Used for specific situations, however, a research base begins to emerge.

Clarke found that the quantity of reading materials available had no effect on reading interests, but that ethnic origin of a sample group of Indian, black, and white adolescents did have an influence. Comparisons between the ethnic groups revealed fifteen areas of significant difference in reading interests with more differences found between black and white students than between black and (American) Indian or between Indian and white (Clarke, 1973).

When Darkatsh analyzed the "most popular" (titles most often checked out) fiction books of nine to twelve year olds, these books had contemporary settings and language, a multiplicity of main characters, ease of readability, and desirable themes (Darkatsh, 1975). When Grover examined variables influencing the selection of library books by second graders, it was found that illustration quality and style, categories of characters, number of pages, readability level, and certain theme categories most affected choice. Book preference was affected by the sex of the child (Grover, 1976). Academically gifted students in grades four to six rated Newbery Award books highest in recreational reading interest and the classics lowest in a study by Stevens (1977), with books from the school library ranking highest in interest when compared to books obtained from other sources. Reading peaked in the fifth grade for boys and in the sixth grade for girls. Boys read over twice as many non-fiction books as girls read. Thirty-one percent of thirty-six values were not viewed as similarly important by children's librarians and seventh grade language arts students. Almost one-half of the values were recognized differently by the two groups in the reading of five Newbery Award books (Ryder, 1978).

A student's participation in specified noncurricular activities outside of the classroom was the most valid predictor of adolescents' reading orientation/interests, followed by gregariousness. High participation subjects had a significantly higher orientation to reading than did lower participation subjects. Females had a higher orientation to reading than did males (Biagini, 1980). A questionnaire that focused on "reading by choice" was administered to rural high school students. Eighty-two percent of the respondents reported that they read in their spare time, with 90 percent of these students indicating that the school library was their primary source of reading materials. Although most of the students had positive attitudes toward reading, reading was rarely selected as a favorite use of spare time (Mellon, 1987).

Influence of Literature

It has long been assumed that literature has the power to affect attitudes and possibly behavior toward self and others. Researchers have attempted to measure such changes by various methods over many years. In Youth Literature (Lukenbill and Stewart, 1988), fifty-four studies employing bibliotherapy are cited. Studies of the use of literature to influence racial and/or ethnic attitudes of children, clustered in the late 1960s and 1970s, indicated both success (Hayes, 1969; Lancaster, 1971; Kimoto, 1974) and failure (Walker, 1971; Schwartz, 1972; Bazelak, 1973; Stenson, 1978).

"Self-concept bibliotherapy" incorporating discussion led by the teacher was measured against the reading of books without discussion with fifth and sixth grade students. It was concluded that the attitude of the teacher is the major factor in whether bibliotherapy will bring about significant differences in children's self-concepts (Roach, 1975). This finding confirms previous studies that support the idea that the attitude of the counselor/bibliotherapist could be more important than the method of instituting change (Altmann and Nielsen, 1974). Two experimental studies with young children also attempted to influence self-concept. Bibliotherapy had a significant effect on self-concept on selected reading readiness measures, but not on the general areas of readiness of kindergarten children. There was a significant correlation between self-concept and reading readiness (Ray, 1983). With first graders there was a significant statistical difference among treatment groups when realistic picture books were seen and heard as a method of changing self-concept (White, 1975). In a more recent study the impact of the portrayal of black traditions in children's picture books was examined and it was concluded that black and non-black self-concepts of third grade children participating in the Michigan study did not change significantly after reading picture books with a high rating in black traditions: music, family, and race pride (Williams, 1979).

An attempt to reduce the fears of kindergarten children through the use of bibliotherapy was unsuccessful in an experimental study using the Link Children's Fear Scale (Link, 1976). A follow-up study was successful in finding a significant difference in post-test scores of those three to five year olds experiencing bibliotherapy and the scores of the control groups (Ongoa, 1979). In a suburban elementary school an experimental study that hypothesized that second and third graders involved in bibliotherapy would demonstrate less school anxiety than those involved in a control group was not supported. In this study a significantly higher level of anxiety appeared in the experimental groups when compared to the control groups (Marrelli, 1979).

The use of bibliotherapy as a strategy for increasing sixth graders' self-reliance was unsuccessful in an experimental study. Although the group receiving bibliotherapy achieved higher mean post-test scores on the California Test of Personality and the Teacher Rating Scale, the differences were not considered statistically reliable (Stephens, 1974).

There was no conclusive evidence that bibliotherapy had an effect on the attitude of third grade students toward their handicapped peers (Beardsley, 1979). There were also no immediate effects upon the attitudes of fourth grade students toward handicapped children regardless of the film or book presentation (Zaniri, 1980).

A study with fifth grade students to determine whether a classroom literature program would change the attitudes of the students toward the aged found that there were no significant differences in the means of the pre- and post-test scores on attitude tests among those who listened to the selections and discussed them, when compared to those who only listened (Schneider, 1978). Two recent studies resulted in conflicting findings: positive change in attitudes toward the elderly (Stone, 1985) and no change in attitudes (Zeleznick, 1985).

Motivation

Many techniques were shown to have some influence in generating library use. Displays, posters, involvement of children in audiovisual production, and the use of media to stimulate interest all had varying degrees of success. However, oral reading, effective booktalking, and introduction of materials appeared to generate the highest degree of success. An experimental study testing teachers' effectiveness in influencing personal reading done by fourth grade students utilized bulletin boards and selective oral reading. Oral reading was more effective than displays (Roney, 1975).

The utilization of book related media (sound filmstrips) was found to be a moderately effective strategy to promote volunteer reading of certain titles according to an experimental study with fourth, fifth, and sixth grade students. Girls were more responsive to use of the media than boys; sixth graders were least affected by the media (Roosevelt, 1978). In a descriptive study that examined the effects of an elementary school library program emphasizing personal reading development, no significant change was observed in the fifth grade students' attitudes toward reading, but there was a slight increase in the number of books read during the final two months of the seven month study. Of the four variables considered—reading achievement, socioeconomic status, sex, and Spanish surnames—sex difference seemed most closely related to reading attitudes and interests, but the evidence was inconclusive (Pointer, 1979). The effects of a lunch time program of recreational activities, including library visits, were studied in an inner-city junior high school. The increase in student visits to the library was not significant; however, there was a significant increase in the number of items borrowed from the library. Eighth grade girls had the highest percentage of borrowers (Sparks, 1981).

Fifth grade low reading ability students were the target group for a local research project on booktalking. Thirty-four booktalks given by the media specialist did influence the choice of books checked out during the three week experiment, and although the low reading ability students continued to read less than the high ability group, their reading increased (Level, 1982). An in-house survey related to booktalks given in a lower middle class, multi-cultural, multi-ethnic Canadian secondary school determined the effects of booktalks. According to the responses, the talks expanded student reading areas by introducing different types of reading and new authors and resulted in students checking out books that were booktalked (Braeder, 1984). The effectiveness of booktalks for high school students was investigated by Bodart (1986). Booktalking did not appear to have an effect on the students' attitudes. The teacher whose students scored highest on the enjoyment factor of the attitude scale also checked out the highest number of books per student. There was a dramatic increase in circulation for the titles booktalked. Gender differences on the attitude scales and in circulation were not significant: while males scored higher than females on all parts of the attitude scale, they checked out substantially fewer books than females.

In a randomized experiment to assess the effectiveness of a special eight week library-oriented treatment designed to improve high school students' understanding of, attitudes toward, and use of the school library, researchers found the library orientation to have a significant effect on students' library use, as well as on their attitudes toward the library and/or librarian. There was no measurable effect on the students' reading attitudes (Schon, Hopkins, Everett, and Hopkins, 1984). Similar studies were carried out with elementary and junior high school students. On the elementary level the findings, although not definitive, seemed to indicate that students' attitudes toward the school library and librarians and reading improved (Schon, Hopkins, Everett, and Hopkins, 1984). On the junior high level there was a significant effect on library use and library and librarian attitudes, although no effect on reading attitudes was indicated (Schon, Hopkins, Everett, and Hopkins 1984-1985).

A case study described the use of production of audiovisual materials to build extrinsic motivation into reading programs for grades five and six and special education classes. All teachers surveyed agreed that the production activities contributed to what students learned in the various curricular areas, and over 90 percent of the teachers had noticed positive effects on student attitudes, creativity, motivation, and self-concept. Responses to a student survey indicated that students came to the library more frequently as they became involved in production, and that the activities stimulated the students to go from pleasure to informational reading (Donoho, 1985). In another study, the effect of posters on children's selection of books in a public library and five elementary schools was measured. Children selected 10 percent more books from the poster table in the public library than from the table without a poster, and 27 percent more books from the poster tables in the school media centers. Children in kindergarten through grade three were more influenced by the visual displays than children in grades four to six, and to a lesser extent, the posters influenced more boys than girls (Watson, Clayburn, and Snider, 1985).

In an attempt to assess the quality of elementary library media programs in the 209 schools named as exemplary by the U.S. Office of Education in 1986, these programs were surveyed by mail questionnaires. The findings indicate that activities designed to increase employment of literature and to promote reading are the bedrock of the elementary school library media program, and that in the best programs children receive individualized attention as they interact with literature (Loertscher, 1987).

Academic Success

Numerous studies have reported the relationship of academic success and the services of school libraries, particularly elementary school libraries. Monahan (1956) found that children with access to a centralized school library read more books of high quality and a greater variety of books than did students who only had access to classroom collections. Among fourth grade students, an experimental group participated in a ten day library training program that included several visits to branch libraries, increased attention to recreational reading, and visits to school classrooms by branch librarians. The purpose of the experiment was to determine if such a program might influence the amount of recreational reading done in the summer and thus offset the traditional summertime decline in reading ability. The experimental group technique was beneficial both in information retention and reading for appreciation (Harmer, 1959). The work of Gaver in the 1950s and 1960s was particularly significant. She concluded that "higher educational gain is associated with schools which have school libraries" (Gaver, 1963). A follow-up study confirmed that students with access to centralized libraries and professional librarians scored higher overall on a standardized test, particularly in the areas of reading achievement and reference skills, than students in schools without libraries (Willson, 1965).

When sixth grade students taught by teachers alone were compared to students taught by both teachers and librarians, the results revealed that scores on a problem solving examination in elementary schools offering library instruction classes were significantly higher than scores in schools without such classes (Gengler, 1965). In a study of academic achievement in 121 Ohio elementary school libraries over a six year period, no significant difference in vocabulary development was found, but students' reading comprehension and knowledge and use of reference materials was superior in schools with good libraries and full-time librarians as compared with those with lesser levels of library service (McMillen, 1965).

When the U.S. Office of Education evaluated the impact of Title II of ESEA, 1966-1968, the findings, although inconclusive, showed that students and teachers felt positive about the use of the media center, but no significant differences in pupils' reading scores emerged (Descriptive Case Studies, 1969). The overall language ability and verbal expression of disadvantaged first grade students were significantly improved as a result of participation in a twelve week library resource program including activities using children's books and storytelling devices (Bailey, 1970). A post hoc evaluation of a three year program that developed instructional materials centers in three schools found significant gains in achievement in the areas of vocabulary and word study skills in the first and second grades and gains in word study skills and arithmetic in grades three through eight. At the high school level academic performance was unchanged (DeBlauw, 1973). Didier's (1982) investigation indicated that the impact of the professionally staffed library media program on student achievement was more clearly visible at the seventh grade level than at the fourth grade level. Student achievement in reading, study skills, and use of newspapers was significantly greater at the seventh grade level in schools with library media personnel compared to schools without professional personnel. In a 1984 review of the literature on reading aloud to children, research was cited showing that reading aloud on a regular basis for an extended period of time can influence reading and learning comprehension, vocabulary and language development, and attitudes toward reading (Stahlschmidt and Johnson, 1984).

Self-Concept

One researcher studied the presence or absence of six conditions identified as promoting students' positive self-concept in selected elementary school libraries. All conditions were present in the libraries studied, thus indicating that the school library can make a difference in the individual child's development of a positive self-concept. Conditions of independence, cooperation, and success were observed, and students found the library media center atmosphere to be positive; felt valued; had many experiences with, and opportunities for, success; cooperated naturally; and found the library media center to be a challenging area (McAfee, 1981).

Reading Research

In a survey of librarians in the nineteenth largest school district in the United States, it was found that librarians are directly involved with reading programs at all grade levels (Master and Master, 1986). Therefore several reports from the field of reading are pertinent. Research pertaining to the learning environments of early readers identified four factors: availability and range of printed materials; reading as part of the environment, both parent reading to child and parent reading alone; facilitation and encouragement of the child's use of pencil and paper; and adult responsiveness to children's attempts to read or ask questions about print (Teale, 1978). Additional research identified the most efficacious ways of parental reading. Young children performed significantly better on prereading tasks when their parents had given them opportunities to talk about and ask questions about the story and to interact orally with them; warm-up questions before reading a book to them, positive reinforcement and encouragement; and post-story evaluative questions (Flood, 1977). An experimental study determined that a librarian-centered reading guidance program can make a difference in reading achievement and attitudes toward reading among elementary school students. The treatment with fifth grade students was positively related to reading achievement scores, reading attitude scores, and the number of books circulated by the school library. Also, the reading attitude scores were positively associated with reading achievement scores (Mosley, 1986).

Personality and Communication Skills of School Library Media Specialists

Since a number of studies indicate that the personality and/or communications style of the librarian is a factor in the success of a school media program, the results of two relevant research projects are added to this review of the literature. In an examination of six exemplary public high school library media programs, the personalities of the librarians were described by using 16 PF, a personality inventory. Descriptors included outgoing, bright, stable, mildly assertive, tender-minded, forthright, self-assured, and controlled (Charter, 1982). Using a modified case study approach and results from four inventories (16 PF, Tennessee Self-Concept Scale, Study of Values, and the Bienvenu Interpersonal Communications Inventory), the personalities and communications behaviors of five successful school librarians, as identified by their peers, were examined. The pattern that emerged included these characteristics: has positive self-concept; projects warmth; is able to be self-sufficient; is confident of individual worth; views change as a positive challenge; is relatively self-disclosing; has no great need for achievement, power, or economic advantage; and is willing to take the risks of being a leader (Herrin, Pointon, and Russell, 1985).

Implications for Practitioners

Although research is somewhat fragmented, there are clear indicators of trends that should be noted and incorporated into practice.

Communication and Interpersonal Relations

Studies demonstrated that the positive attitudes of other professionals in the school (teachers, administrators) generated higher library use. It is important to recognize that the extra-library context is as critical to increasing service as the inner-library context. The school library media center staff must communicate and attract other professionals within the school. The personality and enthusiasm of library media specialists for their services is a critical first step in stimulating higher use.

> Recommendation for practice: Learn to communicate well with peers and supervisors. Show them that the library media services staff and services are excellent, and the children will be affected by their teachers' enthusiasm.

Innovative Materials

Including innovative material (comics) was found to increase use. These findings corroborate studies done in public library settings (inclusion of videos).

> Recommendation for practice: Acquire and promote various formats. Borrow techniques from public library successes. Videos have given new markets to public libraries. Try something new.

Reading Interests

Younger children are attracted by vivid illustrations, older children by themes that reflect their life experiences. Outside interests generate reading in areas pertinent to these interests. A user study—even a simple one—can affect circulation through attention to user interests.

> Recommendation for practice: Marketing again seems to prevail here. Knowing the user groups' special interests is critical. Organize small, rotating collections to meet these needs.

Influence of Literature

There is a belief in the influence of literature on attitudes and self-concept, although the research findings that support this are not strong. If anything, the presenter of this literature rather than the literature itself seems to affect attitude.

> Recommendation for practice: Literature alone does not seem to have exerted a powerful influence on the children studied, but literature in concert with a motivated discussion leader does seem to help in changing attitudes and concepts. Again, the responsibility to develop personal skills based on psychological and sociological understanding of children is critical.

Motivation

Motivation is complex and many isolated studies have demonstrated positive effects on personal reading through displays, posters, involvement in media production, or use of media. However, the overwhelming winner in motivational techniques is a skilled library media specialist who booktalks effectively, generates enthusiasm, and compels the students to learn more.

> Recommendation for practice: The ability of the school media specialist to be enthusiastic and knowledgeable about literature, coupled with identification of appropriate settings in which to introduce the literature, is essential.

> Recommendation for practice: Although personal skills are paramount, there is strong evidence that good marketing techniques do have a positive effect. Studies of public library displays should be examined in relationship to increased circulation.

Academic Success, Self-Concept, and Reading Research

Studies of academic success also include self-concept and reading research. The evidence is fairly strong that the presence of centralized libraries staffed by professionals enhances student success. Although good library support may simply be a reflection of overall better support, this should not be ignored.

> Recommendation for practice: Share the results of studies that indicate that good libraries equate with student success. Present these findings to school administrators, superintendents, and school boards. Argue for additional personnel based on these findings.

Summary for Practice

Although some techniques may be more effective than others, the glaring single finding that emerges is that a school library media professional must be effective in communication with supervisors, peers, and students. Personal skills seem to be the strongest predictor of success—the variable that must be isolated.

Implications for Researchers

The mosaic of research has many pieces in place, but it is still difficult to step back and see the picture as a whole. This is the nature of research. The process is a laborious one and must continue. Listed below are specific conclusions that emerge from a review of the five factors examined.

Communication and Interpersonal Relations

Findings seem to indicate strongly that personality factors are critical in developing the appropriate response to library use on the part of teachers and administrators. But what are these factors? Behavioral studies of librarians in the school setting need to be continued. Sociological mapping in schools where the librarian is perceived as strong in these characteristics should be developed and compared to other settings in which the librarian's personality may be viewed as neutral or negative. Since all other areas examined for this review also return to the skills of the librarian, it is essential that the characteristics of a successful librarian be understood.

Innovative Materials

More studies of the influence of innovative materials are needed. Slender positive findings make this a provocative area for further research. Studies in this area would be empirically simple to devise and execute. The example of comic books could be replicated using other innovative materials.

Reading Interests

User-community knowledge can assist librarians in developing sub-collections that can be easily organized and reorganized as needs arise. Macro-level understanding of the broad sweep and scope of what professionals deem good literature (the classics) may not be appropriate for specific groups of children. Micro-level knowledge of ethnic community composition, outside interests of children, and extra-curricular activity should enhance local use. Studies could be set up that are based on sub-collection development grounded in knowledge of the user-community and compared to collection development along macro-level lines.

Influence of Literature

Again, because reading appears to be stimulated by excellent facilitators, it seems reasonable to follow this line of research. Control groups of effective and neutral or non-effective facilitators of literature should be established and studied. Personal characteristics should be examined in isolation. Is the facilitator a role model, a parental model, knowledgeable about social and ethical issues? What personal qualities characterize success?

Motivation

Personal style of librarians vis-a-vis motivation seems the most fruitful area for research and as such is allied closely to personality studies advocated above. Comparative analysis of successful and neutral or unsuccessful motivation using the librarian as control variable should yield data in this area.

Since merchandising also appears to have some bearing on motivation, it should be easy to develop empirical studies of use through collections displayed in different styles, perhaps utilizing successful techniques from the public library sector (Sivulich, 1989). This type of study is important because it promises to be one of the few areas in which increased library use is not critically dependent upon the personality of the librarian.

Academic Success, Self-Concept, and Reading Research

This is the critical area. There are some indicators that well-staffed, centralized libraries are positive variables in academic success. Since results such as this would appeal more to funders than any other argument, it is important to continue to develop research in this area. These are studies that would require sophisticated researchers capable of isolating variables and conducting regression analyses. Schools that are models in all ways except library service should be sought out for these studies. If the research base can be enhanced to demonstrate firmly that well-staffed school libraries are a crucial variable in academic success, library support can be enhanced. Since other research indicates that personnel are the most crucial factor in success, arguments for more support for personnel might be won.

The overall problem is a circle. Excellent librarians are unlikely to be attracted to settings where resources are minimal. Without excellent librarians, nothing else will fall into place. By conducting research that provides a clear picture of personal excellence, programs of school library media education can modify curricula to develop these skills. These librarians would enhance service in the schools and demonstrate that libraries make a difference to academic success, motivation, and attitude. Once this is proven, the funding should be provided to actualize these ideals.

The challenge to researchers is to demonstrate that librarians and libraries make a difference. The first step is to understand clearly what kinds of librarians make a difference; to focus first on the skills of the librarian. This has emerged as the single most powerful indicator of success in most of the studies examined.

References

Altmann, H., and Nielsen, B. August 1974. Books and Empathy Help Troubled Children. The Canadian Library Journal 31, 384-87.

American Association of School Librarians. 1988. Information Power: Guidelines for School Media Programs. Chicago: American Library Association.

Bailey, Gertrude. 1970. The Use of a Library Resource Program for the Improvement of Language Abilities of Disadvantaged First Grade Pupils of an Urban Community. Ed.D. diss., Boston College.

Bazelak, Leonard P. 1973. A Content Analysis of Tenth-Grade Students' Responses to Black Literature, Including the Effect of Reading This Literature on Attitude towards Race. Ed.D. diss., Syracuse University.

Beardsley, Donna. 1979. The Effects of Using Fiction in Bibliotherapy to Alter the Attitudes of Regular Third Grade Students Toward Their Handicapped Peers. Ph.D. diss., University of Missouri.

Biagini, Mary K. 1980. Measuring and Predicting the Reading Orientation and Reading Interests of Adolescents: The Development and Testing of an Instrument. Ph.D. diss, University of Pittsburgh.

Blazek, Ron. 1975. Influencing Students Toward Media Center Use: An Experimental Investigation in Mathematics. Chicago: American Library Association.

Bodart, Joni. June 1986. Booktalks Do Work! The Effects of Booktalking on Attitude and Circulation. Illinois Libraries 68, 378-81.

Braeder, Darlene. August 1984. Booktalking: A Survey of Student Reaction. Canadian Library Journal 41, 211-15.

Charter, Jody Beckley. 1982. Case Study Profiles of Six Exemplary Public High School Library Media Programs. Ph.D. diss., Florida State University.

Clarke, Polly S. 1973. Reading Interests and Preferences of Indian, Black, and White High School Students. Ed.D. diss., North Texas State University.

Darkatsh, Manual. 1975. An In-Depth Examination of the Distinguishing Characteristics of Newbery Award-Winning Books of Fiction versus Current Popular Books of Fiction for Children. Ed.D. diss., University of Pennsylvania.

DeBlauw, Robert Allan. 1973. Effects of a Multi-Media Program on Achievement and Attitudes of Elementary and Secondary Students. Ph.D. diss., Iowa State University.

Descriptive Case Studies of Nine Elementary School Media Centers in Three Inner City Schools. Title II, Elementary and Secondary Education Act of 1965. 1969. Washington, D.C.: U.S. Department of Health, Education and Welfare, Office of Education.

Didier, Elaine Karin Macklin. 1982. Relationships between Student Achievement in Reading and Library Media Programs and Personnel. Ph.D. diss., University of Michigan.

Donoho, Grace. Spring 1985. Measures of Audiovisual Production Activities with Students. Drexel Library Quarterly 21, 91-104.

Dorrell, Larry Dean. 1980. Comic Books and Circulation in a Public Junior High School Library. Ph.D. diss., University of Missouri—Columbia.

Flood, J. May 1977. Parental Styles in Reading Episodes with Young Children. Reading Teacher 30, 864-67.

Gaver, Mary Virginia. 1963. Effectiveness of Centralized Library Service in Elementary Schools, 2d ed. New Brunswick, N.J.: Rutgers University Press.

Gengler, Charles Richard. 1965. A Study of Selected Problem Solving Skills Comparing Teacher Instructed Students with Librarian-Teacher Instructed Students. Ed.D. diss., University of Oregon.

Grover, Robert J. 1976. The Relationship of Readability, Content, Illustrations, and Other Format Elements to the Library Book Preferences of Second Grade Children. Ph.D. diss., Indiana University.

Harmer, William R. 1959. The Effect of a Library Training Program on Summer Loss or Gain in Reading Abilities. Ph.D. diss., University of Minnesota.

Hartley, Nell Britt Tabor. 1980. Faculty Utilization of the High School Library. Ph.D. diss., George Peabody College for Teachers of Vanderbilt University.

Hayes, Marie Therese. 1969. An Investigation of the Impact of Reading on Attitudes of Racial Prejudice. Ed.D. diss., Boston University.

Herrin, Barbara, Pointon, Louis R., and Russell, Sara. Spring 1985. Personality and Communications Behaviors of Model School Library Media Specialists. Drexel Library Quarterly 21, 69-70. Reprinted in Measures of Excellence for School Library Media Centers, edited by David V. Loertscher. Englewood, Colo.: Libraries Unlimited, 1988.

Hinds, Vira C. 1976. The Utilization of Library Resources by Teachers in Ten Inner-City Schools of New York. Ed.D. diss., Columbia University Teachers College.

Hodges, Yvonne A., et al. 1982. High School Students' Attitudes towards the Media Program—What Makes the Difference? Paper presented at the annual meeting of the Association for Educational Communications and Technology, Research and Theory Division, Dallas, Texas.

Johnson, Harlan R. 1975. Teacher Utilization of Libraries in the Secondary School of Tucson District No. 1. Ed.D. diss., University of Arizona.

Kimoto, Clayton Kazumi. 1974. The Effects of a Juvenile Literature Based Program on Majority Group Attitudes Toward Black Americans. Ph.D. diss., Washington State University.

Lancaster, Joyce Woodward. 1971. An Investigation of the Effect of Books with Black Characters on the Racial Preferences of White Children. Ed.D. diss., Boston University.

Level, June Saine. Winter 1982. Booktalk Power—A Locally Based Research Study. School Library Media Quarterly 10, 154-55.

Link, Mary Anna Shaw. 1976. The Effect of Bibliotherapy in Reducing the Fears of Kindergarten Children. Ed.D. diss., Ball State University.

Loertscher, David V., Ho, May Lein, and Bowie, Melvin M. Spring 1987. "Exemplary Elementary Schools" and Their Library Media Centers: A Research Report. School Library Media Quarterly 15, 147-57.

Lukenbill, W. Bernard, and Stewart, Sharon Lee, comps. and eds. 1988. Youth Literature: An Interdisciplinary, Annotated Guide to North American Dissertation Research, 1930-1985. New York: Garland.

Marrelli, Anne Frances. 1979. Bibliotherapy and School Anxiety in Young Children. Ph.D. diss., University of Southern California.

Master, Nancy L., and Master, Lawrence S. 1986. Perceptions of School Librarians as Curriculum Leaders. University of Nevada and Clark County School District. Text-fiche.

McAfee, Dianne Talmadge. 1981. A Study to Determine the Presence of Observable Conditions of Positive Self-Concept in Elementary School Media Centers. Ph.D. diss., University of Wisconsin-Madison.

McMillen, Ralph Donnelly. 1965. An Analysis of Library Programs and a Determination of the Educational Justification of These Programs in Selected Elementary Schools of Ohio. Ed.D. diss., Western Reserve University.

Mellon, Constance A. February 1987. Teenagers Do Read: What Rural Youth Say about Leisure Reading. School Library Journal 33, 27-30.

Monahan, Marietta. 1956. A Comparison of Student Reading in Elementary Schools with and without a Central Library. Master's thesis, University of Chicago.

Mosley, Mattie Jacks. 1986. The Relationships among a Reading Guidance Program and the Reading Attitudes, Reading Achievement, and Reading Behavior of Fifth Grade Children in a North Louisiana School. Ph.D. diss., North Texas State University.

Ogman, Mildred K. 1977. Deterrents to the Utilization of Media Center Services by Secondary School Teachers. Ed.D. diss., Northern Arizona University.

Ongoa, Esther Ruth. 1979. The Effect of Bibliotherapy Through Listening in Reducing Fears of Young Children. Ed.D. diss., Ball State University.

Pointer, Jean Marie Godwin. 1979. A Descriptive Study of an Elementary School Library Program Emphasizing Personal Reading Development. Ph.D. diss., United States International University.

Ray, Robert Douglas. 1983. The Relationship of Bibliotherapy, Self Concept, and Reading Readiness among Kindergarten Children. Ed.D. diss., Ball State University.

Roach, Lee Edward. 1975. The Effects of Realistic Fiction Literature Upon the Self-Concept of Elementary School Students Exposed to a Bibliotherapy Situation. Ph.D. diss., University of Akron.

Roney, Richard Craig. 1975. The Effects of Two Promotional Teaching Techniques on the Amount of Personal Reading and Selection of Books by Fourth Grade Children. Ph.D. diss., University of Colorado.

Roosevelt, Deborah H. 1978. An Investigation of the Effect of Book-Related Sound Filmstrip Viewing on the Voluntary Reading of Fourth, Fifth, and Sixth Grade Students. Ed.D. diss., Columbia University Teachers College.

Ryder, Mary S. 1978. Personal Values and Values Identified in Newbery Medal Award Books by Students and Children's Literature. Ed.D. diss., University of Denver.

Schneider, Phyllis L. 1978. The Effects of a Literature Program of Realistic Fiction on the Attitudes of Fifth Grade Pupils Toward the Aged. Ph.D. diss., State University of New York.

Schon, Isabel, Hopkins, Kenneth D., Everett, Jamie, and Hopkins, B.R. 1984. The Effects of a Special School Library Program on Elementary Students' Library Use and Attitudes. School Library Media Quarterly 12, 227-31.

Schon, Isabel, Hopkins, Kenneth D., Everett, Jamie, and Hopkins, B.R. 1984. The Effects of a Special Motivational Library Program on High School Students' Library Use and Attitudes. Tempe, Ariz: Arizona State University. Text-fiche.

Schon, Isabel, Hopkins, Kenneth D., Everett, Jamie, and Hopkins, B.R. Winter 1984-1985. A Special Motivational Intervention Program and Junior High School Students' Library Use and Attitudes. The Journal of Experimental Education 53, 97-101.

Schwartz, Carol Suzanne Lewis. 1972. The Effect of Selected Black Poetry on Expressed Attitudes toward Blacks of Fifth and Sixth Grade White Suburban Children. Ph.D. diss., Wayne State University.

Sivulich, Kenneth. March/April 1989. Merchandising Your Library. Public Libraries 28, 97-100.

Sparks, Jane McAmis. 1981. The Effect of a Program of Recreational Activities Made Available in a Junior High School Library upon Use of Library Materials by Students. Ed.D. diss., University of Tennessee.

Stahlschmidt, Agnes, and Johnson, Carole Schulte. Winter 1984. The Library Media Specialist and the Read-Aloud Program. School Library Media Quarterly 12, 146-49.

Stenson, Sharon Anne. 1978. The Effect of a Unit in Chicano Literature on Ninth-Grade Students' Attitudes toward Chicanos. Ed.D. diss., University of Tennessee.

Stephens, Jacquelyn W. 1974. An Investigation into the Effectiveness of Bibliotherapy on the Reader's Self-Reliance. Ed.D. diss., University of Oklahoma.

Stevens, Mary E. 1977. The Recreational Reading Book Choices of Gifted Children in Grades Four, Five and Six in Dade County, Florida Public Schools. Ed.D. diss., University of Miami.

Stone, Mary Ruth Morris. 1985. The Effects of Selected Children's Literature on Children's Attitudes toward the Elderly. Ph.D. diss., University of Alabama.

Teale, W. November/December 1978. Positive Environments for Learning to Read: What Studies of Early Readers Tell Us. Language Arts 55, 922-32.

Vandergrift, Kay E., and Hannigan, Jane Anne. Summer 1986. Elementary School Library Media Centers as Essential Components in the Schooling Process. School Library Media Quarterly 14, 171.

Walker, Patricia Ann. 1971. The Effects of Hearing Selected Children's Stories That Portray Blacks in a Favorable Manner on the Racial Attitudes of Groups of Black and White Kindergarten Children. Ph.D. diss., University of Kentucky.

Watson, Jerry, Clayburn, Marginell Powell, and Snider, Bill. May/June 1985. Persuasive Poster Power. Catholic Library World 56, 423-26.

White, David Ellinson. 1975. The Effect of Hearing and Viewing Realistic Picture Story Books on Self-Concept of First-Grade Students. Ed.D. diss., University of Virginia.

Williams, LilliAnn B. 1979. Black Traditions in Children's Literature: A Content Analysis of the Text and Illustrations of Picture Story Books about Black People in the United States to Determine How Selected Black Traditions Have Been Portrayed and to Determine What Impact These Portrayals Have on the Self Concept of Children Who Are Exposed to the Books. Ph.D. diss., Michigan State University.

Willson, Ella Jean. 1965. Evaluating Urban Centralized Elementary School Libraries. Ph.D. diss., Wayne State University.

Zaniri Toursi, Javed. 1980. The Immediate Effects of Informative Books and Films Upon the Attitudes of Fourth-Grade Students toward Handicapped Children. Ph.D. diss., University of Missouri, Columbia.

Zeleznick, Bernadette A. Borgese. 1985. The Effectiveness of Bibliotherapy on Changing Fourth, Fifth, and Sixth Grade Students' Attitudes toward the Elderly. Ph.D. diss., Temple University.

Part 2

Information Skills

FINAL REPORT BY THE AMERICAN LIBRARY ASSOCIATION PRESIDENTIAL COMMITTEE ON INFORMATION LITERACY

No other change in American society has offered greater challenges than the emergence of the Information Age. Information is expanding at an unprecedented rate, and enormously rapid strides are being made in the technology for storing, organizing, and accessing the ever growing tidal wave of information. The combined effect of these factors is an increasingly fragmented information base—large components of which are only available to people with money and/or acceptable institutional affiliations.

Yet in an information society all people should have the right to information which can enhance their lives. Out of the super-abundance of available information, people need to be able to obtain specific information to meet a wide range of personal and business needs. These needs are largely driven either by the desire for personal growth and advancement or by the rapidly changing social, political, and economic environments of American society. What is true today is often outdated tomorrow. A good job today may be obsolete next year. To promote economic independence and quality of existence, there is a lifelong need for being informed and up-to-date.

How our country deals with the realities of the Information Age will have enormous impact on our democratic way of life and on our nation's ability to compete internationally. Within America's information society, there also exists the potential of addressing many long-standing social and economic inequities. To reap such benefits, people—as individuals and as a nation—must be information literate. To be information literate, a person must be able to recognize when information is needed and have the ability to locate, evaluate, and use effectively the needed information. Producing such a citizenry will require that schools and colleges appreciate and integrate the concept of information literacy into their learning programs and that they play a leadership role in equipping individuals and institutions to take advantage of the opportunities inherent within the information society.

Ultimately, information literate people are those who have learned how to learn. They know how to learn because they know how knowledge is organized, how to find information, and how to use information in such a way that others can learn from them. They are people prepared for lifelong learning, because they can always find the information needed for any task or decision at hand.

The Importance of Information Literacy to Individuals, Business, and Citizenship

In Individuals' Lives

Americans have traditionally valued quality of life and the pursuit of happiness; however, these goals are increasingly difficult to achieve because of the complexities of life in today's information and technology dependent society. The cultural and educational opportunities available in an average community, for example, are often missed by people who lack the ability to keep informed of such activities, and lives of information illiterates are more likely than others to be narrowly focused on second-hand experiences of life through television. On the other hand, life is more interesting when one knows what is going on, what opportunities exist, and where alternatives to current practices can be discovered.

On a daily basis, problems are more difficult to solve when people lack access to meaningful information vital to good decision making. Many people are vulnerable to poorly informed people or opportunists when selecting nursing care for a parent or facing a major expense such as purchasing, financing, or insuring a new home or car. Other information-dependent decisions can affect one's entire lifetime. For example, what information do young people have available to them when they consider which college to attend or whether to become sexually active? Even in areas where one can achieve an expertise, constantly changing and expanding information bases necessitate an ongoing struggle for individuals to keep up-to-date and in control of their daily information environment as well as with information from other fields which can affect the outcomes of their decisions.

In an attempt to reduce information to easily manageable segments, most people have become dependent on others for their information. Information prepackaging in schools and through broadcast and print news media, in fact, encourages people to accept the opinions of others without much thought. When opinions are biased, negative, or inadequate for the needs at hand, many people are left helpless to improve the situation confronting them. Imagine, for example, a family which is being evicted by a landlord who claims he is within his legal rights. Usually they will have to accept the landlord's "expert" opinion, because they do not know how to seek information to confirm or disprove his claim.

Information literacy, therefore, is a means of personal empowerment. It allows people to verify or refute expert opinion and to become independent seekers of truth. It provides them with the ability to build their own arguments and to experience the excitement of the search for knowledge. It not only prepares them for lifelong learning; but, by experiencing the excitement of their own successful quests for knowledge, it also creates in young people the motivation for pursuing learning throughout their lives.

Moreover, the process of searching and interacting with the ideas and values of their own and others' cultures deepens people's capacities to understand and position themselves within larger communities of time and place. By drawing on the arts, history, and literature of previous generations, individuals and communities can affirm the best in their cultures and determine future goals.

It is unfortunate that the very people who most need the empowerment inherent in being information literate are the least likely to have learning experiences which will promote these abilities. Minority and at-risk students, illiterate adults, people with English as a second language, and economically disadvantaged people are among those most likely to lack access to the information that can improve their situations. Most are not even aware of the potential help that is available to them. Libraries, which provide the best access point to information for most U.S. citizens, are left untapped by those who most need help to improve their quality of life. As former U.S. Secretary of Education Terrell Bell once wrote, "There is a danger of a new elite developing in our country: the information elite."[1]

In Business

Herbert E. Meyer, who has served as an editor for Fortune magazine and as vice-chairman of the National Intelligence Council, underscores the importance of access to and use of good information for business in an age characterized by rapid change, a global environment, and unprecedented access to information. In his 1988 book, Real World Intelligence,[2] he describes the astonishment and growing distress of executives who "are discovering that the only thing as difficult and dangerous as managing a large enterprise with too little information is managing one with too much" (p.29).

While Meyer emphasizes that companies should rely on public sources that are available to anyone for much of their information (p.36), it is clear that many companies do not know how to find and use such information effectively. Every day lack of timely and accurate information is costly to American businesses. The following examples document cases of such losses or near losses.

A manufacturing company had a research team of three scientists and four technicians working on a project, and at the end of a year the team felt it had a patentable invention in addition to a new product. Prior to filing the patent application, the company's patent attorney requested a literature search. While doing the search, the librarian found that the proposed application duplicated some of the work claimed in a patent that had been issued about a year before the team had begun its work. During the course of the project, the company had spent almost $500,000 on the project, an outlay that could have been avoided if it had spent the approximately $300 required to have a review of the literature completed before beginning the project.

A manufacturing company was sued by an individual who claimed that the company had stolen his "secret formula" for a product that the company had just marketed. An information scientist on the staff of the company's technical library found a reference in the technical literature that this formula was generally known to the trade long before the litigant developed his "secret formula." When he was presented with this information, the litigant dropped his $7 million claim.

When the technical librarian for an electronics firm was asked to do a literature search for one of its engineers, four people had already been working to resolve a problem for more than a year. The literature search found an article that contained the answer the engineer needed to solve his problem. The article had been published several years before the project team had begun its work. Had the literature search been conducted when the problem was first identified, the company could have saved four man-years of labor and its resulting direct monetary costs.[3]

The need for people in business who are competent managers of information is important at all levels, and the realities of the Information Age require serious rethinking of how businesses should be conducted. Harlan Cleveland explores this theme in his book, The Knowledge Executive.

Information (organized data, the raw material for specialized knowledge, and general wisdom) is now our most important, and pervasive resource. Information workers now compose more than half the U.S. labor force. But this newly dominant resource is quite unlike the tangible resources we have heretofore thought of as valuable. The differences help explain why we get into so much trouble trying to use for the management of information concepts that worked all right in understanding the management of things—concepts such as control, secrecy, ownership, privilege and geopolitics.

Because the old pyramids of influence and control were based on just these ideas, they are now crumbling. Their weakening is not always obvious, just as a wooden structure may look solid when you can't see what termites have done to its insides. Whether this "crumble effect" will result in a fairer shake for the world's disadvantaged majority is not yet clear. But there is ample evidence that those who learn now to achieve access to the bath of knowledge that already envelops the world will be the future's aristocrats of achievement, and that they will be far more numerous than any aristocracy in history.[4]

In Citizenship

American democracy has led to the evolution of many thousands of organized citizen groups that seek to influence public policy, issues, and community problems. Following are just a few examples.

A local League of Women Voters has been chosen to study housing patterns for low-income individuals in its community. It must inform its members of the options for low-income housing and, in the process, comment publicly on the city's long-range, low-income housing plans.

In an upper midwestern city, one with the highest unemployment rate in 50 years, a major automobile company offers to build a new assembly plant in the central city. The only stipulation is that the city condemn property in a poor ethnic neighborhood of 3,500 residents for use as the site of its plant. In addition, the company seeks a twelve-year tax abatement. Residents of the neighborhood frantically seek to find out how they might save their community from the wrecker's ball but still improve their tax base.

A group of upper-middle-class women in the Junior League has read about increased incidence of child abuse. They want to become better informed about the elements of child abuse: What brings it on? What incidents have occurred in their own community? What services are available in their community? What actions might they take?[5]

To address these problems successfully, each of these groups will have to secure access to a wide range of information, much of which—if they know how to find it—can be obtained without any cost to their organizations.

Citizenship in a modern democracy involves more than knowledge of how to access vital information. It also involves a capacity to recognize propaganda, distortion, and other misuses and abuses of information. People are daily subjected to statistics about health, the economy, national defense, and countless products. One person arranges the information to prove his point, another arranges it to prove hers. One political party says the social indicators are encouraging, another calls them frightening. One drug company states most doctors prefer its product, another "proves" doctors favor its product. In such an environment, information literacy provides insight into the manifold ways in which people can all be deceived and misled. Information literate citizens are able to spot and expose chicanery, disinformation, and lies.

To say that information literacy is crucial to effective citizenship is simply to say it is central to the practice of democracy. Any society committed to individual freedom and democratic government must ensure the free flow of information to all its citizens in order to protect personal liberties and to guard its future. As U.S. Representative Major R. Owens has said: "Information literacy is needed to guarantee the survival of democratic institutions. All men are created equal but voters with information resources are in a position to make more intelligent decisions than citizens who are information illiterates. The application of information resources to the process of decision-making to fulfill civic responsibilities is a vital necessity."[6]

Opportunities to Develop Information Literacy

Information literacy is a survival skill in the Information Age. Instead of drowning in the abundance of information that floods their lives, information literate people know how to find, evaluate, and use information effectively to solve a particular problem or make a decision—whether the information they select comes from a computer, a book, a government agency, a film, or any number of other possible resources. Libraries, which provide a significant public access point to such information and usually at no cost, must play a key role in preparing people for the demands of today's information society. Just as public libraries were once a means of education and a better life for many of the over 20 million immigrants of the late 1800s and early 1900s, they remain today as the potentially strongest and most far-reaching community resource for lifelong learning. Public libraries not only provide access to information, but they also remain crucial to providing people with the knowledge necessary to make meaningful use of existing resources. They remain one of the few safeguards against information control by a minority.

Although libraries historically have provided a meaningful structure for relating information in ways that facilitate the development of knowledge, they have been all but ignored in the literature about the information society. Even national education reform reports, starting with A Nation at Risk[7] in 1983, largely exclude libraries. No K-12 report has explored the potential role of libraries or the need for information literacy. In the higher education reform literature, Education Commission of the States President Frank Newman's 1985 report, Higher Education and the American Resurgence,[8] only addresses the instructional potential of libraries in passing, but it does raise the concern for the accessibility of materials within the knowledge explosion. In fact, no reform report until College,[9] the 1986 Carnegie Foundation Report, gave substantive consideration to the role of libraries in addressing the challenges facing higher education. In the initial release of the study's recommendations, it was noted that

> The quality of a college is measured by the resources for learning on the campus and the extent to which students become independent, self-directed learners. And yet we found that today, about one out of every four undergraduates spends no time in the library during a normal week, and 65 percent use the library four hours or less each week. The gap between the classroom and the library, reported by almost a half-century ago, still exists today.[10]

Statistics such as these document the general passivity of most academic learning today and the divorce of the impact of the Information Age from prevailing teaching styles.

The first step in reducing this gap is making sure that the issue of information literacy is an integral part of current efforts at cultural literacy, the development of critical thinking abilities, and school restructuring. Due to the relative newness of the information society, however, information literacy is often completely overlooked in relevant dialogues, research, and experimentation. Moreover, most current educational and communication endeavors—with their long-standing history of pre-packaging information—militate against the development of even an awareness of the end to master information management skills.

The effects of such prepackaging of information are most obvious in the school and academic settings. Students, for example, receive predigested information from lectures and textbooks, and little in their environment fosters active thinking or problem solving. What problem solving does occur is within artificially constructed and limited information environments that allow for single "correct" answers. Such exercises bear little resemblance to problem solving in the real world where multiple solutions of varying degrees of usefulness must be pieced together—often from many disciplines and from multiple information sources such as online databases, videotapes, government documents, and journals.

Education needs a new model of learning—learning that is based on the information resources of the real world and learning that is active and integrated, not passive and fragmented. On an intellectual level, many teachers and school administrators recognize that lectures, textbooks, materials put on reserve, and tests that ask students to regurgitate data from these sources do not create an active, much less a quality, learning experience. Moreover, studies at the higher education level have proven that students fail to retain most information they are "given."

> The curve for forgetting course content is fairly steep: a generous estimate is that students forget 50% of the content within a few months.... A more devastating finding comes from a study that concluded that even under the most favorable conditions, "students carry away in their heads and in their notebooks not more than 42% of the lecture content." Those were the results when students were told that they would be tested immediately following the lecture; they were permitted to use their notes; and they were

given a prepared summary of the lecture. These results were bad enough, but when students were tested a week later, without the use of their notes, they could recall only 17% of the lecture material.[11]

Because of the rapidly shrinking halflife of information, even the value of that 17 percent that students do remember must be questioned. To any thoughtful person, it must be clear that teaching facts is a poor substitute for teaching people how to learn, i.e., giving them the skills to be able to locate, evaluate, and effectively use information for any given need.

What is called for is not a new information studies curriculum but, rather, a restructuring of the learning process. Textbooks, workbooks, and lectures must yield to a learning process based on the information resources available for learning and problem solving throughout people's lifetimes—to learning experiences that build a lifelong habit of library use. Such a learning process would actively involve students in the process of:

- knowing when they have a need for information;
- identifying information needed to address a given problem or issue;
- finding needed information;
- evaluating the information;
- organizing the information;
- using the information effectively to address the problem or issue at hand.

Such a restructuring of the learning process will not only enhance the critical thinking skills of students but will also empower them for lifelong learning and the effective performance of professional and civic responsibilities.

An Information Age School

An increased emphasis on information literacy and resource-based learning would manifest itself in a variety of ways at both the academic and school levels, depending upon the role and mission of the individual institution and the information environment of its community. However, the following description of what a school might be like if information literacy were a central, not a peripheral, concern reveals some of the possibilities. (While focused on K-12, outcomes could be quite similar at the college level.)

The school would be more interactive, because students, pursuing questions of personal interest, would be interacting with other students, with teachers, with a vast array of information resources, and the community at large to a far greater degree than they presently do today. One would expect to find every student engaged in at least one open-ended, long-term quest for an answer to a serious social, scientific, aesthetic, or political problem. Students' quests would involve not only searching print, electronic, and video data, but also interviewing people inside and outside of school. As a result, learning would be more self-initiated. There would be more reading of original sources and more extended writing. Both students and teachers would be familiar with the intellectual and emotional demands of asking productive questions, gathering data of all kinds, reducing and synthesizing information, and analyzing, interpreting, and evaluating information in all its forms.

In such an environment, teachers would be coaching and guiding students more and lecturing less. They would have long since discovered that the classroom computer, with its access to the libraries and databases of the world, is a better source of facts than they could ever hope to be. They would have come to see that their major importance lies in their capacity to arouse curiosity and guide it to a satisfactory conclusion, to ask the right questions at the right time, to stir debate and serious discussion, and to be models themselves of thoughtful inquiry.

Teachers would work consistently with librarians, media resource people, and instructional designers both within their schools and in their communities to ensure that student projects and explorations are challenging, interesting, and productive learning experiences in which they can all take pride. It would not be surprising in such a school to find a student task force exploring an important community issue with a view toward making a public presentation of its findings on cable television or at a news conference. Nor would it be unusual to see the librarian guiding the task force through its initial questions and its multidisciplinary, multimedia search—all the way through to its cable or satellite presentation. In such a role, librarians would be valued for their information expertise and their technological know-how. They would lead frequent in-service teacher workshops and ensure that the school was getting the most out of its investment in information technology.

Because evaluation in such a school would also be far more interactive than it is today, it would also be a much better learning experience. Interactive tutoring software that guides students through their own and other knowledge bases would provide more useful diagnostic information than is available today. Evaluation would be based upon a broad range of literacy indicators, including some that assess the quality and appropriateness of information sources or the quality and efficiency of the information searches themselves. Assessments would attend to ways in which students are using their minds and achieving success as information consumers, analyzers, interpreters, evaluators, and communicators of ideas.

Finally, one would expect such a school to look and sound different from today's schools. One would see more information technology than is evident today, and it would be important to people not only in itself but also in regard to its capacity to help them solve problems and create knowledge. One would see the fruits of many student projects prominently displayed on the walls and on bookshelves, and one would hear more discussions and debate about substantive, relevant issues. On the playground, in the halls, in the cafeteria, and certainly in the classroom, one would hear fundamental questions that make information literacy so important: "How do you know that?" and "What evidence do you have for that?" "Who says?" and "How can we find out?"

Conclusion

This call for more attention to information literacy comes at a time when many other learning deficiencies are being expressed by educators, business leaders, and parents. Many workers, for example, appear unprepared to deal effectively with the challenges of high-tech equipment. There exists a need for better thinkers, problem solvers, and inquirers. There are calls for computer literacy, civic literacy, global literacy, and cultural literacy. Because we have been hit by a tidal wave of information, what used to suffice as literacy no longer suffices; what used to count as effective knowledge no longer meets our needs; what used to pass as a good education no longer is adequate.

The one common ingredient in all of these concerns is an awareness of the rapidly changing requirements for a productive, healthy, and satisfying life. To respond effectively to an ever-changing environment, people need more than just a knowledge base, they also need techniques for exploring it, connecting it to other knowledge bases, and making practical use of it. In other words, the landscape upon which we used to stand has been transformed, and we are being forced to establish a new foundation called information literacy. Now knowledge—not minerals or agricultural products or manufactured goods—is this country's most precious commodity, and people who are information literate—who know how to acquire knowledge and use it—are America's most valuable resource.

Committee Recommendations

To reap the benefits from the Information Age by our country, its citizens, and its businesses, the American Library Association Presidential Committee on Information Literacy makes the following recommendations:

1. *We all must reconsider the ways we have organized information institutionally, structured information access, and defined information's role in our lives at home, in the community, and in the work place.*

To the extent that our concepts about knowledge and information are out of touch with the realities of a new, dynamic information environment, we must reconceptualize them. The degrees and directions of reconceptualization will vary, but the aims should always be the same: to communicate the power of knowledge; to develop in each citizen a sense of his or her responsibility to acquire knowledge and deepen insight through better use of information and related technologies; to instill a love of learning, a thrill in searching, and a joy in discovering; and to teach young and old alike how to know when they have an information need and how to gather, synthesize, analyze, interpret, and evaluate the information around them. All of these abilities are equally important for the enhancement of life experiences and for business pursuits.

Colleges, schools, and businesses should pay special attention to the potential role of their libraries or information centers. These should be central, not peripheral; organizational redesigns should seek to empower students and adults through new kinds of access to information and new ways of creating, discovering, and sharing it.

2. A Coalition for Information Literacy should be formed under the leadership of the American Library Association, in coordination with other national organizations and agencies, to promote information literacy.

The major obstacle to promoting information literacy is a lack of public awareness of the problems created by information illiteracy. The need for increased information literacy levels in all aspects of people's lives—in business, in family matters, and civic responsibilities—must be brought to the public's attention in a forceful way. To accomplish this, the Coalition should serve as an educational network for communications, coalescing related educational efforts, developing leadership, and effecting change. The Coalition should monitor and report on state efforts to promote information literacy and resource-based learning and provide recognition of individuals and programs for their exemplary information literacy efforts.

The Coalition should be organized with an advisory committee made up of nationally prominent public figures from librarianship, education, business, and government. The responsibilities of the advisory committee should include support for Coalition efforts in the areas of capturing media attention, raising public awareness, and fostering a climate favorable for information literacy. In addition, the advisory committee should actively seek funding to promote research and demonstration projects.

3. Research and demonstration projects related to information and its use need to be undertaken.

To date, remarkably little research has been done to understand how information can be more effectively managed to meet educational and societal objectives or to explore how information management skills impact on overall school and academic performance. What research does exist appears primarily in library literature, which is seldom read by educators or state decision makers.

For future efforts to be successful, a national research agenda should be developed and implemented. The number of issues needing to be addressed are significant and should include the following:

- What are the social effects of reading?
- With electronic media eclipsing reading for many people, what will be the new place of the printed word?
- How do the characteristics of information resources (format, length, age) affect their usefulness?
- How does the use of information vary by discipline?
- How does access to information impact on the effectiveness of citizen action groups?
- How do information management skills affect student performance and retention?
- What role can information management skills play in the economic and social advancement of minorities?

Also needed is research that will promote a "sophisticated understanding of the full range of the issues and processes related to the generation, distribution, and use of information so that libraries can fulfill their obligations to their users and potential users and so that research and scholarship in all fields can flourish."[12]

The Coalition can play a major role in obtaining funding for such research and for fostering demonstration projects that can provide fertile ground for controlled experiments that can contrast benefits from traditional versus resource-based learning opportunities for students.

4. *State Departments of Education, Commissions on Higher Education, and Academic Governing Boards should be responsible to ensure that a climate conducive to students' becoming information literate exists in their states and on their campuses.*

Of importance are two complementary issues: the development of an information literate citizenry and the move from textbook and lecture-style learning to resource-based learning. The latter is, in fact, the means to the former as well as to producing lifelong, independent, and self-directed learners. As is appropriate within their stated missions, such bodies are urged to do the following:

- To incorporate the spirit and intent of information literacy into curricular requirements, recommendations, and instructional materials. (Two excellent models for state school guidelines are Washington's "Information Skills Curriculum Guide: Process Scope and Sequence" and "Library Information Skills: Guide for Oregon Schools K-12.")

- To incorporate in professional preparation and in-service training for teachers an appreciation for the importance of resource-based learning, to encourage implementation of it in their subject areas, and to provide opportunities to master implementation techniques.

- To encourage and support coordination of school/campus and public library resources/services with classroom instruction in offering resource-based learning.

- To include coverage of information literacy competencies in state assessment examinations.

- To establish recognition programs of exemplary projects for learning information management skills in elementary and secondary schools, in higher education institutions, and in professional preparation programs.

5. *Teacher education and performance expectations should be modified to include information literacy concerns.*

Inherent in the concepts of information literacy and resource-based learning is the complementary concept of the teacher as a facilitator of student learning rather than as presenter of ready-made information. To be successful in such roles, teachers should make use of an expansive array of information resources. They should be familiar with and able to use selected databases, learning networks, reference materials, textbooks, journals, newspapers, magazines, and other resources. They also should place a premium on problem solving and see that their classrooms are extended outward to encompass the learning resources of the library media centers and the community. They also should expect their students to become information literate.

- To encourage the development of teachers who are facilitators of learning, the following recommendations are made to schools of teacher education. Those responsible for in-service teacher training should also evaluate current capabilities of teaching professionals and incorporate the following recommendations into their programs as needed.

- New knowledge from cognitive research on thinking skills should be incorporated into pedagogical skills development.

- Integral to all programs should be instruction in managing the classroom, individualizing instruction, setting problems, questioning, promoting cooperative learning—all of which should rely on case studies and information resources of the entire school and community.

- Instruction within the disciplines needs to emphasize a problem-solving approach and the development of a sophisticated level of information management skills appropriate to the individual disciplines.

- School library media specialists need to view the instructional goals of their schools as an integral part of their own concern and responsibilities and should actively contribute toward the ongoing professional development of teachers and principals. They should be members of curriculum and instructional teams and provide leadership in integrating appropriate information and educational technologies into school programming. (For further recommendations regarding the role of library media specialists, consult Information Power: Guidelines for School Media Programs prepared by the American Association of School Librarians and the Association for Educational Communications and Technology, 1988.)

- Exit requirements from teacher education programs should include each candidate's ability to use selected databases, networks, reference materials, administrative and instructional software packages, and new forms of learning technologies.

- A portion of the practicum or teaching experience of beginning teachers should be spent with library media specialists. These opportunities should be based in the school library media center to promote an understanding of resources available in both that facility and other community libraries and to emphasize the concepts and skills necessary to become a learning facilitator.

- Cooperative, or supervising, teachers who can demonstrate their commitment to thinking skills instruction and information literacy should be matched with student teachers, and teachers who see themselves as learning facilitators should be relied upon to serve as role models. Student teachers should also have the opportunity to observe and practice with a variety of models for the teaching of critical thinking.

6. An understanding of the relationship of information literacy to the themes of the White House Conference on Library and Information Services should be promoted.

The White House conference themes of literacy, productivity, and democracy will provide a unique opportunity to foster public awareness of the importance of information literacy. (The conference will be held sometime between September 1989 and September 1991.) The American Library Association and the Coalition on Information Literacy should aggressively promote consideration of information literacy within state deliberations as well as within the White House conference itself.

Background to Report

The American Library Association's Presidential Committee on Information Literacy was appointed in 1987 by ALA President Margaret Chisholm with three expressed purposes:

(1) to define information literacy within the higher literacies and its importance to student performance, lifelong learning, and active citizenship;

(2) to design one or more models for information literacy development appropriate to formal and informal learning environments throughout people's lifetimes; and

(3) to determine implications for the continuing education and development of teachers.

The Committee, which consists of leaders in education and librarianship, has worked actively to accomplish its mission since its establishment. Members of the Committee include the following: Gordon M. Ambach, Executive Director, Council of Chief State School Officers; William L. Bainbridge, President, School Match; Patricia Senn Breivik, Chair, Director, Auraria Library, University of Colorado at Denver; Rexford Brown, Director, Policies and the Higher Literacies Project, Education Commission of the States; Judith S. Eaton, President, Community College of Philadelphia; David Imig, Executive Director, American Association of Colleges for Teacher Education; Sally Kilgore, Professor, Emory University, (former Director of the Office of Research, U.S. Department of Education); Carol Kuhlthau, Director, Educational Media Services Programs, Rutgers University; Joseph Mika, Director, Library Science Program, Wayne State University; Richard D. Miller, Executive Director, American Association of School Administrators; Roy D. Miller, Executive Assistant to the Director, Brooklyn Public Library; Sharon J. Rogers, University Librarian, George Washington University; Robert Wedgeworth, Dean, School of Library Service, Columbia University.

This report was released on January 10, 1989, in Washington, D.C.

Further Information Further information on information literacy can be obtained by contacting: Information Literacy and K-12, c/o American Association of School Librarians, American Library Association, 50 East Huron Street, Chicago, IL 60611; Information Literacy and Higher Education, c/o Association of College and Research Libraries, American Library Association, 50 East Huron Street, Chicago, IL 60611.

References

1. Terrell H. Bell, Communication to CU President E. Gordon Gee, September 1986.

2. Herbert E. Meyer, Real World Intelligence: Organized Information for Executives (New York: Weidenfeld & Nicholson, 1987), p.24.

3. James B. Tchobanoff, "The Impact Approach: Value as Measured by the Benefit of the Information Professional to the Parent Organization," in President's Task Force on the Value of the Information Professional (Anaheim, Calif.: Special Libraries Assn., June 10, 1987), p. 47.

4. Harlan Cleveland, The Knowledge Executive: Leadership in an Information Society (New York: Dutton, 1985), p.xviii.

5. Joan C. Durrance, Armed for Action: Library Response to Citizen Information Needs (New York: Neal-Schuman, 1984), p.ix.

6. Major Owens, "State Government and Libraries," Library Journal 101 (1 January 1976): 27.

7. United States National Commission on Excellence in Education, A Nation at Risk: The Imperative for Educational Reform (Washington, D.C.: U.S. Government Printing Office, 1983).

8. Frank Newman, Higher Education and the American Resurgence (Princeton, N.J.: Princeton University Press, 1985), p.152.

9. Ernest L. Boyer, College: The Undergraduate Experience in America (New York: Harper & Row, 1987).

10. "Prologue and Major Recommendations of Carnegie Foundation's Report on Colleges," Chronicle of Higher Education 33 (5 November 1986): 10-11.

11. K. Patricia Cross, "A Proposal to Improve Teaching or What Taking Teaching Seriously Should Mean," AAHE Bulletin 39 (September 1986): 10-11.

12. Edward Connery Lathem, ed., American Libraries as Centers of Scholarship (Hanover, N.H.: Dartmouth College, 1978), p.58.

Bibliography

Patricia Senn Breivik, "Making the Most of Libraries in the Search for Academic Excellence," Change (July/August 1987) 19: 44-52.

Patricia Senn Breivik and Robert Wedgeworth, Libraries and the Search for Academic Excellence. Metuchen, N.J.: Scarecrow Press, 1988. Papers from a National Symposium sponsored by Columbia University and the University of Colorado, New York, March 15-17, 1987.

Larry Hardesty, Nicholas P. Lovrich, Jr., and James Mannon, "Library Use Instruction: Assessment of the Long-Term Effects," College & Research Libraries (January 1982) 43: 38-46.

James A. Hyatt and Aurora A. Santiago, University Libraries in Transition. Washington, D.C.: National Association of College and University Business Officers, 1987.

David W. Lewis, "Inventing the Electronic University," College & Research Libraries (July 1988) 49: 291-304.

"The Literacy Gap," Time, December 19, 1988: 56-57.

Barbara B. Moran, Academic Libraries: The Changing Knowledge Center of Colleges and Universities. Asheeric Higher Education Research Report, No. 8. Washington, D.C.: Association for the Study of Higher Education, 1984.

CURRENT THEMES REGARDING LIBRARY AND INFORMATION SKILLS INSTRUCTION

Michael B. Eisenberg
Associate Professor
School of Information Studies
Syracuse University, Syracuse, New York

Michael K. Brown
Library Media Specialist
Liverpool Public Schools
Liverpool, New York

Introduction

Instruction in library and information skills is widely accepted as one of the major functions of the library media program. Support for this teaching role is found in the mission statement of <u>Information Power</u> (1988, p. 1) and in the first articulated objective:

Mission: To ensure that students and staff are effective users of ideas and information.

Objective 1:   To provide intellectual access to information through systematic learning activities which develop cognitive strategies for selecting, retrieving, analyzing, evaluating, synthesizing and creating information at all age levels and in all curriculum content areas.

Four major themes about library and information skills instruction are assumed within these two statements. These themes represent widespread current beliefs about the value of library and information skills, the nature and scope of skills instruction, and effective approaches to teaching library and information skills:

(1)   Instruction in library and information skills is a valuable and essential part of the school's educational program.

(2)   Essential library and information skills encompass more than just location of and access to sources. The skills curriculum should emphasize general information problem-solving and research processes and the specific skills within these general processes (e.g., selection, analysis, synthesis, and evaluation).

(3)   Library and information skills should not be taught in isolation. The skills program must be fully integrated with the school's curriculum.

(4)   The use of innovative instructional methods and technologies can enhance the teaching of library and information skills.

Few persons associated with the library media profession would disagree with these fundamental assumptions about the instructional role of the library media program. Of course it is worthwhile to provide instruction in library and information skills. And certainly, students today need to learn what to do with information and not just how to find it. Additionally, both experience and intuition lead us to the conclusion that students are more likely to retain and use skills if they are taught in conjunction with actual classroom content. Finally, library and information skills instruction will certainly be improved by utilizing modern instructional technologies and methods.

These four themes represent understandings and assumptions that pervade the literature, state and local standards and curricula, and guidelines for library media programs on all levels. Many seemingly excellent library and information skills instructional programs are built on them. Still, critical and difficult questions must be asked: Do we really know these themes to be accurate? Is there hard evidence to confirm them? Have they withstood careful scrutiny by researchers?

Common practice and intuition are not enough. If teachers, administrators, and school boards are to make a commitment to developing library media programs, they need research facts about the importance of library and information skills to overall student performance and achievement. Also, if library media specialists are to deliver effective skills instruction, they must be able to draw upon documented conclusions about those skills that are most important and the approaches most likely to result in success.

The purpose of this paper is to review the status of each of these themes from a research perspective. What research is available and what do the studies say? Which aspects of these themes have been investigated and what can we conclude? How strong is the evidence supporting these themes, and can we draw reliable and valid conclusions? And if evidence is lacking, what are to be the major questions and issues that must be answered? Time and space make it impossible to cover all related studies here, but an earnest attempt is made to cover a range of relevant research.

Theme 1: The Value of Library and Information Skills Instruction

Because the overall issue of the value of library and information skills instruction for students is so crucial, one would expect to find abundant current research on this topic. Yet there are a surprisingly limited number of studies that directly focus on questions of impact and worth of library and information skills instruction. In her substantive review of over 35 research studies relating to the impact of library media programs on student learning and achievement, Didier (1985) reported results from only six studies that directly focus on the value of skills instruction, none more recent than 1974. Summarizing from all studies, Didier does conclude that various aspects of school library media programs can have a positive impact on student achievement. The research specific to library and information skills instruction confirms that knowledge of library skills can be related to improvements in student achievement, performance on standardized tests, and grade point average. Didier stated that skills instruction and general library media programs can make a positive contribution to "development of reading skills, overall academic achievement, library skills, vocabulary and word study skills, verbal expression, problem-solving ability, and breadth and quality of general reading (p. 34).

In more recent research, Gifford and Gifford (1984) examined the effects of a two-week library skills instruction unit upon 7th graders. Examples of the skills taught were how to care for a book; different parts of a book; student responsibilities when checking out materials; and how to use reference materials, other nonfiction books, and the card catalog. The two evaluation measures were frequency of use of the library media center after the unit and amount of help requested after the unit. "Results of the study indicate that teaching a two-week unit on library usage did significantly increase the total usage of the library (p. 5). It was also found that the experimental group requested assistance significantly less often than the control group, 15 times vs. 51 times.

The positive influence of library media instruction on achievement is supported by Gilliland's (1986) finding that an ongoing library media instruction effort aimed at reviewing and reinforcing "study-locational" skills improved student scores on the study-locational portion of the California Assessment Program test. In her studies on the research process, Kuhlthau (1989) reported that the way students go through the search process affects their confidence and their final products. Increased confidence relates to students learning more about their topics and developing thoughts about the topics. Higher confidence correlates with more focused papers, which are also graded slightly higher.

In her doctoral thesis, Goodin (1987) looked at library research skills and the issue of transferability of skills from high school to college. High school students in college preparatory English classes were divided into experimental and control groups. Both groups received pre-tests on basic college library information knowledge, a research paper assignment, and a post-test. A Likert-type attitude scale was administered to all high school students and again to selected students during their first semester in college. The experimental groups also received a series of lessons on the research process taught by the high school librarian. The program of instruction was based on recommendations of 62 college faculty members. Goodin found that the high school students who received instruction scored significantly higher on the post-test than students who did not. In college, students indicated that they were able to effectively use the skills learned in high school to conduct research for courses. There were no significant differences between groups on the attitude questionnaire, perhaps reflecting the inability of this particular instrument to measure transferability.

In summary, there is some research to support the contention that library and information skills instruction has a positive impact on student achievement and overall skill development. Library media specialists can point to these findings in their efforts to acquire the support and resources needed to develop quality instructional programs.

Additional research is definitely needed to fully explore this theme. Kuhlthau (1989) pointed out that library media specialists have difficulty in measuring the impact of library use on learning and that further research is required on the influence of information search processes on student products. More specific questions for investigation include:

- Does library and information skills instruction contribute to student achievement in specific subject areas as well as to overall student achievement?
- If so, how does one measure the impact of library and information skills instruction on the achievement of specific subject area learning objectives?
- Does library and information skills instruction influence student attitude and motivation?
- To what degree does library and information skills instruction at one level influence performance at subsequent levels?
- To what extent does library and information skills instruction at levels K-12 affect college performance and lifelong learning?
- Does library and information skills instruction require changes in schools' information environments? For example, it seems clear that changes in technology will cause changes in the types of information resources offered. If students develop improved library and information skills, does this require likewise changes in resources, systems, services, and roles of teachers and students?

Theme 2: The Nature and Scope of Library and Information Skills

Understandings in this theme relate to the content side of library and information skills: What does the library and information skills curriculum encompass? What specific skills are to be taught? What are the choices for overall frameworks or models for skills instruction? Is one framework preferable to another? What is the relationship of the library and information skills curriculum to subject area curriculum: where are the boundaries and overlaps?

Traditionally, library instruction focused on skills related to sources: locating, accessing, and using them. These isolated, "library-dependent" skills were frequently taught out of subject context, without any formal articulated curricular framework. Later, library media specialists developed scope and sequences of skills, although most still emphasized a source approach.

In recent years, a new approach to skills instruction has emerged, one that centers on a process approach to library and information skills. This approach is not dependent on any particular source or library. The emphasis is on developing transferable cognitive skills that should increase students' effective use of information in general as well as their use of specific libraries and resources. Recent examples of the process approach include Kuhlthau's (1985b) process model for library research; the "Big Six Skills" information problem-solving framework of Eisenberg and Berkowitz (1988); Cutlip's (1988) view of library media skills within the broad framework of the "Learning and Information Model;" and Stripling and Pitts's (1988) description of library research as a thinking process with 10 steps. All these works share the belief that specific library and information skills should be taught within the context of an overall process.

Unfortunately, with the notable exception of Kuhlthau, these and other process models for library and information skills were developed independently of any formal research. That is, while most have been developed after years of practical experience working with students and meeting their needs, the models are not empirically derived nor tested in any formal field or laboratory study. While this fact does not necessarily detract from the importance or usefulness of these works it does point out a glaring need for verification of process frameworks in real settings as well as the desirability of basing process frameworks on empirically derived models of cognition.

As noted, the one encouraging research effort in this area is Kuhlthau's series of investigations on the information search process. Using a number of methodologies (e.g., case studies, interviews, observations, content analysis), she developed a six-stage model of the research process: initiation, selection, exploration, formulation, collection, and presentation, and also identified thoughts and feelings that go along with each step (Kuhlthau, 1985a). The model holds up over time with the perceptions of students previously studied matching the model even more closely after college (Kuhlthau, 1988). The model has also been confirmed with high school students of high and middle abilities (Kuhlthau, 1989), with further study needed on students of low abilities. For more detail on these important studies, readers are referred to the paper on the search process written for the Treasure Mountain Research Retreat by Carol Kuhlthau.

One other study did attempt to investigate a process-oriented approach vs. a traditional resource-based approach. Dewees (1987) tested two average level 4th grade classes on seven reference skill areas: table of contents, encyclopedia, card catalog, dictionary, table interpretation, index use, and map reading. The group taught using the "Pooh Step by Step Guide for Writing the Research Paper" was significantly higher on overall performance (and higher on each skill area tested) than the group taught library skills using a traditional method, i.e., instruction on individual research skills as separate entities. Findings of the study suggest that a process-oriented approach can be more effective than an approach that focuses on use of individual sources.

These initial conclusions related to a process approach are encouraging. Kuhlthau's findings and related efforts in other areas of library and information science support a process approach to skills instruction. In addition, the outstanding paper by Mancall, Aaron, and Walker (1986), written for the National Commission on Library and Information Science, highlighted research in critical thinking and metacognition that supports a process approach.

These efforts are just a beginning. Few of the studies actually explore the nature and scope of library and information processes, how information processes translate into teachable skills, the variation in processes attributable to group and individual differences, and the link between process and performance. Examples of specific research questions that need to be addressed follow:

- Regarding the various library and information process models developed, what are the relationships (commonalities and differences) among them? Are they simply using different terms to describe the same thing or are there substantive differences? Are they all empirically verifiable? Is there one linking "meta-process?"

- How do the various models relate to learning models already established in other fields?
- How are various process models affected by individual and group differences?
- In terms of practice, how widespread is a process-approach to library and information skills? Are most library media programs source- or process-oriented? Are programs changing? What approach is most prevalent in scope and sequence documents?
- Are particular skills or steps associated with information processes more crucial than others?
- Are particular skills or steps particularly difficult or easy to develop in students?
- What relationships exist between library and information skills processes and other processes in education: critical thinking, writing process, problem-solving?
- What is the relationship between library and information skills, performance, and product?

Theme 3. The Integrated Approach

The phrase "integrated approach" refers to teaching library and information skills in the context of subject area curriculum and classroom instruction. This is a major theme in the current literature, in Information Power (1988), and in various library media curriculum documents (e.g., New York's Secondary Library Media and Information Skills Syllabus, 1986; Pennsylvania's Integrating Information-Management Skills (1988).

Teaching library and information skills independent from subject area curricula is like teaching mechanics students how to use certain tools and then expecting them to be able to use the appropriate tool in a specific situation (e.g., fixing a car). The integrated approach would say, "Bring in your car and I'll show you what the tools can do for you." An integrated approach moves the focus away from the tools and onto accomplishing the task at hand. "It is meaningless to teach locating, organizing, and synthesizing of information without practice. Practice involves using [information-management skills with] content or subject matter; the existing curriculum" (Integrating Information-Management Skills, 1988, p. 4).

Unfortunately, the theme of integration suffers from the same lack of substantiation that is found with the two previous themes. While the desirability of integrating skills instruction with subject area curriculum is widely accepted among library media professionals and educators, there is little documented research to support this view or to support the various approaches offered to effect integrated instruction in elementary and secondary schools.

Some evidence in support of an integrated approach comes from research on bibliographic instruction programs in academic libraries. Kohl and Wilson (1986) reported that almost all studies about bibliographic instruction "have been limited to student self-reports of attitude change or to measuring a student's theoretical understanding of how specific library tools should be used." Unaddressed by research is the more important question about bibliographic instruction and its relationship to students' effective use of information resources in actual course assignments (p. 206). In a study at the University of Illinois at Urbana-Champaign, the authors compared a traditional tool-specific approach to a cognitive approach that focused on helping students develop a relevant research strategy that is individualized/customized/tailored to their specific research assignment. The cognitive approach (course-integrated) for bibliographic instruction did make a statistically significant positive difference in terms of the richness of student bibliographies (graded independently on three criteria by both a librarian and a writing instructor). The ratings of bibliographies with grades assigned to papers were not found significant, most likely because of the many factors other than the richness of the bibliography that influence grades. The Kohl and Wilson study is an important one. As the authors stated, "Obviously further work needs to be done to see if additional research validates the findings presented here" (p. 210).

Patrick's (1985) investigation into instructional involvement of school media programs in 49 schools in the Pulaski (Arkansas) County Special School District does show that interaction with school curriculum is possible in elementary and secondary school settings. Based on data gathered over a 12-month period (October 1983-October 1984), Patrick concluded that "the quantity and quality of library media program instructional involvement can be increased with persistent effort [of the library media specialist] over a long period of time" (p. 66-67). After implementation of a systematic effort to increase library media specialist familiarity with school curriculum (through use of a "curriculum survey form"), it was found that "district-wide, library media program involvement in the curriculum at various levels showed a large increase over the preceding year" (p. 60).

The finding that curriculum involvement is feasible is reinforced by the number of works written to assist practitioners in developing programs that integrate library media instruction and services with classroom content. Walker and Montgomery (1983), Turner (1985), Loertscher (1988), Eisenberg and Berkowitz (1988), and Krimmelbein (1989) all offer well thought out approaches to ensuring that library media skills are curriculum-based. Eisenberg (1984) has established that curriculum mapping is effective for gathering and evaluating information about curriculum. However, while the various approaches appear logical and meet with success in practice as determined through local evaluation, there are no formal research studies assessing the effectiveness or impact of an integrated approach in elementary and secondary schools.

Obviously, there is a need for more research on the integrated approach. Integration of library media skills instruction and services with subject area curriculum is seen as an essential component of effective library media programs. To ensure that this integration occurs, research is needed to establish: criteria and methods for assessing degrees of integration; full understandings of the positive impact of integration; and essential actions to ensure integration. Sample research questions are:

• What is gained in terms of increased student information skills and subject area performance from an integrated approach vs. out-of-context instruction?
• Does integrated library and information skills instruction foster the attainment of subject area curriculum objectives?

- How effective are the various methods of gathering and evaluating curriculum information (e.g., curriculum mapping)?
- What are the key variables for establishing an integrated program? Are certain variables common to existing models for integration (e.g., those of Loertscher, Turner, Eisenberg and Berkowitz, Krimmelbein)? Do successfully integrated programs share common elements?
- What are appropriate methods for assessing the degree of integration of a library and information skills instructional program?
- Is there an interaction between an integrated model and various approaches to skills curricula (e.g., process vs. source approach)?

Theme 4. Alternative Methods of Teaching Library and Information Skills

Unlike the previous three themes, there is considerable research about the relative merits of various methods for teaching library media skills. Some studies report that it is not possible to draw conclusions because of problems with the research methodology (e.g., too many variables, too few subjects, intervening variables). In general, however, most research presents little evidence to support one instructional approach over another.

Iacovou (1987), for example, compared the use of worksheets with the use of computer-assisted instruction (CAI) for additional drill and practice of library skills. The study found no significant difference between the two methods. In fact, actual student achievement appeared to be almost identical in both cases.

Zsiray (1983-1984) also found little difference between a traditional method (lecture) and a computer-assisted approach (microcomputer-based courseware) for teaching a unit on the Abridged Readers' Guide. The lecture and the microcomputer-based methods were found equally effective, although both were "statistically more effective than [an] independent reading approach" in terms of student performance. In addition to student performance, Zsiray analyzed "efficient use of time." Here there was a difference, with the microcomputer courseware taking only 25 minutes compared to a 45-minute lecture (Zsiray, p. 245).

Most studies comparing instructional methodologies find little evidence pointing to one method as superior to another. Hardesty (1984), for example, in a paper presented at the 1984 ALA conference, stated that "there may be fewer differences among the various teaching methods than we commonly believe" (p. 8). He also noted that "Ivor Davies, in his book Competency Based Learning, concluded after examining mountains of data and reviews of the literature that one key point stood out: there are no significant differences in terms of learning among the teaching methods available today" (Davies, 1973, p. 161, in Hardesty, p. 8).

While questions about the performance and efficiency of various instructional methods are interesting, they do not appear to be as critical to the achievement of library and information skills objectives as questions related to other themes. Also, since researchers concerned with instructional design and technology are likely to continue to explore alternative methodologies, it is proposed here that researchers in library media focus on the more pressing questions and issues noted above and monitor investigations into comparative methods by researchers in related educational fields.

Implications for Practitioners

The four themes also have direct relevance for practicing library media specialists. Library and information skills instruction is important and should be an integral part of every library media program. Although more research needs to be done on the impact of skills instruction on student performance, library media specialists can point to evidence that skills instruction has a positive impact on achievement.

In terms of the nature and scope of skills to be taught, there is general agreement that skills instruction should focus on process rather than sources. Practitioners can refer to models of the library research process (Kuhlthau, 1985b, Stripling and Pitts, 1988), library media skills within a broader "learning and information framework" (Cutlip, 1988), and a generalizable information problem-solving approach (Eisenberg and Berkowitz, 1988). All these works share the belief that specific library and information skills should be taught within the context of an overall process. Further research on (a) the common elements among various process models and (b) the relationship between the library and information skills process and other processes in education (e.g., critical thinking, writing, problem-solving) will also greatly assist those in the field.

The "integrated approach" is also an important theme for library media practice. Information Power (1988) and other writings promote the integration of library and information skills instruction with subject area curriculum as an essential component of effective library media programs. The limited research available to date does point to the value of the integrated approach, although more formal research studies assessing the full effectiveness and impact of an integrated approach are undoubtedly needed.

Finally, in terms of comparing alternative methods of teaching skills, most studies find little evidence pointing to one method as superior to another. For practicing library media professionals, it appears that the concerns related to a process-oriented library and information skills curriculum and an integrated approach are more deserving of attention than various instructional strategies.

Implications for Researchers

As noted at the outset of this paper, research investigations must confirm or refute conventional understandings. It is also important to be able to generalize beyond the settings of specific studies to the full range of library media instructional settings. This is accomplished through some kind of research design and replication of studies. Unfortunately, there are only a limited number of empirical research studies relevant to the four themes. These studies do not provide solid verification of assumptions or justification of widespread generalizing beyond the experimental settings.

Therefore, most major research questions related to library and information skills instruction remain unanswered. Of particular urgency are various issues related to the value of library and information skills instruction, the nature and scope of essential skills, and the relationship of skills instruction to classroom curriculum. Some specific concerns identified in this paper as priorities are:

- The influence of library and information skills instruction on subject area objectives, on college performance, and on lifelong learning.
- The impact of library and information skills instruction on the use of information in schools.
- Commonalities and key elements among various process models of library and information skills.
- Relationships between the library and information skills processes and other processes in education: critical thinking, writing, problem-solving.
- The relationship between library and information process and student performance and products.
- The impact of integration of library and information skills and subject area curriculum on attainment of objectives in both areas.
- Key elements in integrated skills instruction.

In writing this paper, the authors recognized another priority that is not always evident: the responsibilities of researchers to practitioners. It is important that researchers ultimately bridge the gap between research and practice. This requires going beyond statistics and data manipulation in reporting results. Researchers need to state directly and succinctly what the research does and does not show as well as the implications for day-to-day library media work. Finally, conclusions about the need for further research must go beyond cliches and point to specific requirements, questions, and approaches.

In conclusion, there is clearly a critical need for serious basic and applied research related to library and information skills instruction. This means tackling the big questions, not just the easy ones. One way of dealing with difficult issues is cooperation among researchers. Together they may be able to determine researchable questions and suggest appropriate methods of inquiry. This is the promise of the Treasure Mountain Research Retreat. The authors hope that this paper contributes to this effort and focuses attention on key concerns related to library and information skills instruction.

References

American Association of School Librarians and Association for Educational Communications and Technology. Information Power: Guidelines for School Library Media Programs. Chicago: American Library Association, 1988.

Cutlip, Glen W. Learning and Information: Skills for the Secondary Classroom and Library Media Program. Englewood, CO.: Libraries Unlimited, 1988.

Davies, Ivor. Competency Based Learning. New York: McGraw-Hill, 1973.

Dewees, Kris B. "The Effect of Teaching Library Skills Using The Pooh Step-by-Step Guide for Writing the Research Paper' at Lieder Elementary School in the Cypress Fairbanks Independent School District. A Research Report." Master's thesis, Prairie View A & M University, 2987. 62p. ED 284577.

Didier, Elaine K. "An Overview of Research on the Impact of School Library Media Programs on Student Achievement," School Library Media Quarterly, (14:1) Fall 1985, pp. 33-38. (Cites Gengler, 1965; Harmer, 1959; McMillen, 1965; Yarling, 1968; Greve, 1974; and Hale, 1970.)

Eisenberg, Michael B. "Curriculum Mapping and Implementation of an Elementary School Library Media Skills Curriculum," School Library Media Quarterly (12:2) Fall 1984, pp. 411-418.

Eisenberg, Michael B., and Robert E. Berkowitz. Curriculum Initiative: An Agenda and Strategy for Library Media Programs. Norwood, NJ: Ablex, 1988.

Gifford, Vernon, and Jean Gifford. "Effects of Teaching a Library Usage Unit to Seventh Graders." Nov., 1984. 6p. ED 254 230.

Gilliland, Mary J. "Can Libraries Make a Difference? Test Scores Say Yes!," School Library Media Quarterly (14:2) Winter 1986, pp. 67-70.

Goodin, M. Elspeth. "The Transferability of Library Research Skills from High School to College." Ph.D. dissertation, Rutgers University, 1987.

Hardesty, Larry. "Use of Media in Library Use Instruction," June 1984. 56p. ED261688.

Iacovou, Mary Susan. "Does Computer Assisted Instruction Affect the Achievement of Third Graders in Library Skills?." May, 1987. 55p. ED286464.

Integrating Information-Management Skills: A Process for Incorporating Library Media Skills into Content Areas. Harrisburg, PA: Bureau of State Library, Division of School Library Media Services, Pennsylvania Department of Education, 1988.

Kohl, David F., and Lizabeth A. Wilson. "Effectiveness of Course-Integrated Bibliographic Instruction in Improving Coursework," RQ (26:2) Winter 1986, pp. 206-211.

Krimmelbein, Cindy Jeffrey. The Choice to Change: Establishing an Integrated School Library Media Program. Englewood, CO: Libraries Unlimited, 1989.

Kuhlthau, Carol C. "Perceptions of the Information Search Process in Libraries: A Study in Changes from High School Through College," Information Processing and Management (24:4) 1988, pp. 419-427.

Kuhlthau, Carol C. "A Process Approach to Library Skills Instruction," School Library Media Quarterly (13:2) Winter 1985a, pp. 35-40.

Kuhlthau, Carol C. Teaching the Library Research Process. West Nyack, NY: The Center for Applied Research in Education, 1985b.

Kuhlthau, Carol C. "The Information Search Process of High-Middle-Low Achieving High School Seniors," School Library Media Quarterly, (17:4) Summer 1989, p. 224-228.

Lashbrook, John E. "Using a Qualitative Research Methodology to Investigate Library Media Skills Instruction," School Library Media Quarterly (14:2) Summer 1986, pp. 204-209.

Loertscher, David. Taxonomies of the School Library Media Program. Englewood, CO.: Libraries Unlimited, 1988.

Mancall, Jacqueline C., Shirley L. Aaron, and Sue A. Walker. "Educating Students to Think: The Role of the School Library Media Program," School Library Media Quarterly (14:3) Fall 1986, pp. 18-47.

Patrick, Retta. "Effect of Certain Reporting Techniques on Instructional Involvement of Library Media Specialists," Drexel Library Quarterly (21:2) Spring 1985, pp. 52-68.

Secondary Library Media and Information Skills Syllabus: Grades 7-12. Albany, NY: The State Education Department, Bureau of Library Media Programs, Bureau of Curriculum Development, 1986.

Stripling, Barbara K., and Judy M. Pitts. Brainstorms and Blueprints: Teaching Library Research as a Thinking Process. Englewood, CO: Libraries Unlimited, 1988.

Turner, Philip. Helping Teachers Teach. Littleton, CO: Libraries Unlimited, 1985.

Walker, Thomas H., and Paula Kay Montgomery. Teaching Library Media Skills. Littleton, CO: Libraries Unlimited, 1983.

Zsiray, Stephen W., Jr. "A Comparison of Three Instructional Approaches in Teaching the Use of the Abridged Readers' Guide to Periodical Literature," Journal of Educational Technology Systems (12:3) 1983-1984, pp. 241-247.

INFORMATION SEARCH PROCESS:
A SUMMARY OF RESEARCH AND IMPLICATIONS FOR
SCHOOL LIBRARY MEDIA PROGRAMS

Carol C. Kuhlthau
Associate Professor
School of Communication, Information and Library Studies
Rutgers, The State University, New Brunswick, New Jersey

Introduction

The challenge for education in the twenty-first century is to prepare students to be able to use information in the workplace, in their personal lives, and as responsible citizens. The report of the ALA Presidential Committee on Information Literacy recommends restructuring the learning process to more actively involve students: "Such a restructuring of the learning process will not only enhance the critical thinking skills of students, but will also empower them for lifelong learning and the effective performance of professional and civic responsibilities."[1]

Education is changing from the assembly-line environment of the industrial age offered by textbook teaching to the data-rich environment of the information age offered by resource based learning. In response to this change, the media center becomes the information center of the school, providing access to a wide range of resources and guidance in the process of learning from them. The concept of the media center as an extension of the classroom providing resources for learning is certainly not a new one, and current trends in education are completely compatible with this concept. It is an idea whose time has come. As a result, a new perspective on library instruction is emerging that incorporates the more traditional skills of locating and using information sources with the process of learning from information.

The information search process is a holistic learning process encompassing the affective experience of students as well as their intellect. Students' experience within the process needs to be clearly understood in order for teachers and media specialists to design library assignments and to plan instruction that encourages rather than impedes learning. The research summarized in this paper concentrates on the information search process from the student's point of view and investigates the user's perception of information seeking. The working definition of the information search process for the purposes of this research is that it is a complex learning process involving the thoughts, actions, and feelings, which takes place over an extended period of time, which involves developing a topic from information in a variety of sources, and which culminates in some sort of presentation of the individual's new perspective on the topic.

This paper describes a series of studies in which a model of the information search process was developed. First the theoretical basis of the model is presented. Next a summary of each study is given, including the research questions addressed, the methods used to examine the problem, and the findings leading to further hypotheses. Finally, implications for future research and practice are discussed.

Theoretical Basis

The theoretical foundation for this work draws from psychology, using schema theory and personal construct theory, as well as from information science.[2,3] An information search is viewed as a process of construction in which people build their view of the world by assimilating and accommodating new information. Personal construct theory describes a series of feelings are associated with the phases of construction. A person initially confronting new information commonly experiences doubt and confusion. These feelings escalate as the person encounters increasingly confusing, sometimes contradictory messages. The experience can become quite threatening, causing the person to consider turning back and abandoning the new idea. Kelly holds that at this point the person forms a hypothesis that moves the process toward testing and assessing the new information in order to form new constructs.

The question of phases or stages in information seeking has been addressed by Taylor, who described four levels of information need: the visceral level, a vague sense of something missing; the conscious level, a clear need for information but inability to express precisely what is sought; the formal level, an ability to state what information is needed; and the compromised level, when the expression of information need is accommodated to the sources available.[4]

The research of Belkin and his colleagues describes an information search as moving from an anomalous state of knowledge (ASK) to a coherent or defined state.[5] Dervin describes an information search as a sense-making process.[6] Mellon's research reveals the prevalence of anxiety in students, particularly at the beginning of the process.[7]

Summary of Five Studies

These theories and my daily experience with students as a library media specialist led to the hypothesis that initiated this research: that from the student's perspective the process of seeking information involves the complex process of construction. The following is a summary of five studies on the information search process in which a model in six stages was developed, refined, and verified.

The first study addressed the problem of high school students' experience in the search process and the question of whether that experience resembled the process of construction as Kelly described it.[8] Twenty-four seniors in advanced placement English classes were tracked during two research paper assignments over a period of one school year. Instruments were designed to elicit perceptions and strategies which are usually unobservable. Data were collected from students' journals, search logs, short pieces of writing, observations, interviews, timelines, flowcharts, and questionnaires. Content analysis was used with categories derived from the theory base, particularly from personal construct theory.

The information search process was found to be similar to Kelly's description of the process of construction. A six-stage model of the information search process was developed describing thoughts, actions, and feelings commonly experienced by students in each stage. The first stage, task initiation, is characterized by feelings of uncertainty of what is expected and apprehension at the task ahead. Students think of possible topics in preparation for selecting one to pursue. In the second stage, topic selection, a feeling of optimism is commonly experienced after a topic has been chosen. The third stage, prefocus exploration, is a difficult time for most students, when they experience confusion and frustration and may even doubt their ability to complete the task. Confusion and doubt are present until a focus begins to emerge. The fourth stage, focus formulation, is the turning point of a search, when students have learned about their topic from the information they encounter and have formed a personal perspective or focus within the topic. In the fifth stage, information collection, which occurs after students have a focused point of view of the topic, they gather information with more confidence and a sense of direction. Interest and motivation were found to increase at this stage. In the sixth stage, search closure, feelings of relief are common, but feelings of anxiety about presentation also begin to be noted. After presentation students often experience satisfaction and accomplishment if all has gone well and disappointment if it has not.[9] This model became the hypothesis for further studies.

The second study addressed the problem of how these students' perceptions of the information search process had changed after four years of college, and how they compared with the model.[10] The same questionnaire eliciting perceptions, which had been administered to this group in high school, was used to provide longitudinal data on their perceptions, with twenty of the original twenty-four responding. Responses after college were compared with the responses students gave in high school, and statistical significance was determined through t Tests. Findings showed that students' perceptions matched the model more closely after college, particularly those regarding focus and process within time. The college students' perceptions of focus formulation had changed significantly from those they had in high school, in the direction indicated by the model. Students came to expect a topic to change and a central theme to evolve during a search for information. They also expected to become more interested as the search progressed.

The third study, further addressed the problem of students' perceptions of the information search process after four years of undergraduate study, and involved a test of the Kuhlthau model over a period of time. In this study, however, an internal view of students' experience in the process was sought. Case studies of four of the college students were developed and compared with case studies of the same students when they were in high school.[11] The methods used for these longitudinal case studies were content analysis of interviews conducted with each participant, and timelines of the search process drawn by the four participants. The case studies revealed a sense of ownership in the process and in an area of expertise emerging after college. Findings also verified the Kuhlthau model generally, but students' descriptions revealed a more recursive rather than strictly linear process, with focus commonly evolving during exploration, formulation, and collection, stages 3 through 5, as the process moved toward closure. These students described the information search process as a purposeful, sense-making process in which they were actively seeking a thread, a story, an answer to questions, or focusing and narrowing.

These studies showed that the model held over time for this select group of students. Further quantitative study was needed to make the model of the information search process generalizable to other types of library users. Study of a larger, more diverse population of high school students was planned, as well as study of users in other types of libraries, such as academic and public.

The fourth study, funded by the Rutgers Research Council, examined the information search process of high, middle, and low achieving high school seniors. The purpose was to verify the Kuhlthau model and to address three questions: Do other high achievers experience a process similar to those in the initial sample? Do low and middle level students experience a similar process? Does the search process relate to teachers' assessment of the product?[12,13]

The study took place in six high schools, with 147 seniors in English classes selected as participants. Students were identified as high, medium, and low achievers by their scores according to national percentiles on standardized tests. A research paper assignment of four week's duration was given. Process surveys were administered at three points in the information search process -- initiation, midpoint, and closure -- eliciting thoughts and feelings at each point. The teachers assessed the students' papers for presence of focus and quantity of sources as well as grade. Statistical analysis was made by using t Tests and ANOVA to determine significance, and Pearson product-moment measures to determine degree of correlation and measures of linear regression. The data from the forty participants identified as low achievers were incomplete and could not be analyzed in the study. There was no significant difference, however, between the high and middle achievers, with the exception of grade: the high achievers received higher grades. Findings showed a significant change in thoughts during the information search process, moving from general background, to specific and more narrowed, to clearer and more focused. There was a similar significant difference in the confidence and feelings during the process, with confidence increasing throughout and feelings moving from confused to confident and relieved. In addition, there was a slight correlation between change in confidence with teachers' assessment of focus in the papers. Change in student confidence also showed some correlation with the grade the teachers gave to the paper. While this study indicates that the model of the search process can be generalized to other students, it also indicates a number of areas for further research, which will be discussed in another section of this paper.

The fifth study in this series addressed the problem of validating the model of the information search process in a wider sample of library users. Up to this point, the research had been confined to high school students and a small sample of college students and had not addressed the question of whether there were similar patterns in the process of users in other types of libraries. In a study funded by a Library Research and Demonstration Grant from the U.S. Department of Education, 385 library users from twenty-one school, academic, and public libraries were studied.[14,15] The instrument employed was a process survey similar to that used in the prior study, revised to include statements taken directly from the original model, which was administered to each participant at initiation, midpoint, and closure. Analysis was made first by descriptive statistics and next by inferential statistics, including measures of significant difference and analysis of variance in Paired t Tests, Chi Square, ANOVA, and Scheffe tests.

Findings revealed a similar process across types of libraries, with background information being sought at initiation, relevant information at midpoint and closure, and with some participants seeking focused information at closure. Descriptions of thoughts were general and vague at initiation, narrowed and clearer at midpoint, with only 50% making focused statements at closure. Confidence increased significantly from initiation to closure. The adjectives most used to describe feelings were *confused, frustrated* and *doubtful* at initiation and *satisfied, sure* and *relieved* at closure. However, the public library users were more confident at initiation than the academic and school participants, and while the academic and school library users indicated similar low confidence at initiation, the college students were significantly more confident at closure than the high school students.

An important finding in this study was that while participants' thoughts and feelings matched the model as anticipated, their identification of tasks did not. According to the model, initiation tasks would be to recognize information need and to identify general topic, midpoint tasks would be to investigate information on the general topic and to formulate a specific focus, and closure tasks would be to gather information pertaining to the specific focus and to complete the information search. Participants, however, reported their task as "to gather" at initiation, "to gather" and "to complete" at midpoint, and "to complete" at closure.

In summary, this series of studies reveals the information search process to be a complex learning process that can be described as occurring in a sequence of stages. Affective symptoms of uncertainty, confusion, and frustration are associated with the vague, unclear thoughts about a topic or question in the early stages of the process. As thoughts shift to clearer, more focused constructs, a parallel shift is noted in increased confidence and the feelings *sure, satisfied,* and *relieved.* Search tasks, however, do not seem to match the state of thoughts and feelings in the early stages of the information search process, and there is evidence of a lack of tolerance for these early formative stages. In addition, although people's thoughts move from vague, general descriptions of topics to clearer, more narrowed ones, many do not make focused statements about their topic at any point in the search process.

Implications for Practitioners

The process approach to information use provides a new perspective on a K-12 library media program, which may be envisioned in the following description. Students come to understand their own search process through guided use of information from elementary school through high school. They learn that thinking, reflecting, and mulling over are an important part of learning from information; that uncertainty is not only all right, it is the beginning of all learning. They take the initiative to find out and the responsibility for telling others. These are basic skills for the information age.

A K-12 process approach begins in elementary school with daily opportunities to find out and tell others, arising from questions and problems in every area of the curriculum. Rather than giving them assignments requiring a few long reports with detailed citations, children's natural curiosity is put into play each day in response to: "What do I want to know? What did I find out? Where did I find it?" In middle school and junior high school, the process approach continues with longer concentrated periods of extended research under the guidance of the teacher and library media specialist on topics that truly engage the students' interest and curiosity. The two key elements at this point are sufficient time to work through the entire process and caring guidance to develop strategies for success in each stage. In secondary school, the process approach is absorbed into assignments across the curriculum, with students pursuing meaning from information to share through presentations in many forms, such as short recaps, debates, papers, essays, videos, plays, portfolios, experiments, proposals, and computer programs. Individual interpretation and personal perspective are stressed, as well as the facts on which they were built, and the citations identifying sources of information used are required.

Research on the information search process originated in practice and sought to build a theory grounded in actual situations in school library media centers. When the findings of this research are presented to library media specialists, their common reaction is an intuitive recognition, an agreement with the results, and an interest in ways to implement programs based on the findings.

Preliminary results from studies of the implementation phase reveal several problems, however. One problem is that traditional library assignments do not encourage the process approach, and sometimes actually impede the process of learning from information, particularly in the early stages. Teachers are sometimes confused about the purpose of library assignments and about what they are actually asking students to do.

Another problem that is surfacing in the implementation studies is lack of time. Rarely is there enough time for students to work through the process under the guidance of librarians and teachers. In most cases, students are expected to accomplish the major part of the assignment independently, even in elementary and middle school. A second problem regarding time is the lack of planning time for team teaching between librarians and teachers. Other problems are also being reported involving the teaming of librarians with teachers. Questions of respective responsibilities are arising, resulting from librarians becoming involved in areas formerly considered the teachers' domain. Librarians are also reporting that they are "being left alone" to complete instruction and guidance. Who is responsible for what needs to be worked out.

Implementation programs are confronting old paradigms, such as "covering the material in the curriculum guide" and "teaching for the test," which obstruct progress in restructuring schools around active, individual learning. Most schools are not structured to accommodate a process approach to individualized learning.

For the most part, however, the library media specialists involved in implementation are encouraged, realizing that change takes time and that they are part of a larger restructuring movement. One reported that "topics created by students amazed the teachers and myself." A common positive reactions that media specialists report is that they have changed the way they approach students, particularly in guiding and encouraging them to focus in: "The stages from confusion to feeling good about a focus actually happened!" They also report a new interest in the end product and are becoming involved in reviewing students' papers or other presentations: "The teacher invited me to class when students shared their research with each other." Following are statements from the media specialists involved in implementation projects reflecting positive outcomes: "Children were able to discuss their fears and felt comfortable going through this!" "Students liked extra attention and library time." "This group seemed to have fewer difficulties and frustrations." "At the end I found them helping each other." "They were the only class that worked well as a group."

This research helps media specialists and teachers understand students' experiences in the information search process. It provides insight for designing library assignments and interventions that actively involve students in using information for learning.

The process approach empowers librarians in new ways and encourages them to address the larger issues of educating for information use and lifelong learning. It offers them a tool for teaming with teachers which, combined with expertise in resources, makes them extremely valuable partners. The time is ripe for restructuring education, and the process approach offers media specialists a way to make a major contribution to the movement.

Implications for Researchers

Research in the school library field, as in other areas of librarianship, has been lacking in two important aspects. First, studies rarely build on prior research findings. With a few notable exceptions, such as the work of Mancall and Drott[16] and Loertscher and Ho[17], research has been fragmented and piecemeal, without connection to prior work or sufficient concentration on one area to build a useful understanding of an issue that can inform practice. Second, for the most part school library media research has not been theory based. Studies have rarely taken into account the psychological, educational, or information theory that informs the questions being addressed. The research into the information search process, on the other hand, builds in a sequence of five studies and is theory based.

This research offers two important implications related to the methodology applied to research on school library media problems. The first is that the combination of qualitative and quantitative methods can be productively applied to study many aspects of a problem over an extended period of time. The research process is related to the information search process in that problems evolve through different stages of formulation. Problems in early formative states may be best addressed by qualitative methods to form testable hypotheses, which can then be measured by more quantitative methods. Qualitative methods also offer an internal view addressing the why of an issue, bringing insight to more quantitative findings. The complex research problems confronting the library media field need to be addressed over a period of time in a series of studies in order to verify and generalize findings that contribute to practice in school library media centers.

The second methodological implication of this research is that it provides an example of the application of relevant theory from other related fields to offer a new way of looking at a problem. Theory from cognitive psychology, information science, and education is particularly fertile ground for school library media research. The research issues addressed in the school library field are not isolated from other fields. Creative connections can lead to new insight and understanding. The model developed in this research provides a new way of viewing school library media practice, and many questions for further research are generated in this work. Following is a discussion of three such questions.

The informal feedback from librarians and teachers using the process approach with low achievers has been encouraging, and there appears to be promise for helping at-risk students. However, the data collected from this sample were incomplete and not included in the analysis, so that the findings cannot be generalized to this population. Further research, using a combination of qualitative and quantitative methods tailored for this group, is warranted. If this research is to affect programs for at-risk students, further study is needed.

The effect of students' experience in the information search process on the outcome or product of their search is an important accountability issue. The fourth study in this series indicated that the way students go through the process affects their written presentation. Further research is needed on this critical issue. Findings indicate that thoughts and feelings change in the information search process as an individual forms new constructs. These new constructs should be evident in the papers that students write at the close of the search. The information search process is the preparation phase of the writing process. Writing blocks, which often result from incomplete thoughts, may be a consequence of a lack of construction during information searching.[18] This important hypothesis needs further investigation because, although writing from sources makes up 80% of school writing, most writing research has concentrated on writing from what is already known rather than writing from what is learned from sources.[19,20]

The issue of implementing a process centered library media program needs study, particularly as it relates to student learning. Several field studies investigating the process approach are in progress. What works, what problems are encountered, impact on student learning, teachers' methods, and librarians' role are some of the areas that need to be studied so that library media programs can be built on rigorous research findings.

Notes

1. American Library Association Presidential Committee on Information Literacy: Final Report. Chicago: American Library Association, 1989. (Thoughtful summary of the deliberations of leaders in education and librarianship on the importance of information literacy to individuals, business, and citizenship, with recommendations for implementing the information age school.)

2. Kulleseid, Eleanor R. "Extending the Research Base: Schema Theory, Cognitive Styles, and Types of Intelligence," School Library Media Quarterly (Fall) 1986, 41-48. (Includes discussion of schema theory and review of recent work in this area.)

3. Kelly, George A. A Theory of Personality: The Psychology of Personal Constructs. New York: Norton, 1963. (Complete explanation of personal construct theory.)

4. Taylor, Robert S. "Question-Negotiation and Information Seeking in Libraries," College and Research Libraries (May) 1968, 178-194. (Seminal paper presenting four levels of information need reflected in reference questions.)

5. Belkin, Nicholas J., Helen M. Brooks, and Robert N. Oddy. "ASK for Information Retrieval," Journal of Documentation 38 (June) 1982, 61-71. (Review of related literature and description of ASK (Anomalous State of Knowledge) hypothesis.)

6. Dervin, Brenda. "Useful Theory for Librarianship: Communication, Not Information," Drexel Library Quarterly (July) 1977, 16-32. (Describes information seeking as sense-making activity that is facilitated by communication.)

7. Mellon, Constance A. "Library Anxiety: A Grounded Theory and Its Development," College and Research Libraries (March) 1986, 160-165. (A qualitative study exploring the feelings of students about using the library for research, finding that up to 85% of students described initial response to library research in terms of fear.)

8. Kuhlthau, Carol C. "Developing a Model of the Library Search Process: Cognitive and Affective Aspects," Reference Quarterly 28 (Winter) 1988, 232-242. (Describes initial exploratory study into the search process of high school students and findings which led to the development of the Kuhlthau Model.)

9. Kuhlthau, Carol C. "A Process Approach to Library Skills Instruction," School Library Media Quarterly 13 (Winter) 1985, 35-40. (Describes Kuhlthau Model of search process and implications for library media specialists.)

10. Kuhlthau, Carol C. "Perceptions of the Information Search Process in Libraries: A Study of Changes from High School Through College," Information Processing and Management 24(4) 1988, 419-427. (In a comparative study, college students were found to hold perceptions that better matched the Kuhlthau Model than those they held in high school, particularly regarding forming a focus and experiencing a process in time.)

11. Kuhlthau, Carol C. "Longitudinal Case Studies of the Information Search Process of Users in Libraries," Library and Information Science Research 10(3) 1988, 257-304. (Case studies of four students reveal an internal view of library research, with comparisons between high school and four years of college.)

12. Kuhlthau, Carol C. "The Information Search Process of High-Middle-Low Achieving High School Seniors," School Library Media Quarterly, in press. (In study of 150 high school students, high and middle achievers were found to experience process described in Kuhlthau Model. Low achievers need further study. Findings indicate impact of process on outcome in student papers and warrant further research.)

13. Kuhlthau, Carol C. "The Information Search Process of High School Seniors: A Comparison of High, Middle, and Low Achievers." Final Report of Study Funded by Rutgers Research Council. Syracuse, NY: ERIC Clearinghouse on Information Resources, Syracuse University, 1989. (Full report of study and presentation at American Association of School Librarians Research Forum, New Orleans, July 1988.)

14. Kuhlthau, Carol C., Betty J. Turock, Mary W. George, and Robert J. Belvin. Facilitating Information Seeking Through Cognitive Modeling of the Search Process. Final Report. U.S. Department of Education, Library Research and Demonstration Grant G00872032387, Available in hard copy, 1989. (Full report of comparative study of information search process of 385 school, academic, and public library users.)

15. Kuhlthau, Carol C., Betty J. Turock, Mary W. George, and Robert Belvin. "Validating a Model of the Search Process: A Comparison of Academic, Public, and School

Library Users," Library and Information Science Research 12(1) (January-March) 1990, forthcoming. (Received 1989 Jesse Shera Award for most outstanding research paper. Describes study confirming Kuhlthau Model of the search process with users in three types of libraries.)

16. Mancall, Jacqueline and Carl Drott. Measuring Student Information Use; A Guide for School Library Media Specialists. Littleton, CO: Libraries Unlimited, 1983. (Description and implications for practice of study funded by USDE verifying and extending findings of earlier exploratory study.)

17. Loertscher, David V., and May Lein Ho. Computerized Collection Development for School Library Media Centers. Englewood, CO: Hi Willow Research and Publishing, 1986. (Implications for practice and recommended applications of findings of a series of studies, some currently in progress, e.g., Bowie, 1988; Montgomery, 1989.)

18. Emig, Janet A. The Composing Process of Twelfth Graders. Urbana, IL: National Council of Teachers of English, 1971. (Study revealing phases in the composing process of students, including prewriting when thoughts were forming in preparation for writing.)

19. Nelson, Jennie, and John R. Hayes. "The Library Revisited: How Students Locate and Evaluate Sources to Be Used in Writing." Paper presented at the National Reading Conference, Tucson, Arizona, December 1988. (Study of sixteen students at Carnegie Mellon University, eight freshmen and eight more experienced writers, which found that the more experienced were issue-driven rather than content-driven in research/writing assignments.)

20. Stotsky, Sandra. "Research and Report Writing Through the Grades: A Critique of Existing Writing Theory and Research and Suggestions for Further Research." Paper presented at Reading Seminar, Harvard Graduate School of Education, March 1989. (Review of research about research process in students, highlighting the Kuhlthau studies of the search process as a breakthrough in describing stages in preparation for writing.)

CRITICAL THINKING: IMPLICATIONS FOR LIBRARY RESEARCH

Kathleen W. Craver
Head Librarian
National Cathedral School
Washington, D.C.

Introduction

Within the past ten years several seminal educational studies, such as the Boyer and College Board reports, the National Assessment of Educational Progress (NAEP), and Goodlad's A Place Called School, have indicated that deficiencies of students in critical thinking constitute a major flaw in American education.[1] The National Commission on Excellence in Education, for example, noted that "nearly 40 percent [of 17 year olds] cannot draw inferences from written material; only one-fifth can write a persuasive essay; and only one-third can solve a mathematics problem requiring several steps."[2] Surveys conducted by the National Assessment of Educational Progress and the National Commission on Excellence have found that students spend most of their time acquiring factual data but do not consistently apply these data to larger concepts of their daily lives.[3]

These reports graphically demonstrate the need for the integration of higher-order thinking skills into school curricula. The reports also provide school systems with a host of recommendations for implementing their instructions in various subject areas. None, however, recognizes that the introduction of the new programs and services that they prescribe will result in an enhanced instructional role for the school librarian. If elementary and secondary school students are to cope successfully with the curricular changes recommended by these reports, it will be essential for school librarians to be cognizant of (1) how critical thinking is usually measured and evaluated, (2) the findings of major critical thinking studies, (3) the implications of this research for the future, and (4) the implications of these studies for library science researchers.

Purpose of Study

The purpose of this article is to synthesize empirical research studies of critical thinking and to discuss the implications of those studies for library information science research. Critical thinking has been identified in four basic areas: reading, writing, group interaction, and speaking. The problems associated with the literature are discussed from the following perspectives: (1) methods used in conducting research, (2) implications for future research studies, and (3) contribution of the literature toward a body of knowledge in this subject. Emphasis has also been placed on neglected aspects of the literature, such as the potential for employing critical thinking strategies in bibliographic instruction and the need for library science educators to initiate research studies specific to the field.

Definitional Problems

The manner in which researchers perceive critical thinking influences how they measure and evaluate it.[4] Within this narrow educational genre there exists considerable disagreement among scholars regarding critical thinking terminology, characteristics, and definitions. Terms such as formal logic, logical thinking, associative thinking, creative thinking, and scientific method have been used as synonyms.[5] There are also major differences in how one characterizes critical thinking. Some researchers describe critical thinking as the pursuit of knowledge, the generation of explanations, the judging of ideas, or the construction of relationships between seemingly unassociated concepts.[6] Others characterize critical thinking as a set of skills that encompasses observation, classification, summarization, and interpretation.[7]

Researchers differ concerning their respective approaches to critical thinking. Some contend that critical thinking does not occur in isolation and therefore cannot be taught as a separate subject. It must be integrated into specific subjects, because critical thinking in science, for example, is essentially different from critical thinking in history. These same proponents of critical thinking also believe that one must possess substantive knowledge of the particular subject before one can engage in critical thinking.[8] Scholars espousing the opposite view, termed the process approach, assert that critical thinking is a sequential process engaged in rather independently of the subject content.[9] This means that one can be instructed in (1) identifying problems, (2) formulating hypotheses, (3) collecting relevant data, (4) evaluating hypotheses, and (5) deriving conclusions regardless of previous subject expertise.[10]

Definitions of critical thinking are equally numerous. They range from Burton's "critical, reflective search for valid conclusions which solve our problems," to Ennis's "reasonably deciding what to believe."[11] The characterizations are formulated by researchers to suit the designs of their respective studies and philosophical framework.

The complications created by the diverse definitions, terminology, and approaches applied to the study of critical thinking have resulted in a series of context-sensitive studies that are difficult to replicate with broader populations and do little to enhance a common critical thinking knowledge base. Many critical thinking studies must therefore be viewed with a degree of caution, since they have not employed standardized research protocols.

Critical Thinking Reading Studies

Most empirical research suggests that critical thinking is related to reading, writing, group interaction, and speaking. Reading, for example, is considered to be one of the optimum means for training the mind to think critically.[12] The following studies describe findings based on reading programs that incorporated elements of critical thinking.

In 1941, Glaser conducted an experiment with eight twelfth-grade English classes in which an experimental group was required to approach problems by defining them, applying logic, using the weight of evidence, and making deductive and inductive inferences. Test scores revealed a mean gain of 71 points for the experimental group and a mean gain of 41 points for the control group. Unfortunately, Glaser used his own test to measure and evaluate the changes. While the test became the forerunner of the now widely-used Watson-Glaser Critical Thinking Appraisal, Glaser could not scientifically attribute his findings to the results of his program, since the test was designed to match it.[13]

Using a similar pedagogical approach, Ennis taught logic to school children. He found that instruction in logic resulted in a statistically significant increase in student scores on critical thinking tests.[14] Ennis used the Cornell Critical Thinking Test, which he and Millman had devised and tested previously, to determine the level of support for his hypothesis.

Both experiments attempted to teach students to reasonably formulate and assess statements by using a schematic approach. In 1965, Livingston developed a course to enhance critical thinking skills. Through the teaching of semantics, Livingston integrated concepts of critical thinking similar to those of Ennis and Glaser. He found that teaching two classes per week for five weeks was sufficient to raise the scores of high school students on the Watson-Glaser Critical Thinking Appraisal.[15]

A year later, Oliver and Shaver employed a social studies model to teach and assess critical thinking. The jurisprudence course focused on analyzing public issues based on knowledge of the American Constitution's principles and concepts. Four hundred students comprised the experimental group. They received instruction in the program throughout the seventh and eighth grades. Oliver and Shaver hypothesized that it was possible to teach critical thinking through a social studies program that required students to define, to classify, and to test statements about such controversial issues as school desegregation and business monopoly. After administering the Wagmis Test (subtests 1, 2, and 4 of the Watson-Glaser Test, Form AM, and parts 6 and 7 of the Michigan Test of Problem Solving, part A) to the experimental and control groups, they found no statistically significant differences between the groups. Oliver and Shaver concluded that specific instruction in reasoning skills may be necessary to develop any significant improvement on standardized tests.[16]

In 1967, Frank experimented with a compromise between the schematic and integrated critical thinking models. In a speech course taught in five high schools, Frank integrated tests of evidence, logical inference, and statement validity into the normal course of instruction. To 103 control and 103 experimental group students, he administered the Watson-Glaser Critical Thinking Appraisal as a pre-test, immediate post-test, and delayed post-test. Test results showed that the experimental group scored significantly higher than the control group on the immediate and delayed tests.[17]

An even more integrated approach to critical thinking was employed by Fuller at the University of Nebraska's Lincoln campus, using a program called ADAPT. Using seven courses in a variety of disciplines, faculty members incorporated critical thinking activities and lessons into their daily classes. To evaluate the project, the Watson-Glaser Critical Thinking Appraisal was administered to ADAPT students and two control groups. ADAPT students were found to have improved as much as one standard deviation over the control group in critical thinking abilities.[18]

At Xavier University in Louisiana, a similar program for minority students, called SOAR, produced significant improvement in an even shorter period of time. In a five-week, intensive, summer training program for pre-freshmen, students focused on five abstract aspects of general problem solving indigenous to science. These included variables control, probability, proportional reasoning, combined reasoning, and recognizing correlations. In addition, students received instruction to improve verbal ability, note-taking, and logical problem solving. At the close of the program students showed average increases in scores on the <u>Nelson-Denny Reading Test</u> ranging from 1.8 grade levels (for those below or equal to the twelfth grade on the pre-test) to 2.2 grade levels (for those below the tenth grade on the pre-test). Testing on the PSAT (Preliminary Scholastic Aptitude Test) revealed similar gains in verbal and reading comprehension scores.[19]

In 1974, Whittrock experimented with relationships among several parts of a text and the association between the text and experience. Using groups of students from elementary school to college age, Whittrock randomly assigned several groups to read and re-read (if they wished) the text only. Other experimental groups were given an "organizer" or summary sentence at the beginning of each paragraph. The last experimental group generated their own organizers and summaries for each paragraph. From various reading comprehension tests, students in the generative group always scored higher on retention and comprehension tests by at least 25 percent, usually by 50 percent, and frequently by 100 percent.[20]

When assessing the impact and applicability of the previous studies, the importance of the ability to read well by the experimental group cannot be overemphasized. Follman and Lowe, for example, in a study to enhance critical thinking and reading with fifth and twelfth graders, reported that students with strong language ability scored high on measures of critical thinking.[21] Standardized critical thinking measuring instruments, such as the <u>Cornell Critical Thinking Test</u> and <u>Watson-Glaser Critical Thinking Appraisal</u>, require a semantic comprehension of words in relation to problems and decisions if the conclusions based on those interpretive mechanisms are to be appropriate. Therefore, students who already possess strong language skills may automatically tend to score higher on standardized measures of critical thinking.

Critical Thinking Writing Studies

While it is essential for researchers to investigate the relationship between reading and critical thinking, it is important to recognize the relevance of writing and reasoning skills. Studies of writing and critical thinking are based on two schools of thought. First, writing improves reading comprehension. Improved reading comprehension thus enhances critical thinking. Second, writing by itself can cause or stimulate critical thinking.

In 1983, Stosky noted, in a review of writing/reading comprehension literature, that from the 1930s to the 1970s, the majority of research that employed writing activities to improve reading comprehension reported significant gains. In addition, the most effective writing activities consisted of summation, abstract writing, outlining, paraphrasing, note-taking, and writing paragraph headings, rather than reading or underlining important passages.[22] Similarly, Nagel found in a 1972 study that eighth grade students showed greater comprehension when they summarized paragraphs in a single sentence compared to a group who read the same materials but wrote nothing. Studies by Taylor and Taylor and Berkowitz with sixth grade and college students, respectively, achieved analogous results.[23]

The assertion that writing itself can influence critical thinking, however, lacks a firm, empirical research base. In a 1977 study of the composition practices of high school students, Emig posited that the act of writing itself involves a unique form of learning.[24] Since it involves various physical processes of the brain, such as hand/eye coordination, as well as mental processes, such as generating ideas, organizing, and evaluating, it promotes the development of a higher level of thinking. This type of research, while it contributes to a theory of writing, does not solve the problem of how writing is itself connected to critical thinking.

Group Interaction Critical Thinking Studies

A third area researchers have studied is the correlation between group activity and critical thinking. Taba, in several critical thinking programs, asserted that group interaction served as a stimulus to critical thinking in the curriculum.[25] Smith, for example, in a study of twelve college classes, noted that student interaction and faculty/student interchange correlated positively with achievement on the Watson-Glaser Critical Thinking Appraisal and the Chickering Critical Behaviors Test.[26] Bloom also found that by increasing classroom participation, the mean class achievement increased by one standard deviation.[27]

In 1970, Maier described a research study in which he observed thirty-four groups with a discussion leader and thirty-three groups without one. He reported that a discussion leader improved group thought processes by acknowledging minority opinions. The leaderless groups were dominated by the vocal majority.[28] Seven years later, Suydam and Weaver summarized their research on mathematical problem solving. They reported that students working in groups of two to four members generally solved more problems than students working alone.[29]

Speaking Critical Thinking Studies

Since speaking assists in creating and molding thought, researchers have hypothesized that speaking may also act as a stimulus to critical thinking. Gail, for example, found that students who participated in class discussions scored significantly higher on tests of fact and higher cognitive learning than did students in the non-discussion control group.[30] Garris noted similar findings about class participation in an experiment comparing two groups. Students who engaged in oral recitation scored significantly higher on the Watson-Glaser Critical Thinking Appraisal.[31]

Researchers have also discovered that the deliberate use of wait time by teachers conveys to students that they are expected to respond intelligently rather than expeditiously. Rowe found at the University of Florida that when faculty members waited at least three seconds, more students gave longer and complex responses, frequently commented on a peer's response, and supported more inferences with evidence and logical argument. Rowe also noted an increase in speculative thinking, the number of questions posed, and the number of proposed experiments. In addition, she found that failure to respond diminished and achievement increased on test items that were considered more complex.[32]

Several researchers have also studied verbal problem solving as a method to increase critical thinking. Devised by Bloom as a tutorial device, the method teams a problem solver with a listener. As the problem solver outlines a logical series of steps toward solution, the listener attempts to discern errors of logic or judgment. Whimbey, for example, found that this method increased student achievement by as much as one standard deviation in subjects ranging from Spanish to physics.[33] In 1983, Worsham and Austin reported that verbal problem solving raised SAT scores of an experimental group by 42 points.[34]

Characteristics of Critical Thinking Research

Despite the fact that more than 2,000 articles have been written about critical thinking since 1985, there have been few empirical studies performed to measure and evaluate it. Little progress has been made regarding the most effective materials and methods to teach critical thinking.

Unfortunately, the majority of critical thinking studies are characterized by several flaws. First, many of the studies are isolated in time and in intellectual origin. The students cited in this article, for example, focused on different independent variables such as the introduction of a course in logic or the integration of a questioning approach into a physics course. While each variable is considered a legitimate aspect of critical thinking, its study in an isolated research setting does not contribute to an empirically developed knowledge base about critical thinking. The lack of replication in these studies gravely diminishes their research significance. The span of years between these studies also reduces their contributions to the research base. Many were performed in the 1950s and 1960s, when course content, teaching methods, and student performances on standardized achievement tests were quite different. None of the studies, for example, acknowledges the possible contaminating influence of a participating teacher's personal pedagogic qualities or enthusiasm for the research project.

A second flaw of the studies concerns methodology. Most of the studies cited employed either the Watson-Glaser Critical Thinking Appraisal or the Cornell Critical Thinking Test to measure and evaluate their hypotheses. While these are considered standardized test instruments to assess critical thinking, they are still context-sensitive and subjective. For example, an item on the Watson-Glaser Critical Thinking Appraisal requires the subject to make a series of political assumptions in order to select a correct response. A political assumption implies that the subject possesses previous "correct" background knowledge that may not even be relevant to his or her ability to think critically.[35]

There is another problem with these tests. On the one hand, they are considered invalid because many items require responses based upon a relatively contextless problem. On the other hand, most experts agree that critical thinking is usually performed by a subject in a context situation where there are a variety of variables or alternatives to be weighed or ranked. To supply the subject with a context-laden problem frequently requires the test taker to bring additional background knowledge to the problem so that it can be solved correctly.

A third problem with these two "standardized" measurements of critical thinking concerns their objective format. Since neither of these tests employs essays, they fail to simulate and hence measure how critical thinking actually occurs in a realistic, problem-solving situation. Although a standardized multiple-choice format is imminently practical for testing large numbers of subjects, it is pedagogically deleterious when assessing the complicated process of critical thinking. What is needed to accurately measure critical thinking is a situation that does not require the application of previous background knowledge but does replicate a real-life problem requiring a higher level of reasoning. Such an instrument, however, is extremely difficult to design.

The available empirical studies on critical thinking do shed light on various aspects of that important process. It is certain, for example, that reading, writing, speaking, and group interaction play important roles in the development of higher order thinking. The ability of researchers to measure and evaluate critical thinking, however, has been significantly restricted by problems concerning valid and reliable test instruments and standardized research protocols. Despite the flaws in critical thinking research, it is clear that techniques such as questioning, tutoring, oral recitation, group discussion, and writing are successful in improving the ability of students to think critically.

Implications for Practitioners

The applications of these findings for library science practitioners are exciting. A library offers a natural setting to employ critical thinking skills with students. It also serves as an excellent laboratory for applying various methods and techniques of critical thinking instruction. Librarians are fortunate in that their subject lends itself to both a content and a process approach. In designing course-integrated bibliographic instruction units, for example, librarians have the opportunity to structure the course content so that critical thinking becomes a necessary requirement of the unit. Librarians may employ such techniques as hypothetical situations in a drug abuse unit, simulations in a chemistry unit, class debate in a political science unit, or a case study in a sociology unit. All of these teaching methods entail (1) defining a problem; (2) identifying its ramifications; (3) searching for the information needed to solve it; (4) exploring multiple solutions, with their ensuing consequences; and (5) making a decision based on the acquisition of subject knowledge. All of the methods can be structured to rely on questioning, group interaction, in-class participation, oral recitation, and writing. These techniques have already been found to improve student critical thinking abilities.

From a process approach perspective, librarians can also integrate a critical thinking component into library science curricula. When librarians design pathfinders, counsel students about term papers, or provide research report instruction, they have an opportune time to teach students a systematic, effective research strategy. This strategy, which employs critical thinking skills, should be transferable to different grades and subjects with varying degrees of sophistication. It can be taught to students from the elementary grades to the college level. A systematic problem-solving approach is considered a characteristic of a critical thinker.

Librarians should provide students with a schema they can impose on any research assignment. Its critical elements should include (1) identification of the main issue and appropriate search terms; (2) recognition of basic assumptions; (3) evaluation of data; (4) evaluation of sources (author's expertise, publisher, etc.); (5) recognition of appropriate facts and persuasive appeals, prejudice, and propaganda; (6) testing of facts meriting conclusions; (7) association of different ideas; (8) acknowledgment of personal bias; and (9) suspension of decision-making until the search is concluded.[36] Librarians can also demonstrate these skills to students by introducing them to appropriate subject matter materials, helping them identify suitable search terms, and teaching them how to search various online catalogs and databases. Depending on student subject expertise, librarians can also teach them how to evaluate the importance of the materials they find.

The emphasis on improving the ability of students to think critically places library practitioners in a unique position to affect change positively. Course-integrated bibliographic instruction units should be designed to reflect both a content and a process approach. Whenever possible, librarians should design units incorporating techniques found to improve critical thinking and methods that require students to experience a situation similar or applicable to real life.

Implications for Researchers

While practicing librarians can easily transfer and apply the findings from critical thinking empirical studies to their own instructional methods, library science researchers face a more challenging task. At present, no empirical research has been conducted in library science and critical thinking. As a result, a virgin territory exists in which many research questions must initially be addressed. Library science researchers are in a unique position to build upon the work performed by researchers in the fields of anthropology, education, and developmental psychology.

Philosophers, educators, and psychologists have defined critical thinking and analyzed its essential characteristics. While the perspectives of each discipline have resulted in varying research parameters and terminology, an analysis of their work reveals substantial overlap. Library science researchers should not expend energy formulating a library science definition of critical thinking, but should instead struggle with creating, measuring, and evaluating critical thinking programs that are applicable to academic, business, and life situations.

Although library science researchers should not concern themselves with definitional problems, they should explore the degree to which critical thinking skills are content specific or independent of content. This area of research has not been effectively resolved. In many of the studies cited, test score gains may have been produced by an instructional program that closely matched the content of the evaluation instrument.

The second problem area for library science researchers concerns methodology. There is substantial disagreement among researchers in other fields about the use of standardized measurements such as the Cornell Critical Thinking Test and the Watson-Glaser Critical Thinking Appraisal to evaluate critical thinking skills. If critical thinking is content-specific, a test that integrates reasoning skills with subject matter needs to be designed. If critical thinking is found to involve a set of generalized skills that can be identified, a test needs to be created that does not require previous background knowledge and that truly measures critical thinking in an isolated context.

Library science researchers should not feel compelled to devise an objective, multiple-choice type instrument to measure critical thinking. The ability to reason at a higher level does not necessarily fit into an either-or format. Researchers should instead develop a broad range of tasks that represent significant library research or subject matter problems. These exercises should require sustained reasoning and permit multiple interpretations or solutions.

In order to design test instruments that measure critical thinking in library science, researchers will have to analyze how students perform research at various stages in their academic development. They will need to identify the "normal" steps a critical thinker takes to locate pertinent information or to successfully solve a research problem. These studies will probably involve research protocols that may record the search process through logs, diaries, journals, or perhaps a "critical moment" format. They may also involve the assessment of student research performance through a series of standardized research questions. Another means of analysis may be to base a model on the functioning of a knowledge expert. By contrasting the research performance of subject experts with that of neophytes, researchers may be able to isolate the types of critical thinking skills required to find information or to successfully complete an assignment.[37]

Although the problems confronting library science researchers with respect to the study of critical thinking are specific to the information science field, they are also generally applicable to other fields of study. Nonetheless, empirical research unique to our field is needed to provide crucial evidence to practicing librarians. Librarians who wish to introduce critical thinking into their curricula will need the results of studies in their own field to justify appropriate curricular modifications.

Conclusion

Nearly two-thirds of Americans currently work in jobs involving the creation, processing, and distribution of information. Millions of people such as attorneys, bankers, and educators are in the "thinking business." As new information technologies are substituted for previous industrial operations, many workers such as machinists, welders, and assemblers will be forced to leave manufacturing and enter the "thinking business." Such a society will require individuals with the ability to think, to reason, to solve problems, to analyze, to make comparisons, to generalize, to digest existing information, and to create new information.[38] Library science researchers will need to know how to improve the ability of students to find, synthesize, and correctly apply information to everyday situations. Additional research is needed in this field before we can provide the answers to such important questions.

Notes

1. E.L. Boyer, High School: A Report on Secondary Education in America (New York: Harper, 1983); College Board, Academic Preparation for College: What Students Need to Know and Be Able to Do (New York: College Board, 1983); The 1979-80 National Assessment of Reading and Literature (Denver, CO: National Assessment of Educational Progress, 1981); and J.L. Goodlad, A Place Called School (New York: McGraw-Hill, 1984).

2. National Commission on Excellence in Education, A Nation at Risk (Washington, DC: U.S. Department of Education, 1983), p. 9.

3. Goodlad, A Place Called School, pp. 236-238.

4. S.P. Norris and R. King, The Design of a Critical Thinking Test on Appraising Observations (St. Johns, Newfoundland, Canada: Memorial University, St. Johns Institute for Educational Research and Development, 1984). ED 260083.

5. E.W. Eisner, "Critical Thinking: Some Cognitive Components," Teachers College Record 66:624-634 (May 1965); and J.W. Thomas and B.S. Taylor, Critical Thinking and Instruction: A Review (Philadelphia: Research for Better Schools, Inc., 1975). ED 177605.

6. E.W. Eisner, "Critical Thinking," pp. 624-634.

7. L.E. Raths, Teaching for Thinking: Theory and Application (Columbus, OH: Charles E. Merrill Books, 1967).

8. J.E. McPeck. Critical Thinking and Education (New York: St. Martins Press, 1981); J.E. McPeck, "Stalking Beasts But Swatting Flies: The Teaching of Critical Thinking," Canadian Journal of Education 9:28-44 (January 1971); W.H. Burton, R.B. Kimball, R.B. Wing, and R.L. Wing, Education for Effective Thinking: An Introductory Text (New York: Appleton-Century-Crafts, Inc., 1960); and D.H. Russell, "Higher Mental Processes," in Encyclopedia of Educational Research, edited by C.W. Harris (New York: Macmillan, 1960).

9. H.W. Gibson, "Critical Thinking: A Communication Model." (Ph.D. dissertation, Washington State University, 1985).

10. B. Skinner, "The Myth of Critical Thinking," Clearing House 46: 372-376 (February 1971).

11. P. Dressel, "Critical Thinking: The Goal of Education," NEA Journal 44:418-4201 (May 1955); W.H. Burton, et al., Education for Effective Thinking p. 18; and R.H. Ennis, J. Millmam and T. Tomko, Manual for Two Tests: Cornell Critical Thinking Test, Level X and Cornell Critical Thinking Test, Level Z (Champaign, IL: University of Illinois, 1983), p. 3.

12. R.G. Stauffer, Teaching Reading as a Thinking Process (New York: Harper & Row, 1969).

13. E.M. Glaser, An Experiment in the Development of Critical Thinking: Teachers College Contributions to Education No. 843 (New York: Bureau of Publications, Teachers College, Columbia University, 1941).

14. R.H. Ennis and D.H. Paulus, Critical Thinking Readiness in Grades 1-12 (Ithaca, NY: Cornell University Press, 1965). See also G.H. Hyram, "An Experiment in Developing Critical Thinking," Journal of Experimental Education 26: 125-132 (October 1957) and K.B. Henderson, "The Teaching of Critical Thinking," Phi Delta Kappa 39: 280-282 (December 1958) for additional empirical studies of logic instruction in secondary schools.

15. H. Livingston, "An Investigation of the Effect of Instruction in General Semantics on Critical Reading Ability," California Journal of Educational Research 16: 93-96 (February 1965).

16. D.W. Oliver and J.P. Shaver, Teaching Public Issues in High School (Boston: Houghton Mifflin, 1966).

17. A.D. Frank, "Teaching High School Speech to Improve Critical Thinking Ability," The Speech Teacher 18: 296-302 (February 1967).

18. R.G. Fuller, Multidisciplinary Piagetian-Based Programs for College Freshmen (Lincoln, NE: University of Nebraska at Lincoln Press, 1977).

19. A. Whimbey, et al., "Teaching Critical Reading and Analytical Reasoning in Project SOAR," Journal of Reading 24: 5-10 (October 1980).

20. M.C. Whittrock, "Learning as a Generative Process," Educational Psychologist 11: 87-95 (February 1974). For confirmation of similar research findings see also R.C. Anderson, R.E. Reynolds, D.L. Schallert, and D.L. Goetz, "Frameworks for Comprehending Discourse," American Educational Research Journal 14: 367-381 (Fall 1977); M. Doctorow, M.C. Whittrock, and C. Marks, "Generative Processes in Reading Comprehension," Journal of Educational Psychology 70: 109-118 (April 1978); and B.J.F. Meyer, "Basic Research on Prose Comprehension: A Critical Review," in Comprehension and the Competent Reader: Inter-Specialty Perspectives, edited by D.F. Fisher and C.W. Peters (New York: Praeger, 1981).

21. J. Follman and A. Lowe, "Empirical Examination of Critical Thinking: Overview," Journal of Reading Behavior 73: 159-168 (Summer 1972).

22. S. Stosky, "Research on Reading/Writing Relationships: A Synthesis," Language Arts 60: 627-642 (May 1983).

23. J. Nagel, "The Effects of a Directed Writing Activity in Eighth Grade Social Studies Instruction on General Reading Achievement and on Social Studies Reading Achievement," (Ph.D. dissertation, Temple University, 1972); K.K. Taylor, If Not Grammar, What?--Taking Remedial Instruction Seriously (East Peoria, IL: Illinois Central College, 1978), ED 159688; and B. Taylor and S. Berkowitz, "Facilitating Children's Comprehension of Content Material," in Perspectives on Reading Research and Instruction, Twenty-Ninth Yearbook of the National Reading Conference, edited by M.L. Kamill (Washington, DC: The National Reading Conference, 1980).

24. J. Emig, "Writing as a Mode of Learning," College Composition and Communication 28: 122-128 (May 1977).

25. H. Taba, Curriculum Development Theory and Practice (New York: Harcourt, Brace and World, 1962); and H. Taba, "The Problems in Developing Critical Thinking," Progressive Education 28: 45-48 (January 1950).

26. D.G. Smith, "College Classroom Interactions and Critical Thinking," Journal of Educational Psychology 69: 180-190 (April 1977).

27. B.S. Bloom, "The 2 Sigma Problem: The Search for Methods of Group Instruction as Effective as One to One Tutoring," Educational Researcher 13: 4-16 (June 1984).

28. N.R. Maier, Problem Solving and Creativity in Individuals and Groups (New York: Brooks Cole, 1970).

29. M.N. Suydam and J.F. Weaver, "Research on Problem Solving: Implications for Elementary School Classrooms," Arithmetic Teacher 25: 40-42 (November 1977).

30. M. Gail, "Synthesis of Research on Teachers' Questioning," Educational Leadership 42: 42-47 (November 1984).

31. C.W. Garris, "A Study Comparing the Improvements of Critical Thinking Ability Achieved Through the Teacher's Increased Use of Classroom Questions Resulting from Individualized or Group Training Programs" (Ph.D. dissertation, Pennsylvania State University, 1974).

32. M.B. Rowe, "Wait Time: Slowing Down May Be a Way of Speeding Up!" Journal of Teacher Education 37: 44-45 (January/February 1986).

33. A. Whimbey, "The Key to Higher Order Thinking Is Precise Processing," Educational Leadership 42: 66-70 (September 1984).

34. A.W. Worsham and G.R. Austin, "Effects of Teaching Thinking Skills on SAT Scores," Educational Leadership 41: 50-51 (November 1983).

35. S.P. Norris, "Synthesis of Research on Critical Thinking," Educational Leadership 12: 40-45 (May 1985).

36. J. Lubans, "Library Literacy," RQ 22: 339-342 (Summer 1983).

37. J. Mancall, S. Aaron, and S.A. Walker, "Educating Students to Think: The Role of the School Library Media Program," School Library Media Quarterly 15: 18-27 (Fall 1986).

38. R.A. Pauker, Teaching Thinking and Reasoning Skills: Problems and Solutions. (Arlington, VA: American Association of School Administrators, 1987).

Part 3

Intellectual Freedom

INTELLECTUAL FREEDOM RELATING
TO SCHOOL LIBRARY MEDIA CENTERS

Dianne McAfee Hopkins,
Assistant Professor
School of Library and Information Studies
University of Wisconsin-Madison

Introduction

Intellectual freedom has been and continues to be a constant source of interest to librarians. While intellectual freedom is usually examined in the research in terms of censorship, i.e., removal or restriction of materials once they have been selected for a given library, the term "intellectual freedom" has a broader, more encompassing meaning. Intellectual freedom has been defined as "the right of any person to hold any belief whatever on any subject, and to express such beliefs or ideas in whatever way the person believes appropriate..." A second, more integral part of the definition, of interest to librarians, is "the right to unrestricted access to all information and ideas regardless of the medium of communication used."[1]

The literature of librarianship is filled with published articles on censorship. Many of these articles reflect the experiences and/or philosophical viewpoints of library practitioners and educators. Where the articles report studies on intellectual freedom, many are actually surveys or status reports on activities in libraries reflecting actual or attempted removal of materials. Where research questions are posed, they often are dissertations designed to fulfill requirements for advanced degrees. All articles cited here by author name can be found in the bibliography.

Research in intellectual freedom is dominated by studies about school library media specialists and centers, with a majority of these studies focusing on secondary level library media programs. The reviewer of intellectual freedom research will also want to be aware of studies in intellectual freedom in other areas of librarianship. Two studies outside school librarianship by Busha and England are summarized in Appendix A, because they are examples of additional studies upon which research in school librarianship can build.

The purposes of this review of research relating to school library media centers are to identify the research that has been done, emphasizing research in the United States; to synthesize selected research studies; and to discuss the implications of and future directions for research in intellectual freedom from the perspective of library media educators in colleges and universities and from the perspective of library media practitioners. The commonly accepted terminology of today is used in this paper. Thus, the terms "school library media specialist," "school library media center," "school library media program," and "school library media educator" are used. The term "librarian" is used when library professionals include those in other types of libraries.

Review of Intellectual Freedom Research

A chronological review of selected studies in intellectual freedom is provided. The chronological review is divided by decade for convenience, beginning with the 1950s and ending with the 1980s. Prior to the 1950s, a study by Eakin is reported.

1950-1959

What is probably the best known and perhaps most influential intellectual freedom study was conducted by Fiske. Fiske sought to look at sources of restrictions on materials in public and school libraries in California. Specifically, she sought to locate, define, and trace the interrelationships of significant factors involved in the selection and distribution of controversial materials under varying circumstances. Fiske examined twenty-six communities in California selected on the basis of size, rate of growth, ethnic composition, geographic location, and type of library service.

Fiske sought answers through a structured interview. In all, 204 interviews were conducted with municipal, county, and school librarians and administrators in forty-eight municipal and county units and forty-six senior high schools in twenty-six communities. Her findings included the following:

- While nearly half the persons interviewed expressed unequivocal freedom-to-read convictions, and only a small proportion believed librarians should take controversiality into account, in practice, nearly 2/3 of the librarians indicated that they did not purchase a book title because of the possibility that the book or its author might be considered controversial.

- Librarians initially designated over 2/3 of the books named as questionable, even though there was no detectable provocation outside the library. Of books questioned, 85% either were not purchased or were restricted in circulation if purchased. Thus, librarians themselves imposed restrictions that limited access to library materials.

- Books complained about by patrons were far less likely to be banned or limited than books questioned by librarians.

- Librarians new to the profession were less restrictive than more experienced librarians.

- School library media specialists felt like second class members of their profession as well as among their faculties. School library media specialists were highly susceptible to the influence of their administrators.

- Persons with professional training in librarianship were more likely to disregard controversiality when selecting materials than those without professional training;

- The press could play a decisive role in the outcome to a challenge.

1960-1969

Farley examined book censorship in senior high school library media centers in Nassau County, New York. His purpose was to look at restrictions on the acquisition of books, to discover patterns of restriction, and to determine responsibility and rationales for restriction in selection and use. The methodology included structured interviews with the head library media specialist in the fifty-four senior high schools. Farley also used a checklist of specific titles deemed to be controversial to check the card catalog for inclusion. His findings included the following:

- The school principal was viewed as influential in determining actions of the library media specialists.

- Library media specialists themselves performed more voluntary censorship than was imposed by others outside the library media center. Fewer than 10% usually or habitually censored controversial books; 30% rarely censored.

- Library media specialists commonly indicated the following reasons for self-censorship: the youth and immaturity of high school students and the belief that some kinds of reading could have ill effects upon character and conduct.

- More experienced library media specialists performed more book censorship than less experienced ones.

1970-1979

The 1970s showed an increase in the number and variety of studies conducted on intellectual freedom and schools. Three are discussed here. Pope focused on sexually oriented materials and their presence in school, academic, and public libraries. He also examined attitudes of librarians toward such materials. Pope sent a questionnaire to 1200 school, academic, and public librarians. The response rate was 60%. Pope found that the extent and type of educational preparation were related to responses on the questionnaire. Librarians with more extensive educational backgrounds were less restrictive than those with less formal preparation; school library media specialists were more restrictive than public or academic librarians. In all three types studied, librarians serving at larger institutions with larger user groups were less restrictive.

Woodworth sought to obtain information on the status of censorship of library media as well as instructional materials in Wisconsin high schools over a three- to four-year period. Questionnaires distributed to all Wisconsin high schools were given to the principal, a library media specialist, and one teacher (chair of English, social studies, or science departments). School board members were also surveyed but were not included in the analysis. Approximately 50% of the teachers and principals returned the questionnaires, while 73% of the library media specialists did. Woodworth's findings included the following:

- Complaints tend to be rejected where the board-approved selection policy was followed.

- Schools resist challenges outside the system, while acquiescing to those inside.

- Fifty-eight percent of respondents reported one or more objections to library or textbook materials.

Woods sought to determine which materials are most likely to be challenged and why. He also sought to provide a status report on challenged materials in the United States. Using the newsletter from the American Library Association's Office for Intellectual Freedom from 1966 to 1975, Woods located 900 censorship cases including public schools at elementary and secondary levels, academic libraries, and public libraries. Woods found an increase in the number of reported challenges in the 1970s. His other findings included:

- Schools accounted for 62% of all educational censorship, with over 2/3 of the school challenges taking place on the high school level.

- A majority (over 59%) of censorship attempts resulted in restriction or censorship.

1980-1989

The 1980s may be viewed as a period of branching out in school library media intellectual freedom studies. While the number of comprehensive studies remains limited, the areas addressed include a ten-year analysis of material reconsiderations in a school district (Stahlschmidt); the study of legal decisions in challenged cases, and implications for the future (Bryson and Detty; Paysinger); a beginning analysis of the use of warning symbols in book reviews (Watson and Snider); a survey of four major book review journals for children and their treatment of controversial materials (Crow); an analysis of components of materials selection policies as they relate to challenges to materials (Bracy); and several status level survey reports. In addition, a study conducted in 1987 (McDonald) focused on attitudes of secondary school library media specialists toward intellectual freedom and censorship, and their level of principled moral reasoning. Another study conducted in 1988 (Hopkins) focused on the identification of factors influencing the outcome of challenges to secondary level school library media center materials. Summaries of several studies conducted in the 1980s follow.

Watson and Snider conducted an exploratory study designed to measure the resistance of teachers and library media specialists to a warning symbol found in book reviews when making book selections for a children's collection. They used forty-five children's book reviews by Ruth Stein published in Language Arts and randomly placed a warning symbol beside nine of the forty-five reviews. One hundred ninety-seven undergraduate and graduate students enrolled in children's literature classes at the University of Iowa and Michigan State University comprised the sample. The findings included:

- A book review warning exerts a negative influence.

- Regardless of the intended reading age, adult book selectors to a great extent reject children's books based on reviews identified by a warning symbol.

Bracy sought to analyze selection policies in Michigan high schools to determine how significant the policies had been in combatting censorship. She used a questionnaire, that focused on the years 1973-1978. The initial sample was 171 public high schools accredited by the North Central Association of Colleges and Schools. Following receipt of permission from principals to query library media specialists. Bracy distributed a questionnaire to 133 library media specialists. Of those 133, 107, or 80%, returned the instrument. Some telephone interviews were also conducted as a follow-up to the questionnaires. Bracy found that the data supported a relationship between restoration of challenged materials to full access and the existence of an endorsed selection policy. An examination of components of the policy showed that materials were retained most often in cases that involved selection policies containing five or more components.

Bryson and Detty and Paysinger looked at legal aspects pertaining to the selection and use of library, textual, and supplementary materials in K-12 schools. Bryson and Detty concluded that even when legal issues appear to be similar or are the same as those in cases already decided by the courts, a different set of circumstances can produce an entirely different decision. Thus, they concluded, drawing specific conclusions from legal research is difficult. Paysinger found that legal conflict over materials used in public schools is growing.

McDonald conducted an exploratory study in 1987 of a random sample of 450 secondary school (grades 7-12) library media specialists in public schools in Iowa, Minnesota, and Wisconsin. The purpose of the study was to explore the relationship between the attitudes of secondary school librarians toward intellectual freedom and censorship and selected demographic variables. One personal characteristic, level of principled moral reasoning, and attitudes toward intellectual freedom and censorship were also examined.

Data were sought through a questionnaire that included an intellectual freedom/censorship attitude scale, a defining issues test, and a demographic survey. Usable responses were received from 328 respondents, yielding a response rate of 72.88%.

Findings indicated significant relationships between attitudes toward intellectual freedom and attitudes toward censorship. Level of education and size of school were significantly related to intellectual freedom attitudes, with library media specialists in schools with more than 1000 students exhibiting fewer restrictive attitudes than those with less than 500 students. Librarians with master's degrees were found to be less restrictive than those with bachelor's degrees. Respondents who had attended ALA accredited schools had significantly higher mean scores on both attitude scales than subjects who had attended other institutions for their educational preparation. Principled morality was found to be only slightly related to intellectual freedom and censorship attitudes.

Hopkins conducted an exploratory study in 1988 of Wisconsin library media specialists in public middle, junior, and senior high schools. The purpose of the study was to identify factors that influenced whether challenged library media materials were retained, restricted, or removed. Data were sought through a questionnaire distributed to a library media specialist in each of Wisconsin's public middle, junior, and senior high schools. Of 606 questionnaires distributed, 534, or 88%, were returned. Findings indicated that the challenge outcome was influenced by the role of the principal in the challenge process, the educational level of the library media specialist, the support of teachers during the challenge, who makes the final decision in the challenge, the degree of use of the approved selection policy; the initiator of the complaint; and support provided to the library media specialist during the complaint. A national study, based in part on the Wisconsin study, will be conducted by Hopkins in 1990. Both the state and national studies are designed to test a conceptual model developed by Hopkins.[2]

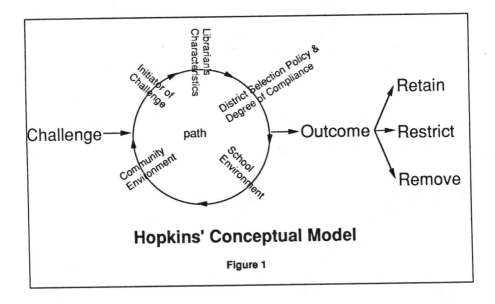

Hopkins' Conceptual Model

Figure 1

Implications for Practitioners

The implications of intellectual freedom research for the practice of school librarianship are several, dealing with how the practitioner interprets and uses intellectual freedom studies and how the practitioner raises questions that need to be addressed through intellectual freedom research. Too many practitioners accept, without question, findings of intellectual freedom research. I believe this is more an issue in intellectual freedom research because the topic interests lay persons and professionals alike. Thus, findings, including questionable ones, are likely to be passed on and publicized. Previous studies, for example, have been used to answer one of the most frequently asked questions: "Is there an increase in challenges to materials?" There has been some question about the studies that have been used as the basis for answering the question.[3] The professional should hesitate to accept generalizations without a careful review of the research report. Implications for continuing and preservice education suggest that a research methods course is a necessary core if the professional is to be discriminating in the analysis of research and if the professional is to articulate research questions that need to be addressed.

Some research findings suggest the importance of internal or external support networks for library media specialists. Where these do not exist, it may be necessary to consider establishing them. Support networks may also be an important research area to address.

While the review of the research does not specifically address this area, it is possible that college and university educators may place too heavy an emphasis on dealing with challenges that come from outside the school, such as from parents, community members, and organized groups. A second area of emphasis seems to be on self-censorship. Pretraining and continuing education opportunities should establish some balance between these factors and those inside the school, such as the influence of the school principal.

Implications for Researchers

The implications for research are examined here in terms of the overall topics that have been generally covered in school library media intellectual freedom research, questions that arise in looking at the studies that have been conducted, and areas for future research to address. An examination of the research that has been conducted indicates that there has been a concentration of studies focusing on variables of the librarian. Studies focusing on librarians have included self-censorship as seen through attitude measures, and collection holdings or nonholdings. The librarians' perceptions of challenges and challenge processes have also been examined. Demographic information such as educational level and age and their relationship to challenges have also been a focus in some studies.

There are several difficulties in the examination of studies for generalizability between studies, not the least of which is the area of definitions. The literature abounds with the use of terms such as "censorship," "intellectual freedom," "attempted censorship," "successful challenge," and "restrictedness." Researchers have used similar terms with different meanings, as well as different terms which, when examined, reveal similar meanings. Thus, simply reading the research poses definitional problems. The intellectual freedom committee of the American Library Association sought to encourage the use of consistent definitions by adopting definitions for the following terms: "oral complaint," "written complaint," "public attack," and "censorship" (see Appendix B). These terms should be examined for their possible use in operational definitions in intellectual freedom studies.

Other difficulties include the rate of return in surveys as well as the combining of findings relating to instructional classroom materials and library media materials. Several surveys base their findings on low rates of return, which make the findings reported questionable. Further, some research looks at the challenge to materials found in school library media centers in terms of the question of voluntary access, as well as challenges to materials used in classroom instruction. Where this has been done, a clear distinction has not always been made between differences in library media materials and materials used in classroom instruction, and clearly separate findings in reports are not always given.

Finally, the subjectivity of the researcher sometimes affects the research, particularly in the reporting of research findings. Subjective, rather than objective, reporting can be found in several reports. In addition, the findings and conclusions are sometimes suspect, in part because of the bias of the researcher.

Other reflections on the research that has been conducted are posed as questions below:

- Do we look at significant research questions?

- Is there clear evidence that the studies are valid and reliable? How have these factors been measured?

- Why does the research focus so often on the secondary school level?

- Can the research question be addressed through measures other than questionnaires? Must the research question be viewed only through the eyes of the library media specialist? Are longitudinal studies appropriate? Are case studies appropriate?

- Is the conceptual basis for the research study clear?

- Have assumptions been stated clearly? Are the assumptions valid?

In terms of future research in intellectual freedom, there are many potential areas of study, both in areas that have already been studied and in areas in which little or no research has been done. One of the intellectual freedom researchers outside the school library media field whose analyses and studies deserve careful attention is Judith Serebnick. Serebnick discusses self-censorship measures, for example, and the need to improve the rigor of checklist-based censorship research.[4] Since self-censorship is an area of special interest to our profession, this area in particular merits careful study.

In her review of research related to censorship in libraries, Serebnick suggests a conceptual framework for further research on selection and censorship in libraries.[5] In the conceptual framework, Serebnick identifies six classes: librarian variables, library variables, community leader variables, community and community action variables, mass media variables, and judicial and legal variables.

Examining our school library media intellectual freedom research base using Serebnick's classes, one can note some attention in the school library media research to librarian variables, including attitudes and demographic variables; to library variables, including organizational, administrative, and legal structure of the library; to selection policies; to mass media variables, particularly book review media; and to impact of judicial decisions regarding censorship and intellectual freedom. There is far less evidence of attention to community leader variables; community and community action variables; mass media variables, such as the influence of information media on challenge outcomes; and judicial and legal variables, including federal, state, and local legislation regarding intellectual freedom.

Additional areas of research concentration, within the context of access, are suggested by Aaron, Molholt, and Rosen. Aaron, for example, included a list of questions based, in part, on theoretical studies developing and evaluating underlying principles of school librarianship; the role of the library media program and staff; and cooperation among various types of libraries. Questions relevant to this discussion include the following: Should all materials be available on the same basis to all people in the school? How can traditional barriers to cooperation be overcome in the school library media area?[6] Rosen summarized research needs for youth services, as developed by the research committees of the Young Adult Services Division and the Association for Library Service to Children, American Librarian Association. Under the areas of intellectual freedom and access to information are the following: Has access to new technologies made information more accessible to youth? Has the cost of this access become a burden necessitating cutbacks in traditional services and personnel that are redefining the role of the youth services librarian? What is available in online database searching for/by teens? What are the information sources for both children and young adults available through networking library services, and what is the match between service and identified needs?[7]

Molholt's discussion of access to information includes research issues in need of attention in the 1990s. For example, she suggested new levels of access for traditional media, such as books; the need to design systems that can respond to users as individuals rather than as classes; and the need to free the intellectual content of both traditional media and obsolete nonmedia from physical constraints.[8]

Still other research areas that might be examined, which focus more directly on challenges to materials, include the dynamics of the reconsideration process as a factor that influences the outcome of a challenge, historical treatment of censorship in schools, pressure groups, and the publishing industry. Extending research beyond the challenge might look at the broader school environment. Research has not sufficiently viewed censorship within the institutional school climate. There is a need to relate intellectual freedom research conceptually to related research areas, including areas such as educational administration.

Finally, research in intellectual freedom needs to be long term. While we can look to dissertations as beginning to address certain research questions, they form the basis of far too much of the intellectual freedom research that has been done. The field of librarianship needs more researchers who are willing to make a life-long commitment to focusing on intellectual freedom research, so that the research can better build upon previous research and address long term, longitudinal issues. At the same time, if intellectual freedom is truly a larger question of access, then our research should also reflect more than the challenge to materials located in school library media centers. The intellectual freedom researcher might begin examining questions of access as addressed in national guidelines of the profession[9] and by McDonald. McDonald views access from intellectual as well as physical perspectives. Among the access issues discussed by McDonald are database searching and interlibrary loan.[10]

Intellectual freedom research relating to school library media centers can be found as early as 1948. In the forty years since then, much of the study of intellectual freedom research has been reflected in dissertations and in status reports issued by organizations and individuals. While research in the 1980s shows attention to varied aspects of intellectual freedom, there continues to be a need for rigorous research that addresses significant questions over time.

Appendix A

Research Summaries

Busha sought to investigate the extent to which public librarians in the east north-central states of the United States accept the intellectual freedom principles and concepts of the Library Bill of Rights and the Freedom to Read Statement. He also sought to determine the attitudes of these librarians toward censorship practices. Further, Busha sought to ascertain the relationship between librarians' attitudes toward censorship and their attitudes about certain characteristic beliefs of authoritarianism. Using a sample of 900 individuals, selected from a population of 3,253 public librarians in Illinois, Indiana, Michigan, Ohio, and Wisconsin, Busha obtained a 70% return, or 624 surveys, for analysis. The most significant result of the study, according to Busha, was "the marked disparity between the attitudes of many librarians toward intellectual freedom as a concept and their attitudes toward censorship as an activity" (p. 147), with 64% of the librarians neither favorable nor unfavorable toward censorship practices.

England sought to discover attitudes and perceptual factors influencing what she called "the censorship activity" of public librarians in six Ontario (Canada) cities. An analysis of library collections was combined with an analysis of statements measuring the perceptions and attitudes of those librarians selecting books for the collections. A questionnaire, an interview, and a checklist of titles comprised the research design. Six hypotheses were studied. Factors examined were attitude toward intellectual freedom, degree of anomy, view of others, personal characteristics, contact with a censorship incident, and the nature of actual collections. Personal and professional characteristics of librarians were examined and found to be significant. The single best predictor of actual censorship in library collections was found to be the librarian's attitude toward intellectual freedom.

Appendix B

Intellectual Freedom Terminology

Censorship: a change in the access status of material, made by a governing authority or its representatives. Such changes include exclusion, restriction, removal, or age/grade level changes, where the intent is to restrict access.

Expression of concern: an inquiry that has judgmental overtones.

Oral complaint: an oral challenge to the presence and/or appropriateness of the material in question.

Public attack: a publicly disseminated statement challenging the value of the material, presented to the media and/or others outside the institutional organization in order to gain public support for further action.

Written complaint: a formal, written complaint filed with the institution (library, school, etc.) challenging the presence and/or appropriateness of specific material.

The above terminology replaces the Intellectual Freedom Glossary, issued in 1985 by the American Library Association's Office for Intellectual Freedom. The new terminology was adopted by the Intellectual Freedom Committee of the American Library Association during its annual conference meeting in San Francisco on June 27, 1987.

Notes

1. American Library Association. Intellectual Freedom Manual. 3rd ed. (Chicago: American Library Association, 1989), ix.

2. Dianne McAfee Hopkins. "Toward a Conceptual Model of Factors Influencing the Outcome of Challenges to Library Materials in School Settings." Library and Information Science Research 11 (July-September 1989), 247-71.

3. Kenneth I. Taylor. "Are School Censorship Cases Really Increasing?"School Library Media Quarterly 11 (Fall 1982), 26-34.

4. Judith Serebnick. "Self-Censorship by Librarians: An Analysis of Checklist-Based Research." Drexel Library Quarterly 18 (Winter 1982), 35-56.

5. Judith Serebnick. "A Review of Research Related to Censorship in Libraries." Library Research (now Library and Information Science Research) 1 (Summer 1979), 114-15.

6. Shirley Aaron. "A Review of Selected Research Studies About School Library Media Programs, Resources, and Personnel," in School Library Media Annual, 1983 (Littleton, Colorado: Libraries Unlimited, 1983), 363-67.

7. Elizabeth McClure Rosen. "Inquiring Librarians Want to Know: Today's Research Questions." Journal of Youth Services in Libraries 2 (Summer 1989), 370.

8. Pat Molholt. "Research Issues in Information Access." School Library Media Quarterly 17 (Spring 1989), 134.

9. American Library Association. Information Power: Guidelines for School Library Media Programs. (Chicago: American Library Association, 1988), 140-148.

10. Frances M. McDonald. "Information Access for Youth: Issues and Concerns." Library Trends 37 (Summer 1988), 28-42.

Bibliography

Aaron, Shirley, "A Review of Selected Research Studies About School Library Media Programs, Resources, and Personnel." In School Library Media Annual, 1983, edited by Shirley Aaron and Pat R. Scales, 303-85. Littleton, Colorado: Libraries Unlimited, 1983.

American Library Association. Information Power: Guidelines for School Library Media Programs. Chicago: American Library Association, 1988.

American Library Association. Intellectual Freedom Manual. 3rd ed. Chicago: American Library Association, 1989.

Association of American Publishers, American Library Association, Association for Supervision and Curriculum Development. Limiting What Students Shall Read. Washington, D. C.: Association of American Publishers, American Library Association, Association for Supervision and Curriculum Development, 1981.

Beineke, John A. "Censorship in Indiana High School Libraries." Phi Delta Kappan 63 (May 1982), 638-39.

Borowiak, Ralph E. "Textbook and Library Censorship in Illinois Public High Schools." Ed.D. dissertation, Northern Illinois University, 1983.

Bracy, Pauletta Brown. "Censorship and Selection Policies in Public Senior High School Library Media Centers in Michigan." Ph.D. dissertation, University of Michigan, 1982.

Bryson, Joseph E., and Detty, Elizabeth W. The Legal Aspects of Censorship of Public School Library and Instructional Materials. Charlottesville, Virginia: The Michie Company, 1982.

Bump, Myrna Marlene. "Censorship Practiced by High School Librarians Prior to Actual Book Selection." Ph.D. dissertation, Kansas State University, 1980.

Burress, Lee. Battle of the Books: Literary Censorship in the Public Schools, 1950-1985. Metuchen, New Jersey: The Scarecrow Press, 1989.

Burress, Lee. "A Brief Report of the 1977 NCTE Censorship Survey." In Dealing With Censorship, edited by James E. Davis, 16-47. Urbana, Illinois: National Council of Teachers of English, 1979.

Burress, Lee. "Censorship in School Libraries." In ALA Yearbook 1983, edited by Robert Wedgeworth, 246-47. Chicago: American Library Association, 1983.

Burress, Lee. Summary Report of a Survey of Censorship Pressures on the American High School,1982. Urbana, Illinois: National Council of Teachers of English, 1983.

Busha, Charles H. Freedom versus Suppression and Censorship. Littleton, Colorado: Libraries Unlimited, 1972.

Chandler, Katherine Mone. "Intellectual Freedom and the Use of Trade Books in the Elementary School: Perceptions of Principals." Ph.D. dissertation, University of Minnesota, 1985.

Crow, Sherry R. "The Reviewing of Controversial Juvenile Books: A Study." School Library Media Quarterly 14 (Winter 1986), 83-86.

Douma, Rollin George. Book Selection Policies, Book Complaint Policies and Censorship in Selected Michigan Public High Schools (ED 078448, RIE Nov. 73).

Douma, Rollin. "Censorship in the English Classroom: A Review of Research." Journal of Research and Development in Education 9 (Spring 1976), 60-68.

Eakin, M. L. "Censorship in Public High School Libraries." Master's thesis, Columbia University, 1948.

England, Claire St. Clere. "The Climate of Censorship in Ontario." Ph. D. dissertation, University of Toronto, 1974.

Ernst, Wanna. "Censorship: An Overview of What Is Happening in School Library Media Centers and Other Areas of Education." In School Library Media Annual, 1985, edited by Shirley Aaron and Pat R. Scales, 9-36. Littleton, Colorado: Libraries Unlimited, 1985.

Farley, John J. "Book Censorship in the Senior High School Libraries in Nassau County, New York." Ph.D. dissertation, New York University, 1964.

Fiske, Marjorie. Book Selection and Censorship. Berkeley, California: University of California Press, 1959.

Fitzgibbons, Shirley, et al. "Selection and Censorship in Indiana School Libraries: Summary Report on the Intellectual Freedom Survey." Indiana Media Journal 6 (Winter 1983), 24-32.

Flagg, Wilma T. "Internal Censorship in Periodicals by Missouri School Librarians in Grades 9-12." Master's thesis, Central Missouri State University, 1986.

Glover, Virginia L. "Censorship in Indiana Public Secondary School Media Centers, 1970-75." Ph.D. dissertation, Purdue University, 1975.

Hopkins, Dianne McAfee. "Censorship of School Library Media Materials and Its Implications, 1982-83." In School Library Media Annual, 1984, vol. 2, edited by Shirley L. Aaron and Pat R. Scales, 10-14. Littleton, Colorado: Libraries Unlimited, 1984.

Hopkins, Dianne McAfee. "Factors Influencing the Outcome of Challenges in Junior, Middle, and Senior High School Library Media Centers in Wisconsin: An Exploratory Study." (Accepted for publication, School Library Media Quarterly, 1990.)

Hopkins, Dianne McAfee. "Toward a Conceptual Model of Factors Influencing the Outcome of Challenges to Library Materials in School Settings." Library and Information Science Research 11 (July-September 1989), 247-71.

Horton, Nancy Spence. "Young Adult Literature and Censorship: A Content Analysis of Seventy-Eight Young Adult Books". Ph.D. dissertation, North Texas State University, 1986.

Immroth, Barbara. "Intellectual Freedom as Practiced by Public and School Librarians in Texas." Collection Management 7 (Fall 1985-Winter 1986), 353-68.

Jenkinson, David. "Censorship Iceberg: Results of a Survey of Challenges in Public and School Libraries." Canadian Library Journal 43 (February 1986), 7-21.

Jenkinson, David. "The Censorship Iceberg: The Results of a Survey of Challenges in School and Public Libraries." School Libraries in Canada (Fall 1985), 19-30.

Kegley, Sissy, and Guerrero, Gene. Censorship in the South: A Report of Four States, 1980-85. New York: ACLU.

McClure, A. Censorship in Ohio: It Is Happening Here. Delaware, Ohio: Ohio Wesleyan University, 1982.

McDonald, Fran. A Report of a Survey on Censorship in Public Elementary and High School Libraries and Public Libraries in Minnesota. Minneapolis: Minnesota Civil Liberties Union, 1983.

McDonald, Frances Beck. "Intellectual Freedom and Censorship Attitudes of Secondary School Librarians and Principled Moral Reasoning." Ph.D. dissertation, The University of Minnesota, 1989.

McDonald, Frances M. "Information Access for Youth: Issues and Concerns." Library Trends 37 (Summer 1988), 28-42.

McKee, Richard E. "Censorship Research: Its Strengths, Weaknesses, Uses, and Misuses." In An Intellectual Freedom Primer, edited by Charles H. Busha, 192-220. Littleton, Colorado: Libraries Unlimited, 1977.

McMillan, Laura Smith. "Censorship by Librarians in Public Senior High Schools In Virginia." Ed.D. dissertation, The College of William and Mary in Virginia, 1987.

Molholt, Pat. "Research Issues in Information Access." School Library Media Quarterly 17 (Spring 1989), 131-35.

National Commission on Libraries and Information Science. Censorship Activities in Public and Public School Libraries, 1975-1985. A Report to the Senate Subcommittee on Appropriations for the Departments of Labor, Health and Human Services, and Education and Related Agencies. Washington, D.C.: National Commission on Libraries and Information Science, 1986.

Paysinger, Nancy Virginia. "An Investigation into the Case Law Pertaining to the Selection and Use of Library, Textual, and Supplementary Materials in American Public Education, Kindergarten through 12th Grade." Ed.D. dissertation, University of Georgia, 1983.

People for the American Way. Attacks on the Freedom to Learn. Washington, D.C.: Citizens for Constitutional Concerns, Inc. (annual report).

Poole, Diana M. "Veiled Knowledge: Censorship in the Public School of British Columbia." Master's thesis, The University of British Columbia, 1986.

Pope, Michael J. Sex and the Undecided Librarian: A Study of Librarians' Opinions on Sexually-Oriented Literature. Metuchen, New Jersey: The Scarecrow Press, 1974.

Rosen, Elizabeth McClure. "Inquiring Librarians Want to Know: Today's Research Questions." Journal of Youth Services in Libraries 2 (Summer 1989), 369-71.

Scott, Dwain Lewis. "Intellectual Freedom in Kansas High School Media Centers." (ED 060886, RIE July, 1972).

Serebnick, Judith. "An Analysis of Publishers of Books Reviewed in Key Library Journals." Library and Information Science Research 6 (July-September 1984), 289-303.

Serebnick, Judith. "An Analysis of the Relationship Between Book Reviews and the Inclusion of Potentially Controversial Books in Public Libraries." Collection Building 1, No. 2 (1979), 8-56.

Serebnick, Judith. "Book Reviews and the Selection of Potentially Controversial Books in Public Libraries." Library Quarterly 51 (October 1981), 390-409.

Serebnick, Judith. "A Review of Research Related to Censorship in Libraries". Library Research (now Library and Information Science Research) 1 (Summer 1979), 95-118.

Serebnick, Judith. "Self-Censorship by Librarians: An Analysis of Checklist-Based Research." Drexel Library Quarterly 18 (Winter 1982), 35-56.

Serebnick, Judith, and Cullars, John. "An Analysis of Reviews and Library Holdings of Small Publishers' Books." Library Resources and Technical Services, 28 (January/March 1984), 4-14.

Stahlschmidt, Agnes D. "The Iowa Plan Revisited: Ten Years Later." Paper presented at the annual meeting of the National Council of Teachers of English, Boston, November 1981. (ED 270125).

Symula, James F. "Censorship of High School Literature: A Study of the Incidents of Censorship Involving J.D. Salinger's The Catcher in the Rye." Ed.D. dissertation, State University of New York at Buffalo, 1969.

Taylor, Kenneth I. "Are School Censorship Cases Really Increasing?" School Library Media Quarterly 11 (Fall 1982), 26-34.

Torke, Keith. "Sex Education Books, Censorship and Colorado High School Libraries: A Survey." Ed.D. dissertation., University of Northern Colorado, 1975.

U.S. Department of Education. Rethinking the Library in the Information Age: A Summary of Issues in Library Research, vols. 1-2. Washington, D.C: U.S. Department of Education, October, 1988.

Watson, Jerry J., and Snider, Bill C. "Book Selection Pressure on School Library Media Specialists and Teachers." School Media Quarterly 9 (Winter 1981), 95-101.

Watson, Jerry J., and Snider, Bill C. "Educating the Potential Self-Censor." School Media Quarterly 9 (Summer 1981), 272-76.

Wildman, Mary Gail. "Challenges to Library Books in the Public High Schools of Mississippi, 1978-85: A Survey of High School Library Media Specialists". Ed.D. dissertation, University of Southern Mississippi, 1986.

Wisconsin Department of Public Instruction. Censorship of IMC Materials in Wisconsin Schools. Part III: Focus on High Schools. Madison: Wisconsin Department of Public Instruction, 1981.

Wisconsin Department of Public Instruction. Schools. Part II: Focus on Elementary Schools. Madison: Wisconsin Department of Public Instruction, 1981.

Woods, L. B. A Decade of Censorship in America: The Threat to Classrooms and Libraries 1966-75. Metuchen, New Jersey: The Scarecrow Press, 1979.

Woods, L.B. "For Sex: See Librarian." Library Journal 103 (September 1, 1978), 1561-66.

Woods, L.B., and Salvatore, Lucy. "Self-Censorship in Collection Development by High School Library Media Specialists." School Media Quarterly 9 (Winter 1981), 102-108.

Woodworth, Mary L. Intellectual Freedom, The Young Adult, and Schools. Revised edition. Madison: University of Wisconsin Extension, 1976.

INTELLECTUAL FREEDOM AND CENSORSHIP RESEARCH: SCHOOL LIBRARY MEDIA RESOURCES

Frances Beck McDonald
Professor
Library Media Education Department
Mankato State University, Mankato, Minnesota

The purpose of this paper is to categorize research needs in the area of intellectual freedom and censorship. Six categories were identified and studies located to illustrate the categories. While no attempt was made to conduct an exhaustive search of the literature, an attempt was made to locate at least one example in each research category. The categories identified were:

1. Censorship
    *   Surveys
    *   Characteristics of Challengers
    *   Case Studies of Censorship Incidents

2. Intellectual Freedom and Censorship: Variables
    *   Librarian Variables
    *   Self-Censorship or Pre-Selection Censorship
    *   Impact of Reviews on Selection
    *   Institutional Variables
    *   Selection Policies: Status, Use, and Result

3. Educational Preparation
    *   Intellectual Freedom Knowledge, Attitudes, and Skills
    *   Intellectual Freedom in the Curriculum
    *   School Library Media Education Faculty Attitudes
    *   Licensure/Certification Requirements

4. Intellectual Freedom: Development of the Concept in School Library Media Programs

5. Rights of Children
    *   Intellectual Rights
    *   Access Rights
    *   Privacy Rights

6. Physical and Intellectual Access to Information

Censorship

The majority of intellectual freedom and censorship surveys describe the following factors: how much, what resources, who initiated, who resolved, process

151

used, and result. Individuals, state departments of education, state professional organizations, and national organizations have reported censorship survey research (see Table 1).

Table 1
Censorship Surveys

Researcher (Date)	Research	Comments
AAP, ALA, ASCD (1981)	Survey	National study
ACLU (1985)	Survey	4 southern states
ALA/OIF	Newspaper reports of censorship activity	Newsletter on Intellectual Freedom
Farley (1964)	Survey	Long Island, NY
Hopkins (1984)	Survey	Status as perceived by national leaders
McDonald (1983)	Survey	Elementary, secondary school libraries (MCLU)
National Coalition Against Censorship	Survey	Court cases
People for the American Way	Survey	Descriptions of incidents
Woodworth (1976)	Survey of attitudes	Included teachers and administrators

Implications for Researchers

A definitive annotated bibliography of all studies, including master's degree theses and alternate plan papers from ALA and NCATE accredited schools and other institutions preparing school library media specialists, is a basic research need. Locating titles of theses and papers should be possible through library school records. Of greater difficulty will be locating unpublished surveys completed by professional organizations and individuals. Identifying studies completed by individuals outside the library media field presents another challenge.

Knowing the who, what, and where of censorship has immediate appeal to school library media specialists, but most studies present little new information. Censorship exists: certain titles occur on every list, some efforts at limiting access to resources result in restriction, other efforts result in removal of resources, and some result in retention of the questioned resource. In spite of predictable results, however, baseline data need to be collected and updated, so survey research will continue to be needed.

Characteristics of challengers. Research in this category explored the motivation, affiliations, and expressions of concern raised by individuals and groups who challenge resources. Jenkinson (1974) identified the agendas and issues raised by local, state, and national groups. Stahlschmidt (1981) studied challenges and the review process in one school district. Moffett (1988) described the textbook dispute in Kanawha County, West Virginia (Table 2).

Table 2
Challenges and Challengers

Researcher (Date)	Research	Comments
Jenkinson (1974)	Content analysis	Narrative report of group characteristics
Stahlschmidt (1981)	Content analysis	Challenge process
Moffett (1988)	Case study	Kanawha County

Implications for Researchers

Content analysis of expressions of concern filed with school officials is needed to define categories of criticism and identify group affiliations. Case studies of censorship incidents are needed to analyze procedures and results and identify strategies used by challengers and school officials. Additionally, case studies could provide information about reactions of community leaders, the press, and other educators. In recent years, social and political changes have shifted the focus of organized groups. Studies of pressure groups are needed to revise outdated information and to determine the accuracy of current speculation that attacks on the curriculum have replaced objections to single titles.

Intellectual Freedom and Censorship: Variables

In 1979, Serebnick presented six classes of variables influencing the selection and censorship of resources: librarian, library, community leader, community and community action, mass media, and judicial and legal. Researchers have investigated librarian variables, mass media variables in the form of reviewing sources, and library variables -- the influence of the principal and selection policies. Attention has not been given to the other categories identified by Serebnick.

Implications for Researchers

Censorship incidents illustrate only one factor explaining access to, and restriction of, information. Other variables need to be examined to isolate the factors that influence selection, availability, and use of resources. Research questions need to be formulated in every class of Serebnick's variables.

Librarian variables were one of the classes identified by Serebnick. She included attitudes and demographic variables in the librarian category. Fiske (1959), Farley (1964), Pope (1974), and Woodworth (1976) discussed demographic characteristics of school librarians in reporting the results of their research. Busha's (1971) examination of the authoritarian attitudes of librarians, although conducted with public librarians, is an example of the type of research needed to determine the personal characteristics of school library media specialists and their attitudes and beliefs about intellectual freedom and censorship. McDonald (1989a) investigated attitudes toward intellectual freedom and censorship, demographic characteristics: and one personal characteristic, level of moral development of school library media specialists (Table 3).

Table 3
Attitudes and Characteristics of
School Library Media Specialists

Researcher (Date)	Research	Comments
Busha (1971)	Attitude survey	Demographics Public Librarians
	Correlation study	Authoritarian beliefs
Farley (1964)	Survey	Demographics
Fiske (1959)	Interviews	Demographics
McDonald (1989a)	Attitude survey	Demographics
	Correlation study	Moral Development
McDonald (in progress)	Correlation study	Authoritarian beliefs
	Attitudes from above	Ego strength
		Family background
		Educational preparation
Pope (1974)	Survey	Demographics
Woodworth (1976)	Attitude survey	Demographics

Implications for Researchers

As key players in the selection and retention of resources, school library media specialists control the information resources available to students. Why have researchers found that school library media specialists were more likely to remove resources when the challenges came from within the school than when the challenges came from outside the school? What factors influence school library media specialists' responses to challenges? Do school library media specialists with different levels of cognitive development, different personal characteristics, and different degrees of ego strength respond differently in access situations? In addition to demographic variables and developmental variables, the backgrounds of school library media specialists must be examined.

Beginning with the Fiske (1959) study, researchers have verified the finding that librarians exhibit censorious attitudes and practice self-censorship. Bump (1980) and Woods and Salvatore (1981) used checklists of resources to determine whether specific titles were available in school libraries. Other researchers looked at review sources. Watson and Snider (1981) examined the effect of warning symbols in reviews on selection decisions. Fiske (1959), Farley (1964), and Pope (1974) all found that there were some items school library media specialists would not buy. McDonald (1989a) and Fiske found inconsistencies in attitudes toward intellectual freedom and censorship, with more librarians agreeing with intellectual freedom in principles rather than in practice. Hopkins (1984) reported that library leaders believed self-censorship to be a major problem (Table 4).

Table 4
Self-Censorship

Researcher (Date)	Research	Comments
Bump (1980)	Survey Checklist	Controversial titles.
Flagg (1986)	Survey	Periodicals. Missouri.
Hopkins (1984)	Survey	National library leaders.
Pope (1974)	Survey	Sex oriented books.
Watson and Snider (1981)	Selection simulation	Review warnings.
Woods and Salvatore (1981)	Checklist-based	Collection Development. National.

Implications for Researchers

Although researchers have established that self-censorship exists, no study has identified factors contributing to self-censorship. Pressures from inside and outside the school need to be examined to determine their effect on selection and restriction decisions. Factors revealed in studies of librarian variables need to be looked at to isolate library, institution, and other variables that contribute to self-censorship.

Institutional variables. Serebnick (1979) included the administrative and legal structure of the institution in her library variables class. Of the institutional variables affecting access to information in a school, the attitudes and behavior of professional colleagues are believed to be key factors. Certainly, the attitudes and expectations of the principal affect the behavior of school library media specialists. Woodworth (1976) investigated attitudes of teachers, administrators, and school library media specialists. Institutional, or library, variables such as the influence of the school principal and amount of selection autonomy were examined by Fiske (1959).

Another library variable identified by Serebnick was the existence of selection policies and reevaluation procedures. Most of the surveys identified earlier included questions about the existence of selection policies and whether policies were followed in resolving the incident. Findings were uniformly mixed, with policies being applied in some incidents and apparently ignored in others. Bracy (1982) analyzed policies to determine what elements were present and how having all the essential elements of a selection policy influenced the outcome of a challenge (Table 5).

Table 5
Institutional Variables

Researcher (Date)	Research	Comments
Bracy (1982)	Survey	Selection policy elements.
Fiske (1956)	Interview	Administrative influences.
Woodworth (1976)	Survey	Administrators, teachers, and librarians.

Implications for Research

Research questions in this category include how professional colleagues influence selection and retention decisions. The climate in the school and expectations of school administrators and teachers need to be examined to determine their impact on collection development and outcomes of challenges. Information is needed about all elements of selection policies, how policies influence the outcome of challenges to resources, and also how objectives and criteria affect the process of selecting resources. Questions need to be asked about why educators follow policies or why they ignore them.

Educational Preparation

In the librarian variable class, Serebnick included the educational preparation of school library media specialists. Although general questions about intellectual freedom content in the curriculum have been asked, no study has focused specifically on the curriculum for pre-service school library media specialists. McDonald (1989a) found differences in attitudes toward intellectual freedom and censorship between respondents from ALA accredited schools and other preparation programs (Table 6).

Table 6
Educational Preparation

Researcher (Date)	Research	Comments
McDonald (1989a)	Attitude survey	ALA school vs. other preparation programs
McDonald (in progress)	Attitudes from above	Subjects from 1989 study
	Survey Correlation	
McDonald (study being designed)	Survey	Faculty

Implications for Research

No research about the intellectual freedom content of the educational preparation of school library media specialists exists. Before studies can be conducted about what students are taught, researchers must identify the essential knowledge, attitudes, and skills needed by school library media specialists in the area of intellectual freedom. A major questions is: are students taught essential intellectual freedom competencies? How are concepts of intellectual freedom incorporated in the library school curriculum? How are students evaluated? Are there differences between ALA accredited schools and NCATE accredited schools? Are there differences between faculty in ALA accredited schools and NCATE accredited schools? Are faculty different in their attitudes, beliefs, and preparation? Do faculty exhibit attitudes and beliefs about intellectual freedom and censorship similar to the attitudes that school library media specialists exhibit?

Another area of investigation relates to requirements for state licensing/certification. Are intellectual freedom and access competencies required? How do the competencies compare with a theoretical list of essential knowledges, attitudes, and skills? What opportunities exist beyond professional preparation to acquire information about intellectual freedom, and do school library media specialists take advantage of professional development opportunities?

Intellectual Freedom: Development of the Concept in School Library Media Programs

Geller (1984) traced the development of the concept of intellectual freedom in public libraries up to the 1939 adoption of the Library Bill of Rights. Historical research about the concept as it has evolved in school libraries has not been done.

Implications for Researchers

Professional documents, records of professional associations, standards, and professional journals need to be analyzed for an historical study of intellectual freedom in schools. Geller provided one model for presenting the results of research describing the development of the intellectual freedom concept.

Rights of Children

The major difference between public libraries and school library media programs in relation to access to information appears to be age of library users and the purposes of the school. One could speculate that beliefs about the rights of children contribute to decisions that school library media specialists make about appropriate resources. Information about the rights of children comes from legal scholars and psychologists. No specific research from the library community has examined beliefs about rights of children. Bryson and Detty (1982) analyzed the implications of judicial rulings on school library resources, and Michaelis (1988) analyzed federal court decisions on the formation of educational policy. Siegel's (1986) questions about the intellectual rights of children have implications for the selection of resources on teaching critical thinking and information skills.

Implications for Researchers

Content analysis of court cases and implications for access to resources appears to be one method of providing information to school library media specialists. Analysis of educational policy is another indication of beliefs about rights of children.

Physical and Intellectual Access to Information

Two categories of research were identified that traditionally have not been viewed as part of intellectual freedom: physical and intellectual access to information. Information Power (1988) stated that the mission of the school library media program was to "ensure the students and staff are effective users of information and ideas," and that mission is accomplished through physical and intellectual access to information. Liesener (1985) described intellectual access to information. Siegel (1986) asked whether critical thinking was an intellectual right. While intellectual access to information is a relatively new concept, the idea of physical access has been the cornerstone of all previous research. Physical access research, however, has been limited to questions about whether the item could be found on the shelves. Physical access includes access to resources outside the school, or interlibrary loan, school library participation in networks, subject access, and availability of electronic databases. Access questions being addressed elsewhere include networking and automation.

References

American Association of School Librarians. Information Power: Guidelines for School Library Media Programs. Chicago: American Association of School Librarians and Association for Educational Communications and Technology, 1988.

Bracy, Pauletta. "Censorship and Selection Policies in Public Senior High School Library Media Centers in Michigan." Ph.D. Dissertation, University of Michigan, 1982.

Bryson, Joseph E., and Detty, Elizabeth W. The Legal Aspects of Censorship of Public School Library and Instructional Materials. Charlottesville, Virginia: 1982.

Bump, Myrna Marlene. "Censorship Practiced by High School Librarians Prior to (Actual) Book Selection." Ph.D. Dissertation, Kansas State University, 1980.

Busha, Charles H. "The Attitudes of Midwestern Public Librarians Toward Intellectual Freedom and Censorship." Ph.D. Dissertation, Indiana University, 1971.

Farley, John J. "Book Censorship in the Senior High Libraries of Nassau County, New York." Ph.D. Dissertation, New York University, 1964.

Fiske, Marjorie (Lowenthal). Book Selection and Censorship: A Study of School and Public Librarians in California. Berkeley: University of California Press, 1959.

Geller, Evelyn. Forbidden Books in American Public Libraries, 1876-1939: A Study in Cultural Change. Westport, Connecticut: Greenwood Press, 1984.

Hopkins, Diane. "Censorship of School Library Materials and Its Implications." In School Library Media Annual 1984, Vol 2. Aaron, Shirley, and Pat Scales, eds., 9-22. Littleton, Colorado: Libraries Unlimited, 1984.

Jenkinson, Edward. Censors in the Classroom: The Mind Benders. Carbondale, Illinois: Southern Illinois University Press, 1974.

Liesener, James. "Learning at Risk: School Library Media Programs in an Information World." School Library Media Quarterly 14 (Fall, 1985), 11-20.

McDonald, Fran. A Report of a Survey on Censorship in Public Elementary and High School Libraries and Public Libraries in Minnesota. Minneapolis: Minnesota Civil Liberties Union, 1983.

McDonald, Frances Beck. "Intellectual Freedom and Censorship Attitudes of Secondary School Librarians and Principled Moral Reasoning." Ph.D. Dissertation, University of Minnesota, 1989a.

Michaelis, Karen Lauree. "Federal Court Decisions and Educational Policy Making: A Review of the Substantive Rights of Students in Public Schools." Ph.D. Dissertation, University of Wisconsin, 1988.

Moffett, James. Storm in the Mountains: A Case Study of Censorship, Conflict, and Consciousness. Carbondale, Illinois: Southern Illinois University Press, 1988.

National Coalition Against Censorship. Books on Trial: A Survey of Recent Cases. New York: National Coalition Against Censorship, 1985.

Pope, Michael. Sex and the Undecided Librarian: A Study of Librarians' Opinions on Sexually Oriented Literature. Metuchen, New Jersey: Scarecrow Press, 1974.

Serebnick, Judith. "An Analysis of the Relationship Between Book Reviews and the Inclusion of Potentially Controversial Books in Public Libraries." Collection Building 1 (1979), 8-53.

Siegel, Harvey. "Critical Thinking as an Intellectual Right." New Directions for Child Development 33 (Fall, 1986), 39-49.

Stahlschmidt, Agnes D. "A Democratic Procedure for Handling Challenged Library Materials." School Library Media Quarterly 11 (Spring, 1983), 200-203.

Watson, Jerry J., and Bill C. Snider. "Book Selection Pressures on School Library Media Specialists and Teachers." School Media Quarterly 9 (Winter, 1981), 95-101.

Woods, L.B., and Lucy Salvatore. "Self-Censorship in Collection Development by High School Library Media Specialists." School Media Quarterly 9 (Winter, 1981), 102-108.

Woodworth, Mary. Intellectual Freedom, the Young Adult, and Schools: A Wisconsin Study. Madison: University of Wisconsin, 1976.

Bibliography

Association of American Publishers. Limiting What Students Shall Read: Books and Other Learning Materials in our Public Schools: How They are Selected and How They are Removed. Washington, D.C.: American Association of Publishers, American Library Association, Association for Supervision and Curriculum Development, 1981.

Bundy, Mary Lee, and Teresa Stakem. "Librarians and Intellectual Freedom: Are Opinions Changing?" Wilson Library Bulletin 57 (April, 1982), 584-589.

Burress, Lee. "Censorship in School Libraries." In ALA Yearbook 1983. Chicago: American Library Association, 1983, 246-247.

Burress, Lee. "Censorship in Wisconsin Public High Schools." In How Censorship Affects the School and Other Essays. Racine, Wisconsin: Wisconsin Council of Teachers of English, 1984, 60-101.

Burress, Lee. Summary Report of a Survey of Censorship Pressures on the American High School, 1982. Urbana, Illinois: National Council of Teachers of English, 1983.

Busha, Charles H. Freedom Versus Suppression and Censorship: With a Study of the Attitudes of Midwestern Public Librarians and a Bibliography of Censorship. Littleton, Colorado: Libraries Unlimited, 1972.

Charter, Jody. "An Open Invitation? Access to Secondary School Library Media Resources and Services." School Library Media Quarterly 15 (Spring 1987), 158-60.

Flagg, Wilma T. "Internal Censorship of Periodicals by Missouri School Librarians in Grades 9 - 12." Master's Thesis, Central Missouri State University, 1986.

McDonald, Frances M. "Access to Information: Professional Responsibility and Personal Response." In Managers and Missionaries: Library Services to Children and Young Adults in the Information Age. Leslie Edmonds, ed. Urbana-Champaign, Illinois: University of Illinois, 1989b.

Serebnick, Judith. "Book Reviews and the Selection of Potentially Controversial Books in Public Libraries." Library Quarterly 51 (October, 1981), 390-409.

Serebnick, Judith. "Self-Censorship by Librarians: An Analysis of Checklist-Based Research." Drexel Library Quarterly 18 (Winter, 1982), 35-56.

Woods, L.B. A Decade of Censorship in America: The Threat to Classroom and Libraries. Metuchen, New Jersey: Scarecrow Press, 1979.

Part 4

Technology and the School Library Media Center

ACCESS TO INFORMATION: THE EFFECT OF AUTOMATION

Catherine Murphy
Director, Library Media Services
Three Village Central School District
Stony Brook, New York

Introduction

This paper focuses on the impact of the online public access catalog (OPAC) upon subject access to information. The OPACs found in school library media centers are more likely to be microcomputer systems, although a number of larger school districts have implemented mainframe online systems, sometimes in cooperation with the local public library. At the present time, there are perhaps 12,000 microcomputer systems in schools, most of them circulation systems, but increasingly these programs are integrated with an online catalog. These figures are estimates from vendors, which I have requested in surveys for other reports published recently (Murphy, 1988, 1989).

The history of microcomputer OPACs in school library media centers dates from 1981, when COMPUTER CAT was developed for Mountain View Elementary School in Colorado. In the next few years, about a dozen vendors entered the school market. This number has remained the same although the list of companies fluctuates. Follett is the frontrunner in sales of microcomputer systems to schools, followed by Winnebago; Utlas, Library Corporation, Columbia, and Data Trek, and other vendors also have school users.

In 1985, when I surveyed microcomputer systems users as part of my doctoral dissertation research (Murphy, 1987), only about 160 sites could be identified by vendors. There has been a strong and steady growth in automation in school library media centers since then, evidenced by my estimates of installations given above, and by the latest figures in School Library Journal's annual report of school library media center expenditures (Miller and Schontz, 1989). Of the 644 respondents to their survey (which was mailed to randomly selected SLJ subscribers), 21% had access to an automated circulation system, 42% planned to develop such a system, 6% had access to an automated card catalog, and 29% planned to develop an automated card catalog.

The school library media professionals implementing these systems are beginning to regard them as more than library management tools. The OPAC database with full catalog records and a system enhanced for public use can revolutionize subject access to collections and provide an instructional tool for critical selection and analysis of information.

In order to consider the actual or potential impact of automation, it is necessary to define the components of subject access. One researcher included the design of the system itself, the bibliographic record, the user, and the additional tools we load into the system to improve access to the record, such as authority file, indexes, and class schedules (Mandel, 1985). Another writer described the parts of an online system that influence access as the files, functions, and communications of the system, and stated that it is the user interface, that reacts with all three components, which is the most important aspect of the system (Hildreth, 1985).

Others have analyzed what can be done to improve access by focusing on the difficulties encountered by subject searchers in online catalogs. For example, these major problems in subject access have been cited: finding the right subject term, knowing what is in the catalog, increasing and decreasing searching results, entering commands, and scanning long displays (Seal, 1986; Markey, 1986). All observers have stressed the interaction between user and system as the major difference between online and card catalog searching.

This paper considers the areas suggested by these writers from the perspective of the state-of-the-art microcomputer OPACs, with a focus on the special needs of the school user. Catalog database development and enhanced subject access are not as well developed in microcomputer systems, nor have they been studied or theorized about to the extent that have big OPAC systems in academic and special libraries. Nor have the needs of online searchers who are children or students received much attention. The next section, about published research and/or theory, therefore includes relevant writings about children's access in the card catalog, and studies or theoretical writings related to the big OPAC systems, in order to project implications for access in school OPACs. Early in the history of the OPAC, two phases of development were described, the minimal and the enhanced access stage (Gorman, 1982). The findings reported next are divided into these two stages.

Bibliographic Records for Children's and Children's and School Library Materials and the Nature of Access

It has been an accepted theory that simplified cataloging is appropriate for children's materials. This special treatment may provide descriptive cataloging that is both limited and enhanced. At its best, simplified cataloging means conformity to a standard adapted to the needs of children and school users. Adhering to a standard means that records can be shared among systems. At its worst, simplified cataloging implies that local rules substitute for a standard under the assumption that local needs are unique. If a standard is not followed, the catalog cannot be networked.

Following are some developments, issues, and research that have been selected as particularly important in the history of cataloging children's and school library materials. The list is not intended to be exhaustive.

Catalog Use Studies

Prior to the Council of Library Resources (CLR) studies beginning in 1981, the research indicated that it was more common to conduct a known-item (author or title) search than a subject search. In Matthews's (1984) summary of this research, known-item searching was also found to be more successful (66%) than subject searching (50%). The emphasis on subject access since the CLR studies is not as surprising to staff in children's and school libraries because they commonly assign more subject headings for fiction as well as non-fiction than do staff in other kinds of libraries.

The reports of card catalog use studies do not include many references to school and children's library participation. An important evaluation of students' searching and in both card and online catalogs was funded by the first Baber research award (Edmonds and Moore, 1988). The results show that success in searching is developmental in both the online catalog and the card catalog, the eighth grade students having performed better than the sixth and fourth grade students in searching for author, title, and subject cards in identifying call numbers. Surprisingly, all participants in this study were not only more successful in searching the card catalog than the online catalog, but they preferred the card catalog over the online catalog.

Library of Congress and the Annotated Card Program

This program was established in 1966 to provide modified Library of Congress Subject Headings and some special classification numbers, as well as annotations, for children's materials. Despite the availability of this standard, school library media specialists appear to prefer the Sears supplementary list. Other less well known subject heading lists such as The Hennepin County, Minnesota Public Library's list (Berman, 1986) have been developed to reflect children's topical vocabulary. De Hart and Meder (1986) also note the Yonkers, N.Y. Public Library and Carolyn W. Lima's A to Zoo list of subject headings for special concepts in children's picture books, as well as earlier ALA publications of subject headings to describe children's literature. Theoretical analysis of cataloging of children's materials centers on the relation of children's to adult cataloging. Should it really be so different that other cataloging tools, classification systems, and subject heading lists are used? Practice indicates that even into the age of automation, the approaches to improved subject access in children's cataloging vary from adult's cataloging. There are now some CD-ROM databases of MARC records that offer Sears headings as an alternative to LC headings, in response to the school market demand. Ideally, the full LC record, complete with annotations, can co-exist with the more appropriate Sears and local headings.

Minimal Level Cataloging

In 1982 the Cataloging of Children's Materials Committee (CCS) of the Resources and Technical Services Division (RTSD) of the American Library Association (ALA), in conjunction with the Children's Literature Section of the Library of Congress, developed special guidelines for standardizing the cataloging of children's materials (works intended for use by children through junior high level, high school level optional). These guidelines recommend adherence to Level 2 descriptive cataloging, provided for by the Anglo-American Cataloguing Rules, 2nd Edition (AACR2), because of the potential for sharing Machine-Readable Cataloging (MARC) in all kinds of libraries. Yet many school practitioners are still developing Level 1 records, which exclude elements such as dimensions, other statements of responsibility (such as illustrator), and series information. Commonsense Cataloging (Miller and Terwilliger, 1983), a text in use in many school and other small libraries, recommends Level 1 under certain guidelines for materials and when the cataloging staff is limited. A recent report of networking activities (Van Orden and

Wilkes, 1989) indicated that slightly more than one-third of the survey participants were following Level 1 guidelines (and the majority also used Sears as the subject authority).

Audiovisual, Software Cataloging

Catalog records for audiovisual materials have not been as readily available in MARC databases. Because these materials are a significant part of school library collections, the lack of MARC records is a major issue. If "home-made" card catalog records for these materials are replicated in the online catalog, important detail may be missing (e.g., running time, content notes). According to the BIBLIOFILE vendor, users in school districts in Montgomery County were sharing original cataloging for audiovisual materials by sending the catalog records to Library Corporation, where the files were combined on a floppy disk and returned to the districts for downloading to the local catalog. Bibliographic Access Network (BAN) is another project generated to share catalog records for materials (including books and other media) not located in the Library of Congress MARC record database. The BAN fiche database, to which a number of state school library systems are contributing and that will be available on a compact disk when it has reached a large enough size, was initiated by the developer of MITINET, a software program which creates records in MARC format (Epstein, 1988).

Research in Conformity to Standards in the Card Catalog

Earlier studies of practices of school library media professionals in cataloging confirm their lack of adherence to standards. In 1977 Rogers (1979a) investigated state supervisors' endorsements of AACR2 for non-print materials and found that there was a lack of awareness of existing codes and guidelines that were accepted by other professionals. She did a follow-up study in 1982 and determined that there was some progress toward standardization (Rogers, 1984). Truett (1984) did a study of the cataloging practices of Nebraska school library media specialists and also found that there was a lack of standardization in the use of rules for choice of main entry. Rogers and others have attributed the school library media specialists' lack of awareness of standards to their isolation from other professionals, lack of clerical help, lack of training in technical services, and the priority of instruction over library management.

Research in Conformity to Standards in the Online Catalog

In my dissertation investigation of cataloging practices of school library media specialists in microcomputer systems (Murphy, 1987), it appeared that these non-standard practices were continued into the online age. The majority of the survey respondents were not aware of MARC, AACR2, or RTSD cataloging guidelines for children's materials. This survey was replicated with the Follett circulation system users, and there was an increase in the number of respondents who endorsed the AACR2 and MARC standard, although the majority were still not aware of the RTSD guidelines (Follett, 1986). Follett's efforts to educate their users and the distribution of the survey almost a year later may account for the increase in awareness. (The author's survey was distributed in 1985, although the dissertation was not completed until 1987.)

Cataloging for Developmental and Curriculum Needs

At the same time that the respondents to the author's survey (Murphy, 1987) were not conforming to AACR2 and MARC, they were creating special headings and notes in the catalog records. The major reason for creating special headings was to access curriculum materials; entries in the notes field were primarily made to indicate the reading level of the material. When this survey was replicated with the Follett circulation system users, the results were exactly the same (Follett, 1986). The use of special terms to catalog curriculum materials in school districts has been noted (Wehmeyer, 1976; De Hart and Meder, 1986). The content of catalog records for curriculum materials in OCLC has also been reported (Kranz, 1987-1988).

Upgrading Circulation Records to Catalog Records

Can a case be made for upgrading brief, non-MARC records in circulation systems to a full MARC catalog database? Some recommend against it, believing that retrospective conversion of the shelf list should be a one time process to implement an integrated system. However, there are thousands of circulation systems now in school library media centers that were implemented with brief records entered manually because the cost was less than a full scale conversion. If these records have an LCCN or ISBN key, they can be matched against a MARC database for an upgrade to standard records (Crawford, 1987). In the case where there are no MARC records available for an item (and the "hit" rate for school library catalog records is not well established), some vendors may create records in MARC format but without descriptive detail. These records will need a second upgrade, which adds significantly to the cost of conversion. Meanwhile, circulation systems are providing users with limited subject access (which Crawford says is better than no access) via "category" fields identifying curriculum units, genre, and other headings.

The Influence of the Technology Standards

The development of new technology, the system itself, appears to be one of the most positive influences on school library media professionals' adherence to standards. The improved capabilities of the hardware and the computer programmers' acceptance of the importance of standards, have increasingly affected conformity. Again, my research (Murphy, 1987) showed that the school library media specialists implementing OPACs that provided for MARC records and other standards were more disposed toward conforming to these standards than the respondents using systems that did not provide for the MARC format. Rogers (1984) also notes the influence of participation in networks upon the members' adherence to AACR2 conventions.

The development of compact disks containing MARC records from the Library of Congress or other sources has made the standard more available and affordable. Union and local catalogs can co-exist on a compact disk, e.g., Western Library

Network's LASERCAT, and can also be used for cataloging as well as for patrons' searches of library holdings.

The Influence of Networking upon Standards

The leadership in some state education departments has provided models for shared databases, collection development and interlibrary loan. The exemplary projects include WISCAT in Wisconsin, TIES in Minnesota, and ACCESS PENNSYLVANIA in Pennsylvania. School library media specialists in these states receive planning assistance and sometimes financial support for retrospective conversion of catalog records. Awareness of mainstream standards and the state-of-the-art in development of automation is communicated.

How Much Standardization is Enough?

The issue of standards continues to be debated in the mainstream library community as well as among microsystem users. One of the realities that tends to be forgotten is that MARC is a communications standard, not a guarantee of content. There are reports about the poor quality of some records received from retrospective conversion vendors. The MicroLIF format for catalog records is a case in point. The format was cooperatively developed by the book and microcomputer system vendors, and although it falls into the category of MARC-compatible (which may describe the internal records in many systems), MicroLIF has been rejected by many prospective buyers because it is perceived as less than the standard. (At the vendor's request I became a member of the MicroLIF Standards Committee, and they have made a recent commitment to provide a full MARC record format.) Crawford (1989) describes the acceptable MARC standard as that which can be imported, adapted if needed within the system, yet also exported. Yet some vendors strip the directory and content designators from the record, supplying generic values when they export records (Mellinger, 1989). The designers of the microcomputer OPACs, and to some extent the mainframe systems are included in this group, do not appear to have completely met the challenge of standards implementation because of technology's limitations, the cost, or other reasons. It is difficult to validate the claims of vendors who state that they do conform to standards.

Designing the OPAC System to Meet the Needs of School Users

The online catalog that has passed through the minimal access stage has a database with records in full MARC format, as much as that is possible, and the enhanced stage will provide new features. Enrichments within the MARC record are sometimes considered too costly or too difficult to implement; the features more often recommended to improve subject access are enhancements in system design and additional tools loaded into the system to link to the MARC record. Mandel, Hildreth, Markey, Matthews, Cochrane, and others have made recommendations for improvements in these areas based on the CLR and other studies.

The top four choices of the OPAC users in the CLR study, out of a possible thirteen features related to improving searching, were the ability to search a book's table of contents, summary, or index; the ability to view a list of words related to search words, the ability to print search results; and the ability to search by any word in the subject heading (Matthews, Lawrence, and Ferguson, 1983). Some of the recommendations made in earlier card catalog use studies, which Cochrane states have not been fully addressed, are similar to the CLR desired features, such as making available contents notes, in-depth subject analytics, and front and back entries from books; other suggestions are for reversed geographic headings, incorporation of classification schemes, and improved user training (Cochrane, 1985).

The developments, issues, and research related to enhancing subject access discussed below touch upon these user recommendations. The list is not intended to be exhaustive.

Integrated Systems

One of the major advantages of an OPAC over a card catalog, identified early in the history of its development, is the ability to provide status information for an item (Matthews, 1983). Because the circulation system is linked to the catalog, the catalog searcher knows instantly whether the book is in, or if it is out, when it is due to be returned. An integrated acquisitions module provides the status of items on order. Local area networks increase access from points outside of the library area; interfaces with union catalogs and full text databases (a development still in the experimental stage) enhance access to resources beyond the local collection. It is possible that some of the circulation systems recently developed may remain at that stage unless it is recognized that the true benefits in access are at the online catalog stage, which provides full MARC records.

Authority Files and Cross References

The issue of responsibility for a standard in authority systems is still being debated. Most of the early microcomputer OPACs were without authority files, and their development is still uneven. Matthews (1984) states that prior card catalog use studies have suggested that catalog success rates are directly proportional to the number of See references, which tell the user to look elsewhere in the catalog; he and Markey recommend the development in online catalogs of See as well as See Also references, which tell the user of the existence of related terms (Matthews, 1984; Markey, 1986). The problem in creating cross references, which are not state-of-the-art in microcomputer systems, is that they are not included in the MARC record and must be loaded separately in a file obtained from the Library of Congress or another vendor or utility. The headings or other entries must then be linked to the appropriate records. As an alternative, some microcomputer systems build the authority files as records are created.

Physical Environment of the Catalog

Some hardware features of the OPAC improve access. The young catalog user has less well developed language skills and is particularly in need of any assistance that replaces typed responses. Touch screens and the mouse/icon combination, even function keys, can make searching easier. The INTELLIGENT CATALOG uses an audio tutor for online help as well as providing a map showing the location of items in the library. Increasing the number of terminals in the library as well as in other areas of a campus or building also improves access.

Communication Features

Hildreth (1985) describes the difficulties of communication in the user interface. These include command and response protocols and display formats, which vary from system to system. The young user may have particular difficulty in moving through menu steps, reading and analyzing the detail of catalog records, identifying call numbers, and even using features that Hildreth declares desirable in system design, such as moving backward and forward among search results, browsing indexes, and retrieving search history.

Searching Strategies

Many of the microcomputer OPACs have now implemented keyword searching, although the fields indexed vary. Keyword searching increases access significantly, sometimes too much, but can be enhanced by Boolean operators to refine searches. Other indexing approaches include right or left truncation (part of the word) and string searching (adjacency). An exciting research study by Lester investigated the extent to which users' subject terms matched Library of Congress Subject Headings (40.1% of the time); she applied three search processes to see how they would have increased matches. When all three were applied, the success rate increased almost 100% (keyword and Boolean were the single most successful strategies) (Roose, 1988). Interestingly, Lester found that name and geographic authority files did little to augment searching by themselves, but were enhanced when keyword and Boolean searching were added. Lester also experimented with searching anywhere in the MARC record and adding a sounds-like spell checker, and results increased again.

Markey also studied subject searching in the online catalog at Syracuse, and found that of the 859 searches made by 188 users in one day, only 154 (18%) exactly matched LCSH, and 5% exactly matched LCSH cross references (Markey, 1986).

Enhancing the MARC Record Contents

Matthews described a potential database called AUGMARC in which additional content could be added to MARC records (Matthews, Lawrence, and Ferguson, 1983). He described the possibilities of using automated data machines to scan the index and/or tables of contents; it is also suggested that the Cataloging In Publication office of the Library of Congress could solicit additional annotations from publishers, or that the library community might request input for certain important titles. The alternatives for enriching the MARC record contents, and there have been experiments such as Cochrane's Subject Access Project (SAP), are to create separate databases or special indexes, and then link them to the catalog record.

There has not been any significant effort to create enriched records for students and children. Some vendors have made efforts to enhance records and make them available (e.g., Follett's database includes grade and reading levels of titles). There are enhancements in school library network records, (e.g., analytics created by individual school library staff), that would be valuable to share.

Adding Classification Schedules and Other Indexes or Thesauri to the Online Catalog

Research has been conducted in an experimental online catalog incorporating subject rich terms from the Dewey Decimal Classification Schedules and Relative Index into the subject searching capabilities of the catalog (Markey, 1986). Earlier research has included the development of PRECIS in Aurora High School in Canada in the 1970s, which allows the catalog user to enter the alphabetical subject heading string at any point (Taylor, 1983). The Children's Media Bank, an online thesaurus that indexed subject subdivisions related to form, curriculum content, and use, was created in 1976-1977 (Hines and Winkel, 1983). Wehmeyer noted the development of computerized lists of terms in university educational systems to index objectives, content, and usage of curriculum materials (Wehmeyer, 1976). These models could provide, or be adapted to, prototype catalogs and be tested by school users.

Implications for Practitioners

The suggestions for practice that affect subject access are delegated to building and district library media personnel, to state education supervisors, to vendors, and to researchers, where appropriate.

1. Although AASL and AECT, and probably most state education departments, have endorsed the MARC communications format as the standard for school library media automated systems, there is no direction at the present time to guarantee minimal content in catalog formats acquired from different bibliographic sources. Minnesota is at least working on such guidelines for school library media centers undertaking a retrospective conversion project.

2. The major issue for building and district library media staff is to select and implement only a system that provides for full MARC cataloging and conforms to other mainstream bibliographic standards.

3. Building and district level library media staff must assume the responsibility for maintaining the integrity of the OPAC database. Editing of records must be in conformity with AACR2 conventions. Archival tapes or disks that reflect current records should be maintained outside of the system.

4. Sources for full cataloging of audiovisual materials should be developed and shared.

5. Enhanced records, which contain annotations, analytics, and other subject rich information, should be developed and shared.

6. Networking of systems, including financial support for local implementation, needs to be developed by state education department leaders.

7. Training in MLS and school media certification programs, as well as in continuing education programs, should include education in technical standards and services.

8. Publications should be solicited that describe state-of-the-art OPAC development and retrospective conversion.

9. Conferences should provide settings for workshops on new technologies and reports about automation experiences. Publication of the proceedings of these conference programs should be encouraged, (e.g., the Retrospective Preconference at AASL in Dallas 1989 proceedings will be published in a forthcoming SLMQ issue).

10. School library media specialists who are implementing systems have the responsibility to communicate to their vendors the ways in which the systems are not meeting the needs of users. Documentation of searches and other aspects of OPAC development will support claims made to vendors via users' group meetings, letters, etc.

Implications for Researchers

The Council of Library Resources established priorities early in the development of OPAC systems. A similar agenda for the school library media community should be prepared by a national group or association.

1. First, establish a foundation for research similar to the Council of Library Resources, which was financially supported by a granting agency and vendors. Identify potential grant-givers for such a foundation to assist the development of research in online catalog use by children and students.

2. Monitor OPAC development in schools by conducting state-of-the-art and evaluative studies of systems.

3. Test the behavior and analyze the user requirements and requests of children and student searchers. Some of the research conducted in the big OPAC systems, such as logs of searches matching searchers' terms and online indexes, with appropriate enhancements to improve access, could be replicated with young users. Research should be carried out in experimental models as well as in existing OPAC in use at school library sites.

4. Encourage school library media specialists to conduct simple research projects locally, such as keeping logs of search terms and successful and unsuccessful matches in the OPAC. These local projects could provide a large pool of information.

5. Investigate state networking systems and report successful models. Report the differences in financing. Evaluate the cost effectiveness of interlibrary loan.

6. Experiment with interfaces between microcomputer systems and free text databases/distributed networks.

7. Investigate and report the most cost effective and efficient methods of retrospective conversion, including the upgrading of circulation records.

8. Evaluate the quality of MARC records supplied from various sources.

9. Investigate the best means for instructing students in online catalog use.

10. Investigate the impact of the online catalog on the role of the library media specialist.

11. Investigate the influence of a computer programmer position in the school on the implementation of OPAC catalogs and networking.

References

Berman, Sanford. "A Selection of Hennepin County Library Subject Headings for Children's Material." In Cataloging Special Materials: Critiques and Innovations, 172-175. Phoenix: Oryx Press, 1986.

Cochrane, Pauline. "Classification as an Online Subject Access Tool: Challenge and Opportunity." In Improving LCSH for Use In Online Catalogs, edited by Pauline A. Cochrane, 148-149. Littleton: Libraries Unlimited, 1986.

-------. Redesign of Catalogs and Indexes for Improved Online Subject Access. Phoenix: Oryx Press, 1985.

Crawford, Walt. MARC for Library Use, 2nd edition. Boston: G. K. Hall, 1989.

-------. Patron Access: Issues for Online Catalogs. Boston: G. K. Hall, 1987.

De Hart, Florence E., and Marylouise D. Meder. "Cataloging Children's Materials: A Stage of Transition." In Cataloging Special Materials: Critiques and Innovations, edited by Sanford Berman, 71-97. Phoenix: Oryx Press, 1986.

Edmonds, Leslie, and Paula Moore. "Fresh Findings: Catalog Use Studies." Author's notes from a report given at ALA Midwinter Conference, San Antonio, Texas, January 11, 1988.

Epstein, Hank. "Improving the Retrospective Conversion Hit Rate for School Libraries: The BAN Fiche." School Library Media Quarterly (Summer 1988): 255.

Follett Software Company. "Online Public Access Catalogs in Public and School Libraries." Report of survey results to the author, who developed the questionnaire for Follett Software Company, June 1986.

Gorman, Michael. "Thinking the Unthinkable: A Synergetic Profession." American Libraries 13 (July/August 1982): 473-474.

"Guidelines for Standardized Cataloging of Children's Materials." Top of the News 40 (Fall 1983): 49-55.

Hildreth, Charles R. "The User Interface in Online Catalogues: The Telling Difference." In Online Public Access to Library Files: Conference Proceedings, edited by Janet Kinsella, 111-132. Oxford: Elsevier, 1985.

Hines, Theodore C., and Lois Winkel. "A New Information Access Tool for Children's Media." Library Resources and Technical Services 27 (January/March 1983): 94-105.

Kranz, Jack. "Cataloging of Curriculum Materials on OCLC: A Perspective." Cataloging & Classification Quarterly 8 (1987/1988): 15-28.

Mandel, Carol. "Enriching the Library Catalog Record." Library Resources and Technical Services 29 (January/March 1985): 5-15.

Markey, Karen. "Searching and Browsing the Library Classification Schedules in an Online Catalogue." In Online Public Access to Library Files: Second National Conference, edited by Janet Kinsella, 49-66. Oxford: Elsevier, 1986.

-------. "Subject Searching in Library Catalogs." In Improving LCSH for Use in Online Catalogs, edited by Pauline A. Cochrane, 243-256. Littleton: Libraries Unlimited, 1986.

-------. "Users and the Online Catalog: Subject Access Problems." In The Impact of Online Catalogs, edited by Joseph R. Matthews, 35-69. New York: Neal Schuman, 1986.

Matthews, Joseph R. Public Access to Online Catalogs. New York: Neal Schuman, 1984.

Matthews, Joseph R., Gary S. Lawrence, and Douglas K. Ferguson. Using Online Catalogs: A Nationwide Survey. New York: Neal Schuman, 1983.

Mellinger, Michael J. "Automation Standards: Myth vs. Reality." Library Journal 14 (June 1, 1989): 72.

Miller, Marilyn L., and Marilyn L. Schontz. "Expenditures for Resources in School Library Media Centers, FY '88-'89." School Library Journal 35 (June 1989): 31-40.

Miller, Rosalind E., and Jane C. Terwilliger. Commonsense Cataloging, 3rd edition. New York: H. W. Wilson Co., 1983.

Murphy, Catherine. "The Microcomputer Stand-Alone Online Public Access Catalog in School Library Media Centers: Practices and Attitudes Toward Standardization." Ph.D. dissertation, Columbia University, 1987.

--------. "A Primer on Automating the School Library Media Center." Electronic Learning 8 (May 1989): 34-37.

--------. "The Time is Right to Automate." School Library Journal 35 (November 1988): 42-47.

Rogers, Jo Ann V. "Mainstreaming Media Center Materials: Adopting AACR2." School Library Journal 27 (April 1981): 31.

-------. "NonPrint Cataloging: A Call for Standardization." American Libraries 10 (January 1979): 46-48.

-------. "Progress in Access to Non-Print Materials." School Library Media Quarterly 12 (Winter 1984): 127-135.

Roose, Tina. "Online Catalogs: Making Them Better Reference Tools." Library Journal (December 1988): 76-77.

Taylor, Audrey. "Alternatives in Action: The Aurora COM/PRECIS Experience." School Libraries in Canada 13 (Winter 1983): 3-8.

Truett, Carol. "Is Cataloging a Passe Skill in Today's Technological Society? Library Resources & Technical Services 28 (July/September 1984): 268-275.

Van Orden, Phyllis J., and Adeline W. Wilkes. "Networks and School Library Media Centers." Library Resources and Technical Services 33 (April 1989): 123-133.

Wehmeyer, Lillian. "Cataloging the School Media Center as a Specialized Collection." Library Resources & Technical Services 20 (Fall 1976): 315-325.

NETWORKING:
STUDIES OF MULTITYPE LIBRARY NETWORKING WITH
IMPLICATIONS FOR SCHOOL LIBRARY MEDIA PRACTICE

Barbara Froling Immroth
Associate Professor
Graduate School of Library and Information Science
University of Texas, Austin

Introduction

Information Power takes a strong position on school library media centers in networks. Challenge number 5 is "to participate in networks that enhance access to resources located outside the school" (1988, p. 12). The concept of providing adequate resources, intellectual access to information resources and access to information beyond the school permeates the document. However, no research studies directly pertaining to school libraries and networks are cited in the selected readings or selected research studies.

Summary of Studies

Several dissertations with content relating to school library media programs in multitype networks have been written. Immroth (1980) studied the school programs in the Colorado Regional Library Service Systems (RLSS). Her research questions included:

1. How do the Colorado RLSS compare with the components in the theoretical definitions of networks?
2. How well do school library media specialists fit into the organizational pattern?
3. In what ways have the Colorado RLSS successfully overcome the barriers inhibiting cooperation in the networks?

A matrix of network components was constructed from writings about networking theory and practice. Six characteristics used to describe a general multitype network, according to Swank, were identified: information resources, readers or users, schemes for the intellectual organization of documents or data; methods for the delivery of resources, formal organization, and bidirectional communications networks. The matrix of network components was then matched to the components described in the NCLIS report of the Task Force on the Role of the School Library Media Program in the National Program to develop definitions of a general multitype network. State documents were examined to obtain background and support information. Site visits were made to twenty librarians and networkers in the state for preliminary background information.

Potential and actual network participants were queried by questionnaire about their multitype network involvement and asked to rate the usefulness of a list of

175

twenty-five resources or services. The information from the respondents was compared to the model listing the characteristics of networks and to the national plan for the inclusion of school library media programs in multitype networks.

The comparison of theory and practice in this study led to the following conclusions: the Colorado RLSS have been successful in overcoming some inhibiting barriers, and strong leadership from the top has led to the inclusion of school media programs as equal members of the network. Professional isolation has decreased through joint participation in activities of mutual interest. Users usually received materials fast enough to satisfy their needs. Distance did not deter libraries from exchanging materials; over three-quarters reported exchanges with libraries over twenty-five miles away. In sum, an examination of the actual experience of the participants in Colorado demonstrated the ability of a multitype library network to successfully include schools.

Dissertations by Walker, Weeks, Turock, and Lunardi have further implications for school library media programs in networks. Turock (1981, p. 6) had two objectives:

1. Identify and measure variables in multitype library networking, determine their interdependence, uncover problems, and suggest modifications.

2. Propose a model, based on the evidence, useful for research and development.

A case study was taken of the Rochester Area Resource Exchange (RARE), in which Turock had been an administrator. Data on the performance factor were collected on-site in a field study and checked by comparison with current and archival records. Five variables affecting the performance factor were volume of use, percentage of filled requests, patterns of activity, response time, and increased access to unique periodicals. Data on the organization factor were collected in twenty structured interviews of a cross section of participants. Seven variables affecting the organization factor were planning, governance, funding, communication-delivery, configuration, administration, and success. Data on attitude were collected from statements about performance, organization, and success on a mailed questionnaire from a stratified random sample of network participants. Data about the three factors were related to success and to each other and used in the creation of a model for the development and evaluation of multitype networks.

The data on performance indicated that 89.3 percent of requests for all school system interlibrary loans were filled (Turock, p. 72). The schools accounted for a total of one percent of requests received by other types of libraries (p. 76). Most school requests (67 percent) are being filled within the originating school system (p. 76, 78). Informal activity was defined as borrowing from another library within one's own district or directly from a local public library. Using informal "phantom systems," over 87 percent of the requests were filled in seven days or less (p. 83). A new high school Union List of Serials indicated that over 50 percent of the serial titles requested by public libraries could have been filled by school libraries. School systems were able to fill 70.6 percent of article requests from schools; 97 percent of school periodical requests could be filled from network sources (p. 88). The data on organization indicated that, first, perceptions of multitype network success are highly related to those of funding and communication and delivery; and, since no significant relationships were found among the seven indicators, each measured separate, individually important factors. Second, legislation was an important influencing factor on librarians. Third, funding disagreements needed to be resolved for both compensation mechanisms and continued commitment. Attitudes differed according to the library system of which the participants were members, in that they were most satisfied with their own type of system. Those who were getting something of benefit from the network were satisfied with it.

Walker's (1982) work examined the patterns of student and teacher interlibrary borrowing. A case study of the Howard County (Maryland) public school system's use of the Maryland Interlibrary Organization (MILO) was performed by the school system supervisor of media services. Walker's research questions were:

1. What are the general patterns of interlibrary borrowing in the Howard County public school system, in terms of total system interlibrary loan requests, request totals by school level, user category, individual school, and monthly totals?
2. What are the general patterns of interlibrary borrowing in terms of the types of requests initiated?
3. What is the general subject distribution of requests (by Dewey decimal category) for interlibrary loans?
4. How current are interlibrary loan materials requested?
5. What are the "service variables" related to MILO requests, such as turn-around time and fill rate?
6. What other variables affect interlibrary borrowing?

Descriptive data were obtained from three major sources: (1) interlibrary loan request forms, (2) an attitudinal questionnaire for library media specialist, and (3) a network use questionnaire. The ILL request forms provided bibliographic information, subject classification, date of request, fill date, the date after which material would not be useful, the request type, and administrative information. In addition, the school district required the name and position of the borrower and the school or office originating the request. The attitudinal survey instrument, with a Likert-type rating scale, was administered to all media specialists in the school system at an in-service meeting at the end of the study. The network use questionnaire, included with all materials borrowed through MILO ILL, was to be completed by each user.

Data from the ILL request forms showed significant differences among students at different grade levels in the types of requests placed, subject distribution, and currency of requests. High school students were the heaviest users, followed by elementary teachers and central office professionals. In the four-month period under study, there were 703 requests from a user population of more than 25,000. Of the total requests, 74.25 percent were for monographic material. High school students most frequently requested material for use in a classroom assignment in English, science, or social studies and from Dewey classes 800, 600, 500, 900, and 300. Teachers most often requested material for use in college courses in the Dewey 300 class (social sciences, including education) and the Dewey 600 class (topics related to the education of those with medical and psychiatric handicaps). Central office professionals requested materials for use in administrative decisions exclusively from the Dewey 300 and 600 classes. Attitudinal data from a questionnaire administered to school library media specialists showed that specialists differed significantly by school level only in the degree to which they encouraged students to use the microfiche MILO union catalog. No significant association in paired ranks was found between the attitudes toward MILO borrowing expressed by specialists and the number of requests from their schools. Data collected from the network use questionnaire showed that students differed significantly by grade level and from teachers in their indications of whether materials arrived in time to be of use, the courses for which materials were used, their sources of information about MILO, and the manner in which citations were located. Teachers differed significantly from central office professionals in reasons for use and sources of information about MILO, subject areas of requests, means of locating citations, and alternative sources for needed materials.

Weeks's dissertation (1982), a study of attitudes, examined three hypotheses:

1. Individuals who participate in a multitype library network, those who participate in a single type unaffiliated library network, and those who do not participate in a formal network organization will differ at a statistically significant level (.05) on a scale designed to measure attitudes toward library networking.

2. Individuals on these three levels of participation will differ at a statistically significant level (.05) on a scale designed to measure attitudes toward technology.

3. There exists a significant statistical correlation between attitudes toward technology and attitudes toward library networking expressed by school library media specialists. Five variables were considered to influence attitudes toward library networking and technology: years of experience, level of education, type of school assignment, degree of involvement in professional organizations, and participation in continuing education opportunities. The variable of the number of technologies available in a library media center (LMC) was also studied in regard to attitudes toward technology.

A mailed questionnaire was used to collect demographic data about school library media specialists employed in public schools in New York State and to provide information about their attitudes toward library networking and technology. A Networking Attitude Scale (NAS) and a Technology Attitude Scale (TAS) were formed from responses. After analysis of the relationships between the demographic variables and the attitudes shown on the NAS and the TAS, Weeks reached four major conclusions: (1) most school library media specialists in New York State have generally positive attitudes toward the concept of library networking, although individuals who are participating in the multitype library network pilot projects indicated the most positive reactions toward the concept; (2) the four network services that were considered by respondents to be most important for school LMC programs--interlibrary loan, delivery systems, reference services, and development of union catalogs--are currently available in the library pilot projects in New York State; (3) school library media specialists indicated that they held generally positive attitudes toward technology, and participation in a library network did not appear to influence these attitudes; (4) the correlation between the two sets of attitudes did not indicate a great deal of overlap between the two concepts. The findings in this study suggest that attitudes concerning the two concepts must be studied separately (Weeks, 1982, pp. 175-77).

A dissertation written by Lunardi in 1986 studies the effect of the LSCA Title III on stimulating public school library participation within cooperative library networks. Twenty-four networks in forty-two school libraries in eighteen states were surveyed. The seven variables used were fiscal, legal, attitudinal, governance, planning, evaluation, and technological concerns. Lunardi found that school librarians are contributing network members and that network membership improves and extends the services offered to students and teachers. He asserted that network membership is one way school librarians adapt to the changing environment, and that LSCA Title III is vital to this process.

Partridge's dissertation, completed in 1988, was summarized as follows by Diane D. Kester:

Purpose. The major purpose of her study was to identify the major obstacles to cooperation as perceived by school library media specialists in Mississippi. A second purpose was to determine if school librarians who had membership in the Coastal Mississippi Library Cooperative (CMLC) perceived fewer barriers to cooperation than school librarians who were not members.

The study. Her population included the librarians from all types of libraries in the six county membership in CMLC. She also included a random sample of the public librarians and school library media specialists in the remainder of the state. The questionnaire sent to the school library media specialists focused on the barriers to cooperation as identified by Nolting. The questionnaire to the librarians in the CMLC region focused on the perception of their participation in CMLC. Four interviews were also conducted with public librarians.

Results. The t-test was performed on the barriers to cooperation and revealed that there were no significant differences between school library media specialist non-members and members of CMLC. Chi-square tests were used on the demographic portion and revealed that of four variables (number of students, phone in the media center, computer in the media center, and computer in the school) and the dependent variable, membership in CMLC, the number of students served, and a phone in the media center were positively correlated significantly. One large barrier identified was communication: the lack of information about networking services, expectations, and experience in cooperation. The low response rate on the return of the questionnaires prevented Partridge from accepting the stated hypothesis.

Findings. Partridge found that school library media specialists perceived that eight of the twenty-four traditional barriers were present in Mississippi. Half of these barriers were categorized as lack of information and experience. Psychological barriers had declined. Non-network members perceived more barriers than network members.

Two dissertations concerning networking were being written at the end of 1989 by Diane D. Kester, University of North Carolina at Chapel Hill and Thomas W. Zane, Brigham Young University.

In 1987 the Center for Education Statistics of the U.S. Department of Education published two reports with information on this topic. Statistics of Public and Private School Library Media Centers, 1985-86 showed that about half of public schools and 28 percent of private schools provided interlibrary loans to students. The mean number of loans received per school was 30 in both public and private schools (Statistics, 1987a, p. 43). Network membership or participation was not measured in the survey. Only 11 percent of public and 6 percent of private school LMCs provided off-site data retrieval for teachers (p. 45). In the "Summary of Recent Federal Legislation in Support of School Library Media Centers," LSCA Title III is mentioned as providing funding for interlibrary cooperation and networks including school libraries, although no questions about participation were asked. In the latest CES report on school libraries, little attention was given to school libraries in networks. The other CES report published in 1987 was Survey of Library Networks and Cooperative Library Organizations: 1985-1986. Compared with data collected in 1977-78, participation of public school libraries in networks has grown 48 per cent (Survey, 1987b, p. 7). There were 257 networks with 18,152 public school libraries participating, or an average of 70.6 per network with school library membership in 1985-1986 (p. 18, Table 2).

Miller and Moran's first study of expenditures for school LMCs, for fiscal years 1982-1983, did not report on network participation, nor did the study of FY 1983-1984. In 1985-1986 no mention is made of network participation, but it is reported that 52 per cent of the LMCs have a telephone available in the library; 6 per cent have an automated card catalog and 27 per cent have plans to develop an automated card catalog. In the report for 1987-1988 a small number of schools report resource sharing and network participation among school libraries within a district and with other types of libraries (Miller and Shontz, 1989).

Many status reports of network participation appear in the literature. Successful experiences and proposed projects can be found in state and national journals. One cutting-edge example, representative of school participation in networks, is Epler's (1988) report of networking in Pennsylvania. This report demonstrates a creative approach to integrating online searching into the school library media curriculum and bringing schools into the resource sharing network through the establishment of Linking Information Needs-Technology, Education, Libraries, referred to as LIN-TEL. Training sessions and a support system assisted school librarians in integrating online searching into the school curriculum. Resource sharing was achieved by means of a state database on CD-ROM. Schools could apply for retrospective conversion of records through a rigorous proposal process. In 1987 the CD-ROM disc held 1,000,532 records (Epler, p. 52). For an expenditure of under $9,000 per school, 161 high schools joined the project, with more joining in following years. State level leaders were able to negotiate contracts providing necessary equipment and services at one-third the estimated cost to local level units negotiating individually (p. 54).

Two reviews of research articles showed little recent writing about school LMCs in networks. School Library Media Annual, 1986 (Aaron, 1986) has three listings under "Network systems" and four listings under the subheading "State statutes" in the index (p. 428). The State Government section has a subsection, "Resource Sharing and Library Services and Construction Act (LSCA) in 1985" (p. 71-72). In the section "Research Studies Dealing with School Library Media Programs from the ERIC Files: July 1984-June 1985," Minor reviews Immroth's and Rogers's studies about networking (p. 401). In the section "State Laws Pertaining to School Library Media Programs," Aaron and Walk report:

> Two areas seemed to receive more attention in state statutes than other topics. They were (1) joint school and public libraries to serve the needs of school children and residents of a community and (2) interlibrary cooperation and networking activities among different types of libraries to produce more effective, cost-efficient services to community members, including elementary and secondary school students (p. 90).

In the most recent edition of SLMA (1988) there are no listings under "network" in either the index or table of contents.

In the broader area of networking, many papers and studies have been prepared. Pat Molholt's "Library Networking: The Interface of Ideas and Actions" (1988), written for the Office of Library Programs, U. S. Department of Education, Office of the Assistant Secretary for Educational Research and Improvement, discusses the overarching issues that need to be addressed in order for interlibrary cooperation to continue to be viable: increased functionality, performance reliability, consistent user assistance, access, and participation in governance. The EDUCOM Networking and Telecommunications Task Force's (1989) paper on networks discusses benefits, access and use, services, research and development, structure and management, and financing. A number of benefits are listed, including maintaining U.S. leadership in research and education and improving competitiveness in world markets. It states that "over time, the experience gained on the network will provide opportunities for improvement of the nation's entire educational system" (p. 3). School library media specialists need to be aware of these issues and the decisions being made regarding them in order to be in a position to provide their users with intellectual and physical access to the information they require.

Implications for Practitioners

It is known from the status reports and ASCLA and CES surveys that more schools are joining and using networks. A major implication for practice is that school librarians must formalize the teaching of networking by looking for clients, teachers willing to integrate network skills into the curriculum. Students are going to need information-seeking skills to be competitive with other students who have mastered these skills.

A second implication is that school librarians need to learn the skills of searching and using networks. Certification requirements may need to be updated to include these competencies; schools training school librarians need to include the skills in the curriculum. State libraries and state departments of education need to provide continuing education for practitioners to familiarize them with searching and networking skills.

A third implication is the need for the individual school librarian to be creative about joining available networks. As the Pennsylvania example demonstrates, the schools participating in the network are those with the librarians willing to learn the skills and write the proposals.

Another major implication is the need for more participation by schools in networks. The networks need to be expanded at the local/state level in order to provide the information and documents that students will be requesting using their enhanced information-seeking skills. As school librarians teach students to explore the network, other libraries will need to be informed of the expected student demands for information. It is known from reports of academic libraries that the current interlibrary loan system is overburdened. What would happen if every high school freshman in the country requested two items through interlibrary loan to satisfy a research need? Would school librarians be accused of carrying out one of the great "communist plots" of the 1990s, leading to the breakdown of the interlibrary loan system? What would that do for our image? What would it do for increased information skills for students? In addition to these general implications, specific implications from the research follow.

- Schools should develop local collections so that normal information needs can be met locally and schools can be contributing network members.

- Bibliographic directories to access local collections need to be developed so that all users of the system will be made aware of the specific resources available in the public schools.

- Factors of cost, distance, and release time must be taken into consideration in planning professional meetings so that school library media specialists will be able to attend.

- Overlap of multitype systems services with services of educational cooperatives needs to be resolved, as both are serving the same users and both are supported with public funds.

- Local school library media specialists need help in creating an awareness of the positive benefits of systems membership in local school administrators, local school board members, and school staff.

- The multitype systems should develop and provide continuing education in shared use of materials purchased with federal funds.

- Communication equipment should be available to school users. Knowledge about operation of equipment and wider information resources available through its use should be available through continuing education.

Turock (1981) states that the greatest increase in activity (borrowing) will be experienced by the school libraries themselves as they join multitype operations (p. 157). LMCs will need to plan for the change in workload. She suggests that the phantom systems be studied and "made part of the formalized structures" (p. 158). Lending as well as borrowing will be expected: LMCs must be prepared to be contributing members of the network. "Rewards, in terms of fiscal support, might be better based on the performance delivery of members than on their participation alone" (p. 159). Legislation influences librarians; whether the reverse is true is questionable. However, librarians must address the development of model legislation around which multitype networks might be built, or be forced to contend with inadequate or inappropriate mandates in the future (p. 164). Another need is for the creation of funding schedules based on school library involvement and financial mechanisms for strengthening those delivery resources (p. 165). Decentralized avenues to resource sharing not only increase speed but also encourage local connections among libraries of different types and move closer to the ideal of information provision developed around the concept of total community library service (p. 166). "Evaluation of attitude ... was useful in targeting barriers that were operating in a specific setting as well. Barriers so discovered could then receive focused effort to reduce or overcome them" (p. 170). "Introducing a change model into a situation as diverse as multitype networking then, is a complex political as well as management or research undertaking" (p. 175).

Walker (1982) asserts that library media specialists would "welcome additional training in methods of encouraging student use, methods of integrating instruction in interlibrary borrowing into classroom units" (p. 155). He also suggests that the cost per request ($8 to $10 for a total of $12,000 for the project year) "would not substantially improve the library media collections of the 49 schools in the district, but access to a vast collection of information far beyond the scope of local means to provide" would be a greater benefit to users (p. 157).

Implications for practice from Weeks's (1982) findings include the following: most school library media specialists have generally positive attitudes toward the concept of networking, and participants in multitype projects had the most positive reactions toward the concept (p. 175). The four network services that were considered to be the most important for school library media center programs-- interlibrary loan, delivery systems, reference services, and development of union catalogs--are currently available (p. 176).

Implications for Researchers

Information Power

Information Power (1988, p. 13)asks several questions that could be the basis for extensive research:

- Which functions and services are best provided by local systems and by commercial vendors, and which are best provided by utilities and networks?

- How can traditional attitudinal and other barriers to resource sharing be overcome?

- How do library media programs fully and effectively participate in networks that meet the needs of members of the school community?

- How does the library media specialist use resource sharing to promote the concept of lifelong learning?

- How does the library media specialist promote partnerships with community agencies and businesses to broaden students' learning opportunities?

A current state-of-the-art survey is needed to update the NCLIS and AASL Networking Committee reports on present involvement of school libraries in networks and use of technology. This information could be gathered as part of the CES data proposed to be collected annually. More detailed information is needed about appropriate legislation and funding. Evaluation of current practice in networking is also needed. The dissertation writers suggested several general areas of further research: replication of their studies; expansion of the study to another geographic area or type of library group; and further testing after refinement of the instruments taking into account the present results.

Immroth

Areas needing attention in order to further reduce barriers to cooperation could be compared with similar areas in other states:

- The perceptions of academic, public, and special librarians on the place of school library media specialists within the RLSS could be compared to the perceptions of the school library media specialists.

- A resource assessment could be undertaken to identify resources that school library media programs have to offer to other system members.

- A follow-up study of the SLM program within the RLSS could be made now that schools have had more time to become involved with the system.

- Similar evaluative studies in other states could be made to determine alternative patterns of use.

- A study of lending patterns within the network would be useful to determine the need for access to school collections.

- A study of potential users, who they are and what they actually need, would be useful in planning for continued and expanded resources and services.

- A study determining variations among the regions in effective use of resources and services could be made.

- A study of the actual involvement and effectiveness of school library media specialists on multitype information network governing boards could be made.

- A study to determine effective means of training users in awareness of resources and services and use of the system could provide models for such training (pp. 137-39).

Lunardi

Lunardi (1986)suggests six areas for further research: (1) public school library services and material loans among network libraries, (2) network library services and material loans among public school libraries, (3) the contractual agreements used for public school library participation in networks, (4) the evaluation procedures used, (5) the effectiveness of state libraries among networks, (6) the participation of private and/or parochial school libraries in networks (pp. 178-79).

Partridge

Partridge (1988) suggests that further research should be done on the perceptions of technology, the amount of course work (library education) geared toward technology, perception in school systems, and perceptions of other barriers to cooperation.

Turock

Turock (1981) suggests testing her model in two ways: on multitypes across the country that are adding school libraries, and on multitype arrangements generally, with and without school library members (p. 176). She stresses the importance of reviewing the research against a systems approach by "1) placing the multitype library in the context of its operating environment and 2) the political dimension in the development of the multitype" (p. 177). She cites "a need to analyze the characteristics of libraries entering the networks, their constraints, supports, social and economic situation, to investigate their services, available expertise, resources and their expectations in regard to networking" (p. 178). She also suggests the need for in-depth public policy research "to get below the level of rhetoric, political and professional, to learn how policy-making in external environment affects internal operation" (p. 183).

Walker

Walker (1982) suggests the need for further research into the reasons for the wide variation in the number of requests placed per school (Walker, 132). He cites the need to understand the influence of the school librarian's attitudes on the use patterns of user groups (p. 134). He also stresses the need for "methods of encouraging student use, methods of integrating instruction in interlibrary borrowing into classroom units" (p. 155).

Weeks

Weeks (1982) suggests a comparison of school library media specialists in Colorado and Indiana with those in New York to determine if length of time in a network affects attitudes (p. 178). She also suggests studying the attitudes of public, academic, and special librarians toward networking and technology and comparing them with the attitudes of school librarians (p. 178).

In summary, although there has been little research on school library media programs in networking, it is known through the research that has been done and from the numerous status reports of operating networks that there are implications for practice and many areas for further research. As noted by the emphasis given to networking in Information Power (1988), it is safe to say that school librarians must become more involved in teaching students, teachers, and administrators searching and must networking skills, and find ways to become more active in networks to provide access to information needed by their clients. Preservice and continuing education for school library media specialists is needed in the concept of networking and in presenting the case for implementation of networking to administrators and school boards.

References

Aaron, Shirley L., and Pat R. Scales, eds. School Library Media Annual, 1986, Volume Four. Littleton, Colorado: Libraries Unlimited, 1986.

American Library Association and Association for Educational Communications and Technology. Information Power: Guidelines for School Library Media Programs. Chicago and Washington, D.C., ALA and AECT, 1988.

EDUCOM Networking and Telecommunications Task Force. "The National Research and Education Network." Princeton, New Jersey, 1989. Photocopy.

Epler, Doris M. "Networking in Pennsylvania: Technology and the School Library Media Center." Library Trends Summer 1988: 43-55.

Immroth, Barbara Froling. "The Role of the School Library Media Program in a Multitype Library Network." Ph.D. diss., University of Pittsburgh, 1980.

Lunardi, Albert Anthony. "The Library Services and Construction Act, Title III: Public School Library Participation within Cooperative Library Networks." Ed.D. diss., University of San Francisco, 1986.

Miller, Marilyn L., and Barbara B. Moran. "Expenditures for Resources in School Library Media Centers FY '82-'83." School Library Journal October 1983: 105-114.

--- "Expenditures for Resources in School Library Media Centers FY '83-'84." School Library Journal May 1985: 19-31.

--- "Expenditures for Resources in School Library Media Centers FY '85-'86." School Library Journal June-July 1987: 37-45.

Miller, Marilyn L., and Marilyn L. Shontz. "Expenditures for Resources in School Library Media Centers, FY '88-'89." School Library Journal June 1989: 31-40.

Molholt, Pat. "Library Networking: The Interface of Ideas and Actions." Rensselaer Polytechnic Institute, 1988. Photocopy.

Partridge, Margaret Ann. "Factors Related to Mississippi School Library Media Centers in Multitype Cooperation." Ph.D. diss., University of North Texas, 1988.

Smith, Jane Bandy, ed. School Library Media Annual, 1988, Volume Six. Englewood, Colorado: Libraries Unlimited, 1988.

Task Force on the Role of the School Library Media Program in the National Program. The Role of the School Library Media Program in Networking. Washington, D.C.: National Commission on Library and Information Science, 1978.

Turock, Betty Jane. "Performance, Organization, and Attitude: Factors in Multitype Library Networking." Ph.D. diss., Rutgers University, 1981.

U.S. Department of Education. Office of Educational Research and Improvement, Center for Education Statistics. Statistics of Public and Private School Library Media Centers, 1985-86 (with historical comparisons from 1958-1985). Washington, D.C.: Government Printing Office, 1987a.

U.S. Department of Education. Office of Educational Research and Improvement, Center for Education Statistics. Survey of Library Networks and Cooperative Library Organizations: 1985-1986. Washington, D.C.: Government Printing Office, 1987b.

Walker, H. Thomas. "A Study of the Participation of a Public School System in a Large Public and Academic Library Consortium." Ph.D. diss., University of Maryland, 1982.

Weeks, Ann Carlson. "A Study of the Attitudes of New York State School Library Media Specialists Concerning Library Networking and Technology." Ph.D. diss., University of Pittsburgh, 1982.

EDUCATIONAL COMPUTING RESEARCH: STATUS AND PROSPECTUS

Gary Marchionini
Associate Professor
College of Library and Information Services
University of Maryland at College Park

Introduction

Educational technology is an applied field, with research in the field including human-machine interaction. The microcomputer has opened a wide variety of information processing technologies that have moved rapidly into schools and school library media centers at all levels. Data collected by the Office of Technology Assessment (1988) and the Center for Social Organization of Schools (Becker, 1986a, 1986b) indicate that almost every public school in the U.S. has at least one computer and that student-to-computer ratios average about 30 to 1 for all schools. High schools have slightly lower and elementary schools have slightly higher ratios. Electronic Learning (Bruder, 1988) reported that there are about 1.5 million computers in K-12 schools, that 12 states have computing competency requirements for students, and that 23 states have computing requirements for teacher certification. Becker (1986a, 1986b) reported that school library media centers have a median of two computers and that they are used for a variety of instructional applications. While computers are commonly found in schools and school library media centers, results are mixed regarding the effects of computing on learning and instruction.

This analysis aims to clarify what the research says about educational computing and to raise issues for both practitioners and researchers in the application of technology as a human- machine interaction. Most of the research has addressed either knowledge acquisition in specific traditional subjects or particular learner or system characteristics. What has become increasingly apparent in cognitive science research is the critical nature of interactions among user, system, and task. The organizational scheme for this analysis is based on the notion that a fundamental problem in educational computing research is understanding how increasingly complex interactions with machines, bureaucracies, and procedures affect our abilities to reason and learn. Thus, the educational computing research is organized herein according to who initiates and controls the interactions.

Two general types of interactions are directed learning and self-directed learning. Directed learning assumes that an external entity (the teacher, system, or expert) has some knowledge that the learner wishes to acquire and that the learner cooperates in effecting the transfer of that knowledge. Thus, directed learning is knowledge driven because the knowledge to be learned can be organized optimally by the expert. Additionally, directed learning facilitates assessment of learning because knowledge acquisition outcomes can be stated in advance. This type of learning is most common in formal schooling, and is characterized by directed interactions that are initiated and controlled by the expert. Directed learning was the first type to be automated, since initiation and primary control can be readily

189

predetermined and programmed. Moreover, most educational computing efforts have been to apply computers to the expert's packaging of the knowledge. Although considerable research has been conducted in this area and some benefits have been demonstrated, much work remains to be done in improving computer strategies for helping learners to intentionally acquire knowledge offered by others.

Self-directed learning assumes that the learner initiates and controls learning to satisfy an interest or solve a problem. Thus, self-directed learning is learner-identified goal or problem driven. It typically takes place at work, in libraries and library media centers, and at home. Of course, when learning is initiated by the learner rather than the instructor or system, the outcomes are not fixed in advance by the instructor or system, and thus it is difficult to build a priori assessment mechanisms. Measures in self-directed learning depend on learner judgments about outcomes or post hoc assessments made by instructors after learning has occurred. What seems most essential about self-directed learning is the process itself, since this is the type of learning students will typically do outside of school; knowing how to solve problems and satisfy information needs is thus the instructional objective rather than specific knowledge acquisition. There have been repeated calls for more attention to learning how to learn and process-oriented higher order thinking skills. Although research efforts in self-directed learning indicate that learners can succeed in solving the problems at hand, there is no clear evidence of transfer of the process to other problem areas. One clear trend in actual practice, however, is that computer applications that are generic problem solving tools are being applied increasingly to simulate and promote self-directed learning (Becker, 1986a, 1986b; see also issues of The Computer Teacher, Electronic Learning, etc., for practitioner suggestions for applying computing tools to instruction).

Directed Learning

Early applications of computers in learning were drills or tutorials for mathematics or language arts facts and skills. Literature reviews in the 1970s (Edwards, et al., 1975; Jamison, Suppes & Wells, 1974; and Vinsonhaler & Bass, 1972) provided hope for educational technologists that computer drills and tutorials could help students learn math and language facts and skills. Kearsley, Hunter & Seidel (1983) provided an optimistic assessment of the research literature, reporting nine outcomes, beginning with "There is ample evidence that computers can make instruction more efficient or effective" and ending with "We have just scratched the surface of what can be accomplished with computers in education." A series of meta-analyses of the educational computing research literature conducted by Kulik and his colleagues at the Center for Research on Learning and Teaching at the University of Michigan (Bangert-Drowns, Kulik & Kulik, 1985; Kulik, Bangert & Williams, 1983; Kulik, Kulik & Cohen, 1980; Kulik, Kulik & Bangert-Drowns, 1985) dominated the first half of the 1980s. Their findings indicated that computer-based learning is faster than paper and pencil based learning, that low ability learners can benefit from drills and tutorials, and that high ability learners can benefit from programming and problem solving applications.

These 15 years of reviews gave comfort to teachers, school library media specialists, and administrators who were bringing microcomputers into schools. However, Clark (1985), Becker (1987), and others have argued that the studies reviewed and included in the meta-analyses were methodologically varied and that many of them were flawed by not controlling critical instructional variables such as time on task. Moreover, they argued that results of these studies may not be applicable to the current computing milieu, since those studies included in the meta-analyses were conducted with timesharing computer systems rather than the now-ubiquitous microcomputer. Becker (1987) reported some positive effects in his review of studies using microcomputer technology, but cautioned against over-optimism because of limited numbers and variable quality of research. He called for additional field studies and established a three-year series of such investigations to better assess the learning outcomes of present practice.

Although a large number of studies have been conducted, a rather parsimonious summary is that computers can help students learn facts and skills faster than with traditional methods, that average-ability students do not learn fewer facts and skills by using computers, and that most students have positive attitudes toward computers. Low ability and high ability students, and those with special needs can benefit from computer-based learning that is appropriate for their needs. A review of research reviews by Stennett (1985) noted the lack of evidence for which particular features of computer-based learning were responsible for positive effects. Krendl & Lieberman (1988) in their review noted trends toward research based upon psychological theory, more precision in defining variables and effects, and variety in research methods. They also called for more attention to research on group uses of computing, for investigations of informal (self-directed) learning, and to examine negative effects of computing. Work on intelligent tutoring systems (Park, Perez & Seidel, 1987) promises to improve and expand the quality and availability of software for directed learning. Advances in networked computers will allow these larger programs and knowledge bases to be delivered in schools, thus extending the need for controlled studies of directed learning interactions.

Self-Directed Learning

Many researchers have noted that computers are cognitive tools, and have argued for teaching students how to use them as cognitive amplifiers (Kozma, 1987; Papert, 1980; Shavelson & Salomon, 1985). Computing tools such as programming languages, word processing packages, database management systems, spreadsheets, and hypermedia systems seem to be natural environments for embedding problems and activities that can be especially useful for simulating self-directed learning (Marchionini, 1988). Although this is a provocative idea, measuring cognitive amplification beyond memory and skill execution is difficult, and research results are mixed at best. Nonetheless, many educators are providing such computing tools to students for accomplishing simple or complex tasks in a variety of problem areas.

One of the earliest tools used for both directed and self-directed learning was programming languages, and the considerable research that has been conducted is reviewed first below. Assessments of word processing as an aid in learning how to write are considered next. Studies of the uses of database management and other retrieval systems for social studies and information retrieval--of particular interest to school library media specialists--are then reviewed.

Programming

Programming a computer demands careful specifications of data organization and procedural actions. Such activity requires careful planning, systematic selection and sequencing of instructions, and repeated testing and modification--all activities that intelligent citizenship demands. It seemed reasonable in the earliest days of educational computing that programming could be a powerful tool students could use to construct models for problems in mathematics, science, and other fields while practicing higher order thinking skills. Papert (1980) invented the Logo programming language for this very purpose, and many elementary schools now teach Logo to promote higher order thinking skills and metacognition. Papert argued that a rich computing environment would allow learners to direct their own learning in productive and transferrable ways.

Many researchers have addressed the learning and use of Logo in schools. Although it seems clear that upper elementary school students can learn to program, it has not been demonstrated that the skills of programming actually transfer to other situations. A series of studies done by Pea and his colleagues at Bank Street College Center for Children and Technology (Pea, 1983; Pea & Kurland, 1983; Pea & Kurland, 1984) suggest that transfer does not take place and that minimal learning effects are gained by Logo programming. They argued for guided discovery approaches to Logo programming, in which activities are structured for students so that they can accomplish tasks within the context of instructional goals. Maddux (1989) provided a measured response to the negative research effects reported by the Bank Street group. He suggested that a programming environment such as Logo offers several benefits and should be studied and used in more controlled and structured ways.

Programming is taught for reasons besides the promotion of thinking skills. As a vocational subject, it is increasingly important in high school curricula, and has been used in mathematics and science curricula for directed learning of traditional algorithms and procedures. Since programming is developing a procedure to operate a machine, a good understanding of the procedure is required to create a working program. Some mathematics educators have advocated such an approach, although research results to date have shown no clear advantages in controlled experiments (Hatfield & Kieren, 1972).

Word Processing

Word processing has become one of the primary applications of computers in offices and homes. In addition to the obvious use of word processing technology to learn vocational skills, much attention is given to using word processing technology to help students learn composition and writing skills. A common expectation is that, since word processing frees writers from retyping or "repenning" their work, they will produce more revisions and thus a more refined final product.

Collier (1983) found that college students made more simple word revisions with the word processor but more conceptual revisions with paper and pen. Hawisher (1987) found that college subjects actually made more revisions with paper and pen, and Daiute (1985) found few differences in numbers of revisions among graduate students and elementary students. Dalton & Hannafin (1987), in a comparative study of seventh graders, found that word processor use had little effect on the quality of writing for able students but had some positive effects for low-achieving students. Baer (1988) reported that seventh-grade students had better attitudes toward writing when using word processing than when using paper and pen. Krull & Hurford (1987), in their review of writing productivity, reported equivocal results about the degree to which word processing improved the quality of writing, but noted that writers who use word processing generally believe that their writing is improved by its use. Costanzo (1989) pointed out that even though there is no strong evidence that word processing improves the quality of writing, it serves the needs of students with special needs. The approaches, styles, topics, and abilities of writers change as they move from elementary school through college, and Costanzo suggests that future research should consider how word processing can best support these changes.

Database Management and Information Retrieval

Databases are used increasingly to manage the massive amounts of information available to workers and learners. Powerful search systems for local databases (e.g., AppleWorks files, CD-ROMs) and for remote ones (e.g., Dialog, BRS, CompuServe) are becoming increasingly common in schools. Although there have been many calls for the use of databases in social studies, there are few research studies reported.

Rawitsch (1988) compared eighth-grade students' use of a social studies database in paper and pencil and electronic forms. He found that, when they used the computer, students were somewhat more successful in solving problems that required comparing data, but they took more time. Students did prefer using the computer to doing the problems on paper. In assessing student "work style" as structured or unstructured, Rawitsch found that those with structured styles were more efficient in using the computer. A subsequent study by Rawitsch, Bart & Earle (1988) compared the uses of an electronic database and a computer simulation in promoting hypothetical-deductive reasoning by seventh graders, but found no statistically significant differences on post-test scores.

Beishuizen (1987) created and tested a computerized coaching system for searching two databases. While conducting their searches, those who were coached performed better in the loosely structured database, but there were no differences between this group and the uncoached group on the highly structured database. He also reported that some students were annoyed at interruptions by the "coach" and that students who used a breadth-first strategy on a subsequent database tended to do better than those who used a depth-first strategy.

Callison & Daniels (1988) found that high school students were able to apply a powerful retrieval system to search online databases. They found that students who were most successful tended to be enthusiastic about getting started with their searches, conducted multiple searches, and used print indexes to select terms, and that some students worked independently while others worked in groups.

Marchionini (1989) studied third through sixth-grade students' use of a full-text, CD-ROM electronic encyclopedia. He found that, although upper elementary students performed faster and more successful searches, young children were also generally successful in completing searches with a powerful Boolean retrieval system.

In a series of formative evaluations for an electronic learning tool kit (Inquire), Hawkins et al. (1988) compared junior high students to graduate students when using the system. They found that junior high students asked about the same number of questions, but they were less hierarchically connected than the graduate students' questions; they copied rather than abstracted while taking notes; they missed significant information and included irrelevant information; and they generally did less information integration as they used the system. This study also found that high ability students benefited more from using the system than average or low ability students. As more electronic databases come into schools, more research is needed to determine how best to apply these databases to support specific coursework activities as well as to develop generic information literacy skills and concepts.

Emerging Tools

Computing tools known as hypertext or hypermedia systems are gaining considerable attention from educators and information specialists. Together with powerful storage technologies, these systems allow users to access massive quantities of multimedia information in rapid and flexible ways. It has been argued that hypermedia systems are well-suited to self-directed learning because they allow a myriad of links among information units that mirror human associative memory (Jonassen, 1988). Although no controlled research results are available, several large-scale projects are in use or under development. The Intermedia system has been successfully used in courses in English literature and biology at Brown University (Landow, 1988; Yankelovich, Haan, Meyrowitz & Drucker, 1988), and the Perseus Project at Harvard is designed for use in a variety of courses related to the ancient Greek world (Crane, 1988). Hypertext versions of literary works have been used in high school English courses (Harris & Cady, 1988), and hypertext shells such as the Project Jefferson Notebook (Chignell & Lacy, 1988) allow teachers or library media specialists to create their own hypertext databases. Although it is too soon to judge the effects of hypermedia systems on learning and teaching, practitioners and researchers alike should pay critical attention to the successes and failures of these emerging tools.

Implications for Practitioners

The results of research have not demonstrated that computing is superior to existing methods of teaching and learning, but rather that it is a viable alternative when properly matched to students and topics. The Office of Technology Assessment Report (1988) suggests a multi-faceted approach to applying computing:

Emphasizing a single use of technology now could stifle much needed innovation, initiative, and experimentation. OTA concludes that Federal programs should allow, perhaps encourage, flexibility of use by different districts (pp. 12-13).

Applying computing in education requires practitioners to do four things. First, they must invest time in learning generic hardware and software principles. Rapid changes in computer technology mean that computer literacy is a process rather than a destination, educators must continually update their skills and knowledge by building on fundamental principles of human-computer interaction.

Second, practitioners must create lessons that optimize the uses of computing. It will remain a challenge for school library media specialists to collaborate with teachers to develop as well as deliver instruction. Educational computing offers a window of opportunity for extending this collaboration, since all school personnel are struggling to apply these new tools in effective and efficient ways.

Third, practitioners must plan the organizational patterns for students and workstations. At present, there is no evidence of optimal organizations for getting students, computers, and software together. We do not know what topics and types of learning activities are best facilitated by a library or a science laboratory model. Moreover, there is scant evidence for mapping individual or group computing to instructional situations. As more computers become available in schools, practitioners are in an ideal position to consider these organizational questions.

Finally, practitioners must reflect on the effects on the overall curriculum and their own teaching styles and performance. One way to systematically assess these effects is to collaborate with researchers interested in the problems of educational computing. Overall, the best advice is the same principle computer designers are finally recognizing: Know your user! Teachers, school library media specialists, administrators, and school districts should proceed according to their individual interests and strengths so that computing can become another tool in the repertoire for teaching and learning.

Implications for Researchers

The Association for Educational Communications and Technology marked the occasion of changing the name of its major journal from Educational Communications and Technology Journal to Educational Technology Research and Development (Vol 37, No.1, 1989) with a special issue dedicated to discussions of the directions of research and practice for the educational technology field. Winn

(1989), Clark (1989), and Reigeluth (1989) each argued for a prescriptive approach to research rather than a descriptive one.

Acceptance of educational technology as an applied field has implications for the questions researchers address and the methodologies they apply. Questions of **what** and **how** must at least be understood so that questions of **why** can be addressed. Like educational research in general, educational computing research must be rooted in the theories of psychology, cognitive science, and sociology before it can mature. These theories can serve to support the prescriptions in the near future, the results of which will establish a theory of human-computer learning. Accordingly, the following are some illustrative basic questions that this author believes must be answered on the road to a mature theory of educational technology.

1.	What are the effects of human-machine interactions?
1.1	What are the long-term effects of regular interactions with machines?
1.2	How are these interactions different across people? systems? tasks?
1.3	What are the characteristics of interactions initiated and controlled by people? by machines?

2.	What are the relationships among task, learner, instructor, and system?
2.1	Tasks
2.1.1	What types of knowledge and tasks lend themselves best to directed learning? self-directed learning?
2.1.2	What new tasks must be addressed in today's curricula as a result of technology?
2.2	Learner
2.2.1	What learner characteristics are appropriate to machine interactions?
2.2.2	How does technology affect knowledge acquisition?
2.2.3	How does technology affect metacognitive processing?
2.2.4	How does technology affect attitudes and motivations?
2.3	Instruction
2.3.1	How does technology affect classroom interaction and collaboration?
2.3.2	How does technology affect assignments?
2.3.3	How does technology affect teacher styles and performance?
2.4	Systems
2.4.1	What computer system characteristics are specific to users and tasks?
2.4.2	How is technology best organized, delivered and supported in schools?
2.4.3	How are the roles of teacher and learner affected by highly interactive technology?
2.4.4	What are the social and political implications of highly technological centers of learning?

These questions are by no means meant to be exhaustive, nor are they mutually exclusive. Rather they provide a flavor of the kinds of questions researchers are asking. Furthermore, the answers to each raise important followup questions that motivate explanations of **why** effects were found.

Cognitive science is having a powerful impact on education in general and on educational technology in particular. This will likely continue as researchers press their efforts to understand how computers can act as cognitive amplifiers and augmenters. Continued efforts will be made to apply artificial intelligence techniques to educational computing, and since much effort has been directed toward the study of collaborative work, parallel efforts are beginning to assess the impact of computers on collaborative learning. An area that requires attention is the social impact of educational computing: how it affects individuals in small groups as well as the larger school climate and society as a whole. One example of such work is the study by Schofield & Verban (1988) that examined the factors in schools that mitigate computer applications. Additional investigations of equity, grouping, and collaboration are necessary for a comprehensive theory of human-computer learning to emerge.

To address such questions, more varied methodologies must be accepted by the research community. Rather than shaping the questions to fit a particular methodological paradigm, the questions should determine which method is most appropriate. Field studies, case studies, naturalistic observations and interviews, and surveys are being applied productively to address general and complex research questions, to identify additional research questions, and to develop categories and taxonomies of critical factors. There is general agreement that there need be no more media comparison studies, but carefully designed, controlled experiments are needed to test competing hypotheses in an emerging theory of educational computing. Because the computer is a malleable medium for modeling the world, it has been applied in a variety of ways to improve teaching and learning. To assess the effects of these varied applications on complex human activity requires a broad range of methodological tools carefully applied by inquisitive and diligent researchers.

References

Baer, V.E. (1988). Computers as composition tools: A case study of student attitudes. Journal of Computer-Based Instruction, 15(4), 144-148.

Bangert-Drowns, R.L., Kulik, J.A. & Kulik, C-L.C. (1985). Effectiveness of computer-based education in secondary schools. Journal of Computer-Based Instruction, 12, 59-68.

Becker, H.J. (1987). The impact of computer use on children's learning: What research has shown and what it has not. Center for Social Organization of Schools, The Johns Hopkins University.

Becker, H.J. (1986a). Instructional uses of school computers: Reports from the 1985 national survey, Issue No. 1 (June). Center for Social Organization of Schools, The Johns Hopkins University.

Becker, H.J. (1986b). Instructional uses of school computers: Reports from the 1985 national survey, Issue No. 3 (November). Center for Social Organization of Schools, The Johns Hopkins University.

Beishuizen, J. (1987). A computer coach for information retrieval. In J. Moonen & T. Plomp (Eds.), EURIT 86: Developments in educational software and courseware, pp. 21-27. Oxford: Pergamon Press.

Bruder, I. (1988). Electronic Learning's 8th annual survey of the states, 1988. Electronic Learning, 8(2), 38-45.

Callison, D. & Daniels, A. (1988). Introducing end-user software for enhancing student online searching. School Library Media Quarterly, Spring, 173-181.

Chignell, M. & Lacy, R. (1988). Integrating research and instruction: Project Jefferson. Academic Computing, 3(2), 12-17, 40-45.

Clark, R.E. (1989). Current progress and future directions for research in instructional technology. Educational Technology Research and Development, 37(1), 57-66.

Clark, R.E. (1985). Evidence for confounding in computer-based instruction studies: Analyzing the meta-analyses. Educational Communications and Technology Journal, 33(4), 249-262.

Collier, R.M. (1983). The word-processor and revision strategies. College Composition and Communication, May, 149-155.

Costanzo, W. (1989). The electronic text: Learning to write, read, and reason with computers. Englewood Cliffs, NJ: Educational Technology Publications.

Crane, G. (1988). Redefining the book: Some preliminary problems. Academic Computing, 2(5), 6-11.

Daiute, C. (1985). Writing and computers. Reading, MA: Addison-Wesley.

Dalton, D. & Hannafin, M. (1987). The effects of word processing on written composition. Journal of Educational Research, 80(6), 338-342.

Edwards, J., et al. (1975). How effective is CAI? A review of the research. Educational Leadership, 33, 147-153.

Harris, M. & Cady, M. (1988). The dynamic process of creating hypertext literature. Educational Technology, 28(11), 33-40.

Hatfield, L. & Kieren, T. (1972). Computer-assisted problem solving in mathematics. Journal of Research in Mathematics Education, 3(2), 99-112.

Hawisher, G. (1987). The effects of word processing on the revision strategies of college freshmen. Research in the Teaching of English, 21(1), 145-160.

Hawkins, J., et al. (1988). Inquire: Final Report to the National Science Foundation, Application of Advanced Technologies Program. Grant No. MDR-8550339.

Jamison, D., Suppes, P. & Wells, S. (1974). The effectiveness of alternative instructional media: A survey. Review of Educational Research, 44, 1-61.

Jonassen, D. (1988). Hypertext principles for text and courseware design. Educational Psychologist, 21(11), 269-292.

Kearsley, G., Hunter, B. & Seidel, R.J. (1983). Two decades of computer based instruction projects: What have we learned? T.H.E. Journal, January, 90-94; February, 88-96.

Kozma, R.B. (1987). The implications of cognitive psychology for computer-based learning tools. Educational Technology, November, 20-25.

Krendl, K. & Lieberman, D. (1988). Computers and learning: A review of recent research. Journal of Educational Computing Research, 4(4), 367-389.

Krull, R. & Hurford, J. (1987). Can computers increase writing productivity? Technical Communication, Fourth Quarter, 243-249.

Kulik, J.A., Bangert, R.L. & Williams, G.W. (1983). Effects of computer-based teaching on secondary school students. Journal of Educational Psychology, 75(1), 19-26.

Kulik, J.A., Kulik, C-L.C. & Bangert-Drowns, R.L. (1985). Effectiveness of computer-based education in elementary schools. Computers in Human Behavior, 1, 59-74.

Kulik, J.A., Kulik, C-L.C. & Cohen, P.A. (1980). Effectiveness of computer-based college teaching: A meta-analysis of findings. Review of Educational Research, 50, 525-544.

Landow, G. (1988). Hypertext in literary education, criticism, and scholarship. Providence, RI: Institute for Research in Information and Scholarship, Brown University.

Maddux, C.D. (1989). Logo: Scientific dedication or religious fanaticism in the 1990s? Educational Technology, February, 18-23.

Marchionini, G. (1988). Electronic problem scenarios: Integrating computers into instruction. Journal of Education for Library and Information Science, 29(3), 165-176.

Marchionini, G. (1989). Information-seeking strategies of novices using a full-text electronic encyclopedia. Journal of the American Society for Information Science, 40(1), 54-66.

Office of Technology Assessment. (1988). Power on! New Tools for Teaching and Learning. Washington, DC: Congress of the United States.

Papert, S. (1980). Mindstorms. New York: Basic Books.

Park, O., Perez, R. & Seidel, R. (1987). Intelligent CAI: Old wine in new bottles, or a new vintage? In G. Kearsley (Ed.), Artificial intelligence and instruction: Applications and methods. Reading, MA: Addison-Wesley.

Pea, R. (1983). Logo programming and problem solving. Paper presented at the AERA Annual Conference, Montreal, April.

Pea, R. & Kurland, D.M. (1984). Logo programming and the development of planning skills. Technical Report 16, Bank Street College of Education, Center for Children and Technology.

Pea, R. & Kurland, D.M. (1983). On the cognitive prerequisites of learning computer programming. Technical Report 18, Bank Street College of Education, Center for Children and Technology.

Rawitsch, D. (1988). The effect of computer use and student work style on database analysis activities in the social studies. Research Bulletin #1, Improving the Use of Technology in Schools: What We Are Learning. MECC/University of Minnesota Center for the Study of Educational Technology.

Rawitsch, D., Bart, W. & Earle, J. (1988). Using computer database programs to facilitate higher-order thinking skills. Research Bulletin #1, Improving the Use of Technology in Schools: What We Are Learning. MECC/University of Minnesota Center for the Study of Educational Technology.

Reigeluth, C.M. (1989). Educational technology at the crossroads: New mindsets and new directions. Educational Technology Research and Development, 37(1), 67-80.

Schofield, J. & Verban, D. (1988). Barriers and Incentives to Computer Usage in Teaching. Technical Report 1, Learning and Development Center, University of Pittsburgh.

Shavelson, R.J. & Salomon, G. (1985). Information technology: tool and teacher of the mind. Educational Researcher, 14(5), 4.

Stennett, R. (1985). Computer assisted instruction: A review of the reviews. London Board of Education (Ontario). Educational Research Services. ED 260687.

Vinsonhaler, J. & Bass, R. (1972). A summary of ten major studies of CAI drill & practice. Educational Technology, 12(7), 29-32.

Winn, W. (1989). Toward a rationale and theoretical basis for equational technology. Educational Technology Research and Development, 37(1), 35-46.

Yankelovich, N., Haan, B., Meyrowitz, N. & Drucker, S. (1988). Intermedia: The concept and the construction of a seamless information environment. IEEE Computer, 21(1), 81-96.

Part 5

Miscellaneous Topics

STATE, REGIONAL AND DISTRICT-LEVEL MEDIA PROGRAMS

Carole J. McCollough
Assistant Professor
Library Science Program
Wayne State University, Detroit, Michigan

Introduction

This summation reviews the literature on the management of state, regional and district-level school library media programs from the period beginning with the publications of the 1975 standards, <u>Media Programs: District and School</u> to the 1988 guidelines, <u>Information Power</u>.

The 1975 <u>Media Programs</u> standards serve as an articulation of a multileveled organizational structure for school library media services. The document describes the role of the media program director/supervisor as the interface between the educational program and the application of media and technology to instruction. The director role at the state, regional and district levels assumes responsibility for "decision-making related to setting overall goals, analyzing curriculum, selecting instructional modes, and establishing and maintaining responsible evaluative processes" (<u>Media Programs</u>, 1975).

National Studies Assessing the Library Media Administrative Role

Two studies covered in this investigation provided a national overview of district-level library media services. The first, published by Elsie Brumback in 1984, was conducted to assess levels of leadership and program effectiveness in state agencies. The second, conducted by Stephanie Nelson in 1987, sought to 1) gain a perspective on the number of district-level media directors nationwide, 2) identify the activities and services media directors were involved in, and 3) measure the impact of district-level directors on library media programs.

Brumback's (1984) analysis of state-level leadership provides a retrospective view of state library media services leading up to the 1982 U.S. Department of Education funded study, "State Education Agency Responsibilities and Services for School Library Media Programs." The study identified the strengths and needs of participating states. Of particular interest to this investigation were the political and policy implications found in the major conclusions of the report. These conclusions indicated:

- The placement of the library media unit within the state agency affects its involvement and effectiveness.
- All states do not have state adopted standards or guidelines for school media programs.
- The state agency, with the exception of one or two states, is limited in its ability to mandate library programs that meet established criteria.

- All states do not mandate that schools have libraries or media centers.

- The demise of ESEA Title IVB funds will reduce state staffs, eliminate support services, curtail travel, and reduce overall effectiveness of library media programs at the state level.
- The majority of participating states (nine) do not provide coordinated and unified programs of library media services.

The identification of current district library media directors in the second study revealed a significant reduction in numbers. Nelson's findings support a perceived pattern of reductions in administrative positions attested to regularly by the professional association leadership.

Further findings from the Nelson study indicate that the district supervisor's role is frequently viewed as one of support rather than administration. The district supervisor, more often than not, does not serve as a decision-maker in matters of program and personnel evaluation or budget management. In addition, many traditional responsibilities in the areas of production and the acquisition and maintenance of materials have been assumed by other departments.

Findings on the changing structure of the supervisory function indicate a strong need for a district-by-district role definition of the library media director. Nelson suggested further 1) the need for a clear articulation of how the media director fits into the organizational structure of school districts and 2) self-examination by district directors of the tasks and services performed, and how these activities affect the overall quality of the building-level media program.

State Surveys of Library Media Programs, Personnel and Services

Three state studies conducted to determine the state of the art as a framework for policy and program decision-making provide useful models for assessing existing knowledge about district-level management of library media programs. The Library of Michigan convened a task force of school, public, special and government librarians to investigate interdependent activities and concerns. The final report, Information at Risk: Michigan Libraries in the 1990's (1988) focused on the primary issue affecting all types of libraries: state and local funding.

A survey based on an instrument developed by Marilyn Miller and Barbara Moran was used by the task force to analyze school library media centers. The survey was sent to a sample of 648 school library media centers in the state. Results pointed to a state of limited resources and uncertain support of school library media centers. The lack of media specialists at the elementary level was one of the major indicators of limited support. The report further indicated the disparity in funding for school library media centers from district to district. Amounts ranged from $.00 to $30.00 per pupil.

The school media section of the final report concluded that without an advocate at the state level, responsible for school library media supervision and coordination, the problems affecting programs and services throughout the state would continue. Eleven recommendations relating to school library media centers called for interdepartmental cooperation between the Library of Michigan and the Department of Education; promotion through incentive funding of multitype networks that include school library media centers; a media consultant at the state level; support and implementation of the national guidelines, <u>Information Power</u> and state supported staff development activities.

The Ohio State Department of Education (1967) chose to adopt a leadership position in promoting school library services. A task force was underwritten to produce operational guidelines for developing a quality library media program in Ohio schools. The stated goals of the document were to 1) provide a rationale for integration of the school library into the total education program, 2) delineate the dimensions of service of a dynamic K-12 library program, 3) identify the essential components of an effective K-12 library program, 4) provide a practical guide for planning a district library program, and 5) stimulate thinking about emerging trends and developments in library science and educational technology.

Effective administration was identified as a primary component among those interrelated dimensions that contribute to dynamic library programs. Two areas of administrative responsibilities considered essential for a successful district-level program included the development of appropriate policies and planning, monitoring and projecting the program budget.

The Ohio guidelines described five components of a comprehensive library program: district leadership, competent personnel, carefully selected resources, functional and inviting facilities, and a broad-based community support system. The guidelines also assigned major responsibility for facilities planning to the district library supervisor, from identifying and securing national, state and regional planning resources to providing leadership in writing educational specifications.

The Wisconsin state survey of 1982 was prepared from a 1981 investigation of Wisconsin's 433 school districts conducted by the Bureau of Instructional Media Programs. The report represents the state of the art in Wisconsin and was presented in 14 composite tables. The tables provided statistical evidence of such criteria as responsibilities of the district media director, board approved instructional media policies, the range of district-level media services provided, the extent of resource sharing, and the identification of district collections and union catalogs.

The Wisconsin report concluded with a profile of district media directors. The profile documented Wisconsin school districts that have part-time directors and building-level professionals with district responsibilities. It also noted percentages of media directors with multiple certifications [school library media, audiovisual, instructional technology], all awarded by the state. Of the 369 media directors identified, 79% held certificates at the coordinator, director and supervisor levels.

These composites of statistical data provide the framework for a needs assessment in the areas of staff development, program services, and media resources for the Wisconsin State Board of Education. Ohio's operational guidelines go further toward identifying essential components of effective media programs. Finally, the Michigan study serves as an advocacy document for state leadership in library media programs and services.

Investigations of Leadership, Roles and Responsibilities

The greatest number of studies reviewed for this report focused on activities of the district-level media director. The studies discussed in this report provide fresh insights about factors relating to the managerial role of the district supervisor.

Rogus (1986) has developed lists of "foci" (essential areas of library media supervisor responsibility) from a synthesis of standards documents, library media texts and leadership research. His checklists "Taking Care of Self," and "Informal Staff Development Activities" were developed to fulfill time management/self-analysis objectives. Rogus' checklists emphasized specific demands of the library media setting, including honoring priorities, task achievement, and group maintenance for effective leadership.

Bingham (1983) analyzed educational supervision from the historical perspective, noting the relationship of supervision to changing models of school organization. Three approaches to supervision were described: scientific, clinical and artistic. Bingham listed eight interactive operational essentials for effective supervision:

- board-level support and funding,
- an organizational framework that defines and protects supervision functions,
- performance evaluation within the teacher's goal structure,
- curriculum specialists as resources to principals and teachers,
- superintendent-level priority, attention and provision for supervision,
- preservice/inservice training and supervision of supervisors,
- clinical supervision within the teacher's goal structure,
- supervisor as mentor, trainer and collaborator with principals.

Bingham's report concluded with a description of the direct, indirect and central office responsibilities and managerial services of the district media supervisor.

The realities of declining enrollments and U.S. Department of Education projections of enrollment expectations indicate clearly that the expansionist period of American public education has ended, or that it is at least in a holding pattern. The impact of pupil enrollment on the administration of district-level media services is a concern to all who face and/or anticipate its relationship to funding and programming. Brown (1984) suggested an analysis of social, financial and residential factors to determine enrollment patterns.

One operational reality of declining enrollment figures is the deployment of personnel. This issue was discussed by Brown together with creative options that address staff reductions. The list includes jobsharing, permanent library media substitutes, and recertification for other teaching fields.

Kulleseid's (1982, 1985) seminal research on survival and empowerment provided new insights into communication patterns, change agent strategies, power structures and program survival characteristics. While many policies and contractual procedures were found to be counterproductive, collective bargaining agreements were reported as essential components of program survival. Of particular importance in this review were findings relating the instructional development role of the media professional. Research reports indicating that Kulleseid's study population did not view instructional development tasks as critical to survival of library media program support in declining situations suggest a vastly different set of priorities than those identified in the Information Power (1988).

Nelson's (1987) research looked at influences library media directors have on media program development. The study uncovered some observations that have a special relevance to this review. Extrapolating from the investigations of Davis (1976), Hanna (1979), Frary (1979), and Maxwell (1979), Nelson noted:

> The role of the district library media director [has] evolved with basically no direction, and the role in each district was essentially created by the individual in the position...the district library media director's job was further complicated by a mix of supervisory, consultative and administrative tasks. The job titles assigned district-level library media personnel had little to do with the roles actually assigned, developed and assumed (p. 15).

Education/Competencies of District Media Directors

The introduction to the 1978 Drexel Library Quarterly issue dedicated to district-level library media services suggested that most library media directors came to their positions with little or no specialized professional preparation (Chisholm; Lowrey and Case; Meyers; Meyers and Barber; Portteus; Aaron; Woolls). The Wisconsin Survey of library media programs and practices (1982) included the identification of building-level practitioners with district-level responsibilities. The Wisconsin findings strongly suggested that there are persons performing administrative jobs without formal preparation. Additional findings from Held's investigation, reported later in this section, support the Wisconsin reports and indicate a continuing necessity to monitor the preservice and inservice needs of district library media directors.

Held's (1986) study of the perceptions of school library media leadership of present and future functions of district media directors replicated in part the study of functions conducted by Curry (1977) in Virginia. In the Held study findings, library media educators indicated a decrease in involvement in research and production, and the service functions of logistics.

Study participants in the Held research investigation from library education identified instructional technologies and computer generated learning products as primary areas where additional competencies would be needed in the future. Additional knowledge and skill training identified by the administrative leadership included organization and personnel management, curriculum planning; and the selection and evaluation of media materials.

Implications for Practitioners

State Studies

1. Several states have conducted studies to assess school media programs, resources, personnel, budgets, policies and networking activities (Ohio, 1986; Wisconsin, 1982; Michigan, 1988). In one case the study provided a framework for developing state guidelines. Other studies have served to identify needs, determine compliance with national guidelines, chart progress and stimulate innovative thinking about trends.

2. There are two major structures in place that determine the governance and fiscal management of school districts, broadly defined by geographic considerations. The first is characterized by shifting demographics, declining tax bases and a large urban bureaucracy. The second features a predominance of suburban districts. Populations in the second group show evidence of large numbers of new immigrants from the Far East, Caribbean, and Central American countries.

3. All states do not have state adopted standards or guidelines for school library media programs (Brumback, 1984).

4. The organizational structure of the library media unit within the state agency directly affects its effectiveness (Martin, 1982).

5. The demise of ESEA Title IV B funds [has] eliminate[d] support services and reduced both staffs and overall effectiveness of library media programs at the state level (Martin, 1982).

6. Many states do not provide coordinated/unified programs of library media services. (Martin, 1982).

7. Most states do not mandate a position for a media director at the district level (Kulleseid, 1985).

Leadership, Roles and Responsibilities

8. Critical elements of district-level leadership have been identified as:

   - written philosophy that indicates the district's commitment to quality library service;
   - board adopted policies;
   - written, long range goals;
   - instructional affiliations with area information resource institutions and agencies (Ohio Department of Education, 1986).

9. The responsibility for facilities planning, writing educational specifications and identifying core instructional resources for new and remodeled media centers rests with the district media director/supervisor (Ohio Department of Education, 1986).

10. Library media director/supervisors must be prepared to deal with the management of decline by presiding over library closings, transferring collections and redeploying personnel (Brown, 1984).

11. Position descriptions can be used to clarify job expectations, maintain consistency throughout a district; inform others of the roles, functions, and services of media personnel; and foster a sense of commitment, responsibility and personal investment in their work (Ohio Department of Education, 1986).

12. There is an emerging awareness evident in state departments of education that evaluation procedures for library media specialists must be different than those used for classroom teachers (Turner, 1986).

13. Districts with media director/supervisors provide more professional services than districts without (Eberhard, 1974).

Administration and Policy Issues

14. There is evidence of increasing public interest in the selection of library materials and a tendency to challenge professional expertise on the basis of community values (Kulleseid, 1985).

15. The library media professional has almost no formal authority in the creation and implementation of fiscal policies and procedures affecting programs at any level of the school system (Kulleseid, 1985).

16. There is continuing debate over the efficiency and viability of the centralized processing services provided at the district level (Brodeur and Heinich, 1980).

Education and Competencies

17. District library supervisors require knowledges, skills and competencies in the areas of organization, instructional development, staff development and personnel management, evaluation, research skills, public relations, interpersonal communication skills and fiscal management (Krentz, 1986).

18. There is a need to focus more attention on developing competencies in organization management, integrating new technologies, the development of computer systems and products and the utilization of media research (Held, 1986).

Implications for Researchers

It is clear from the research reviewed for this report that the research output specifically targeted toward state, regional and district-level programs, services and leadership has decreased significantly since the rich period right after publication of the 1975 standards (Media Programs). There is a need to reassess the position papers published in the 1977 (Butler and Stenzier, Mancall and Barber) and 1978 issues of Drexel Library Quarterly that provided the timely philosophical framework for state, regional and district-level leadership.

The shift from quantitative standards in Media Programs (1975) to the qualitative approach that characterizes the Information Power (1988) guidelines suggests a research agenda with a decidedly environmentally based perspective:

1. There is a need to extend state of the art studies to each state in the union.

2. In the wake of reports that many regions have eliminated state and district-level director positions, there is a need to identify the reality and impact of coordinated services on quality library media programs.

3. There is a need to collect data on how library media directors adapt to the political realities of local organizational structures and economic variables. We need to identify those behavioral patterns, negotiation strategies, and responses to institutional change that are in place. Information on how successful library media directors are bridging the gap between the ideal and the pragmatic is critical.

4. The research that has identified exemplary library media programs must be replicated for state- and district-level programs. Environmentally specific definitions of excellence must be collected.

5. The focus in Information Power (1988) on the instructional development role of the library media professional calls for detailed descriptions and analyses of the decision-making processes in place for instructional development.

6. Models for analyzing school culture and system organization must be developed locally to get a handle on the operational power structures identified by Kulleseid (1985) as instrumental to managing change.

7. Library media director networking interface models must be developed to implement the expanded information resource provision goals identified in Information Power (1988).

8. There is a need to reassess the central services provided at the district level in the wake of the currently available technologies. Consideration of local access to regional resources must be analyzed.

9. There is a need for identification and delivery of continuing education needs at the director level.

References

Aaron, Shirley L. "The Media Supervisor and Collective Bargaining." Drexel Library Quarterly 14 (July 1978): 95-101.

American Library Association and Association for Educational Communications and Technology. Information Power: Guidelines for School Library Media Programs. Chicago: ALA, AECT, 1988.

American Library Association and Association for Educational Communications and Technology. Media Programs: District and School. Washington, DC: ALA, AECT, 1975.

Bingham, Rebecca. "The Role of the District Library Media Supervisor in Today's Educational Setting." In School Library Media Annual, Vol. 1. Littleton, CO: Libraries Unlimited, 1983.

Brodeur, Doris, and Robert Heinich. Report of the 3rd Annual Survey of the Circulation of Non-Print Educational Media in Public Schools, 1979-1980. Bloomington, IN: University of Indiana, 1980. ED 202456.

Brown, Dale W. "Declining Enrollment and School library Media Services." School Library Media Annual, Vol. 2. Littleton, CO: Libraries Unlimited, 1984.

Brumback, Elsie. "State Level Media Leadership: Changing to Meet the Times." In School Library Media Annual, Vol. 2. Littleton, CO: Libraries Unlimited, 1984.

Butler, Naomi W., and Yale Stenzier. "The Planning and Modification of Library Media Center Facilities." Drexel Library Quarterly 13 (April 1977): 62-69.

Chisholm, Margaret E. "The Supervisor and Instructional Planning." Drexel Library Quarterly 14 (July 1978): 37-44.

Curry, Lowell Roger. "A Study of the Media Function as Perceived by School Principals and District-Level Media Administrators." Ed.D. diss., University of Southern Mississippi, 1975.

Davis, Sally Ann. "Role of the SLM Director." Ph.D. diss., University of Wisconsin, 1975.

Eberhard, Heyson C. "A Study of Kansas Elementary School Library Media Centers with District School Media Directors Compared to Elementary School Library Media Centers without District Media Directors from 1966-1972." Ed.D. diss., Oklahoma State University, 1974.

Frary, Mildred. "District-Level Supervision." School Library Media Quarterly 7 (Spring 1979): 182-186.

Hanna, Mary Ann. "State-Level Supervision." School Library Media Quarterly 7 (Spring 1979).

Held, Frederick W. "The Present and Future Functions of the Public School District Media Director." Ed.D. diss., Indiana University, 1986.

Krentz, Roger Franklin. "A Study of Selected Competencies of Full-Time School District Media Directors." Ph.D. diss., University of Wisconsin, 1986.

Kulleseid, Eleanor Ransom. Beyond Survival to Power for School Library Media Professionals. Hamden, CT: Library Professional Publications, 1985.

Kulleseid, Eleanor Ransom. "A Study of Survival: Three New York City Elementary School Library Media Centers and Their Support Components." D.L.S. diss., Columbia University, 1982.

Library of Michigan. Information at Risk: Michigan Libraries in the 1990's. Lansing, MI: Library of Michigan, 1988.

Lowrey, Anna M., and Robert N. Case. "Measuring Program Effectiveness." Drexel Library Quarterly 14 (July 1978): 12-23.

Mancall, Jacqueline C., and Raymond W. Barber "The Supervisory Network." Drexel Library Quarterly 13 (April 1977): 24-35.

Martin, Betty, and Frances Hatfield. The School District Library Media Director's Handbook. Hamden, CT: Library Professional Publications, 1982.

Maxwell, James G. "Regional-Level Supervision." School Library Media Quarterly 7 (Spring 1979): 186-188.

Meyers, Judith K. "Research Responsibilities of the School Supervisor." Drexel Library Quarterly 14 (July 1978): 113-127.

Meyers, Judith K., and Raymond W Barber. "The Media Supervisor and the Selection Process." Drexel Library Quarterly 14 (July 1978): 45-64.

Nelson, Stephanie. "The Influence of the District Library Media Supervisor on Library Media Program Development in the United States." Ed.D. diss., Utah State University, 1987.

Ohio Department of Education. Quality Library Services, K-12. Ohio Department of Education, Division of Elementary and Secondary Education. Columbus, OH: Ohio Department of Education, 1986. ED 274355.

Portteus, Elnora M. "Supervisory Interface: Reality and Action." Drexel Library Quarterly 14 (July 1978): 65-77.

Rogus, Joseph F. "Supervisory Savvy: Strengthening Performance as a School Library Media Supervisor." School Library Media Quarterly 14 (Spring 1986): 133-137.

Turner, Philip M. "The Involvement of State Education Agencies in the Evaluation of School Library Media Specialists." School Library Media Quarterly 15 (Fall 1986): 63-64.

Wisconsin State Department of Public Instruction. District Level Instructional Media Programs in Wisconsin Public Schools, A Status Report. Madison, WI: Wisconsin State Department of Public Instruction, 1982. ED 233689.

Woolls, Blanche. "District Level Program Evaluation." Drexel Library Quarterly 14 (July 1978): 24-35.

Bibliography

Adams, Helen R. School Media Policy Development: A Practical Process for Small Districts. Englewood, CO: Libraries Unlimited, 1986.

Biagini, Mary K. A Model For Problem Solving And Decision Making: Managing School Library Media Programs. Englewood, CO: Libraries Unlimited, 1988.

Bingham, Rebecca T. "Components of Effective Supervision at the District Level." School Library Media Quarterly 7 (Spring 1979): 191-194.

Dane, Chase. "Managing the School Media Library." In Current Concepts in Library Management. Edited by Martha Boaz. Englewood, CO: Libraries Unlimited, 1979.

Gillespie, John T. A Model School District Media Program; Montgomery County as a Case Study. Chicago: American Library Association, 1977.

Hardin, Sue Hunt. "Guidelines for the Establishment of School District Level Media Centers in the United States." Ed.D. diss., University of South Carolina, 1977.

Lloyd, Helen, feature editor. "Leadership—Beyond the Building Level; School Library Media Supervision at the State, District, and Regional Levels." School Library Media Quarterly 7 (Spring 1979): 173-194.

Otzman, Ruth. "District Media Directors: The Goal Is Leadership." Media Spectrum 7 (Second Quarter 1980): 5-6.

Pretlow, Delores Z. "The District Media Center: Development and Testing of a Purchasing Model for Selected School Districts." Ed.D. diss., George Washington University, 1982.

Pretlow, Delores Z., and Beverly J. Bagan. "May We Help You?" School Library Media Quarterly 13 (Winter 1985): 56-58.

Prostano, Emanuel T., and Joyce S. Prostano. The School Library Media Center. 3rd ed. Englewood, CO: Libraries Unlimited, 1982.

Strack, Robert C. "The District Media Supervisor: Personnel, Planning and Technical Duties Are Major." Wilson Library Bulletin 75 (May/June 1979): 115-116.

Taggert, Dorothy T. Management and Administration of the School Library Media Program. Hamden, CT: Library Professional Publications, 1980.

Woolls, Blanche. Managing School Library Media Programs. Englewood, CO: Libraries Unlimited, 1988.

Woolls, Blanche, and David Loertscher, eds. The Microcomputer Facility and the School Library Media Specialist. Chicago: ALA, 1986.

Yesner, Bernice L., and Hilda L. Jay. The School Administrator's Guide to Evaluating Library Media Programs. Hamden, CT: Library Professional Publications, 1987.

RESEARCH RELATED TO THE EDUCATION OF
SCHOOL LIBRARY MEDIA SPECIALISTS

Daniel Barron
Coordinator, School Library Media Program
College of Library and Information Science
University of South Carolina
Columbia, South Carolina

Introduction

This paper presents an extensive bibliography of literature concerning the education of school library media specialists. It has been divided into ten areas, including certification, competencies, courses, distance learning, institutes, the Knapp School Library Manpower Project Report, level of education, needs, program evaluation, and teacher education. The bibliography includes both description and analysis of reported research and selected other literature concerning the education of school library media specialists. The term research is used to describe investigations in which it was clear that some hypothesis was tested or a set of research questions was answered. Other literature includes thought pieces and reports of practice that are significant to the discussion, but cannot be classified as research. The citations for this study were gathered from the ERIC, LISA, and Dissertation Abstracts Online data bases; a review of the research reported in all issues of School Library Media Annual; and other related textual files and collections.

Each data base was searched using a strategy involving combinations and truncations of the terms *training, preparation, adult education, adult learning, library education, librarian, school librarian*, and *media specialist*. The numbers reported below include the total number of citations resulting from the search terms listed.

1. training/preparation/library education and librarians: ERIC=1334, Dissertation Abstracts=85, and LISA=1870.

2. training/preparation/library education and school library media specialists: ERIC=385, Dissertation Abstracts=50, and LISA=98.

3. adult education/learning and training ... and librarians: ERIC=37, Dissertation Abstracts=2, and LISA=17.

4. adult education/learning and training ... and school library media specialists: ERIC=4, Dissertation Abstracts=1, and LISA=0.

Further analysis reveals that very little research has been done related to the education of librarians generally and school library media specialists in particular.

Analysis of the Citations and Sources

A total of 322 citations and sources were selected for further analysis from more than 500 items thought to be potentially relevant. A number of items were eliminated because they were reports, editorials, and other shorter pieces that were not research and did not offer any direction for further study. Since the search was limited specifically to those sources concerning the education of school library media specialists, additional information with some transfer value may not have been selected because the focus of the search was so specific. Only 93 of the 322 items retrieved could actually be classified as research. An examination of all of the items related to the training, preparation, or library education of school library media specialists confirms this. International publications were deleted because of the wide differences in systems of education.

Actual copies of all sources were obtained whenever possible, but analysis was occasionally conducted using only the abstracts located in the data base search. The bibliography is listed alphabetically beginning with certification and closing with teacher education. Within the areas, citations are arranged in alphabetical order by author. Not all items listed are referred to in the text. ERIC and LISA access numbers are listed for a number of items in the bibliography for items that may not be readily available in hard copy.

The following terms were used to sort the citations and sources:

CERTIFICATION (processes and requirements)
COMPETENCIES (requirements for performance)
COURSES (individual courses or combinations short of a program)
DISTANCE (distance learning)
INSTITUTES (non-degree related education)
KNAPP (Knapp School Library Manpower Project)
LEVEL (level of education as a predictor of performance)
NEEDS (educational needs of personnel)
PROGRAM EVALUATION (evaluation of programs of studies)
TEACHER EDUCATION (needs of teachers and other educators)

Information in each of these categories is presented below.

Certification

The items listed in this section are the products of writers and researchers dealing with the political or bureaucratic process by which an individual is permitted to practice the profession. Most of the studies have focused on an examination of requirements of state departments of education for certification, especially in relationship to some ideal as identified by the writer or researcher. This area is important to library media educators because the initial certification of school library media specialists may depend upon specific course work that their program of studies must provide. Certification may be related also to whether an array of courses or the entire program has been approved by the state.

Citations consisted of articles listing requirements of individual states such as those formerly written by Franklin and continued by Perritt. Studies by Kosters and Franklin examined a specific area, non-book media. They recommended increased course work in this area.

Competencies

Most of the writing reported on this topic is descriptive of how various districts, states, and other groups have developed lists of what they think a school library media specialist should be able to do. Some are descriptions of entry level requirements, while others are lists that are to be used to write job descriptions and develop criteria for performance evaluation. Most appear to be based on the perceptions of practitioners, their supervisors, and library media educators, representing a current practice approach to library media education.

History tells us that Dewey developed a list of competencies for his first education program based on observations of what librarians were doing at the time. This approach has been repeated. Examples of this approach include the Knapp Library Manpower Project (to be discussed later); Daniel's competency-based education project at Syracuse; Pfister's study for the state of Florida; and the controversial "King Report," submitted by Griffiths. Daniel and Ely also report the results of implementing an education program based on the identified competencies.

Deer surveyed library media education programs and public school administrators. Media education programs were studied to determine what curricular changes had taken place and administrators were queried to ascertain the competencies they most desired in an employee.

Hawley used a different approach. She identified a service and teacher use of the media program, and then traced one of the predictors of teacher use to the variable "the extent to which the library media specialist is involved as a councilor with the teacher." From this analysis she suggests that those preparing school library media specialists and teachers should re-evaluate their curricula and develop programs to help foster better cooperation. Other studies with a similar approach include those of Turner, who focused on instructional design competencies, and Hawley, who studied the need for communication skills among media managers.

Research and thinking in this area raise the question of whether library media educators should concentrate their efforts on programs that prepare people to perform the tasks and functions as they actually operate in the work place, or to prepare graduates to go out to change current practice in order that ideal program development might take place. Or should they do both?

If graduates are to go out with the expectation of changing things, they may fall into the same categories as those addressed in the conclusions reached by Kulleseid. In her study, she found that the library media specialists had very little formal decision-making power at any level. The informal influence, through entrepreneurial behaviors associated with voluntary expansion of professional roles and increased frequency of communication with students, teachers, parents, administrators and other professionals, had the most positive impact on program survival. The question here is, "How do library media education programs prepare people for this type of program development?"

Another question is of holistic or inclusive competencies. Are there overall competencies that all library media information professionals share? Is it possible to identify a generic core or foundation, or are the types of libraries, media programs, and information agencies too specific for a common pool?

Courses

References in the literature to course offerings in library education for school library media specialists are mostly descriptions of special courses in topic areas such as the exceptional child, curriculum design competencies, microcomputer technology, and online searching. Articles cover the reason for the course, its implementation, and evaluation. While some of these courses are intended to address the unique needs and circumstances of special population groups, many minority groups and special areas in the school community are not included. Most of these articles are not research studies, but merely describe courses taught in very traditional ways, and none of the reports located gave any indication that success measures of non-traditional or innovative educational methods have been undertaken.

Distance Learning

Using telecommunications technologies such as computers and television to deliver library media education is a relatively recent undertaking. The literature includes thoughtful analyses such as that by Wyatt, who proposes a model for distance education based on a description of existing technologies, but with no examples from distance education programs that are actually in existence. Barron's article describes existing programs and reports of selected research in this area.

Since this mode of teaching and learning is very new, use of distance learning for continuing education is just now beginning to appear in the literature. A number of needs analysis reports indicate that practicing library media specialists find it difficult to get to existing and continuing educational programs, but only Ostrom mentioned distance education specifically in her report.

Institutes

Institutes were particularly popular forms of education during the 1960s and 1970s, when they were heavily funded through federal programs such as NDEA and ESEA. A sample of reports from these efforts is given, and they will not be too helpful from an evaluation standpoint. Most are descriptions of objectives, content, implementation, evaluation, and syllabi or other materials used at a particular institute. Writers do not report if, how, or how much the institute met the stated goals and objectives. A conclusion to be drawn from an analysis of this literature is that practitioners prefer short, intensive, carefully organized educational experiences on specific topics related to their daily operations and concerns.

Knapp School Library Manpower Project

The Knapp School Library Manpower project is a landmark study in both development of school library media services and training for the profession. Because of the importance of this study, although it is twenty years old, it has been included in this review of the literature.

Funded by the Knapp Shoe Company and administered by the American Association of School Librarians, one phase of the project identified competencies of exemplary school library media specialists. These were placed into a list of observable behaviors, and education programs were designed to offer experiences that would allow graduates to demonstrate these competencies. The results were then evaluated. This project represents one of the first reported approaches to systematically developed programs. It also gave the school library media professional preparation programs greater national visibility than had any other single project. Another outcome was the publication of The Behavioral Requirements Analysis Checklist, a competency list that is still valid.

Level of Education

Researchers have queried the relationship of level of education to school library media program development. Wert, in one of the first comparative studies, found that a direct relationship exists between the amount of formal library education of a high school librarian and the librarian's performance on the job. School librarians with more library education developed more extensive programs of reader services than did the group with less education, and the amount of time the librarian spent on reader services and in student/teacher use of the library directly correlated to the amount of education.

Hodowanec and Didier found that the nature and extent of the school library media specialist's education does have a significant positive impact on programs and services. Bowie found a positive correlation between the level of training and school library media specialists' perceptions related to instructional development, planning and evaluation, and professionalism. Coleman found that school library media specialists with master's level training reported significantly higher value ratings for selected values taken from the 1975 guidelines, Media Programs: District and School.

McGee found that the number of literature courses taken was a better predictor of the use of certain types of literature with grade school children than the degree awarded. McMillan found that amount of education was not a predictor of how restrictive school library media specialists were in their approaches to intellectual freedom and censorship issues, but concluded that more time needs to be spent in the preparation programs related to these areas.

Fleming found that the level of preparation of library media specialists in his North Carolina study appeared not to have a great deal of influence on the respondents designation of degrees of importance for present and desired services. Royal found few relationships between the level of education and responses of school library media specialists to perceived competencies needed to develop instructional activities. He did find that graduate level persons were consistently more positive in their responses to questions posed about the competencies.

Graff reports that library technical assistants and professional personnel had similar perceptions of their continuing education needs but took different roles and responsibilities in Utah schools. Sitter found a significant difference in the perceptions of professionals and clerical personnel related to the need for teaching library media and information skills in Colorado. Skelley concluded that more inservices were provided by those library media specialists who had more training in how to plan and implement inservice programs.

Needs

The educational needs of various groups of school library media specialists have been studied. Most often, these reports have taken the form of needs assessment surveys and thought pieces. Perritt and Heim argue that ALA-accredited program preparation should be the basis for all training for those serving in children's and young adult services positions.

Allen and Bush, in a survey of schools with ALA-accredited programs, attempted to determine the relative status of children's and young adult education. The genesis of the study was the popular notion that faculty and administrators in these schools had ignored or given little attention to school library media education. Allen and Bush report that a number of needs exist and that some of the concerns are real, but there is evidence that the schools, especially the selected ones, are making an effort to meet the needs of these professionals. They conclude that there is reason for optimism.

Mancall and Bertland reported on the first AASL national needs assessment for continuing education. They then recommended action based on the respondents' statements of what topics they perceive to be most important and the way they prefer the instruction be delivered. These two researchers found that online searching, integrating media and literature into the curriculum, information skills development, collection evaluation, and systematic program management were among the most desired topics. Short one-day workshops at conferences, regional workshops, summer and weekend workshops, and electronic delivery of courses were among the most desired formats for continuing education.

Three reports by Rogers and Kim are cited. They studied the specific library education needs of Ohio, while Stone and Turner focused on the specific needs related to a single competency, instructional design. Most of the studies indicate a specific need for a specific group, and are not transferable to a more global population or the more holistic educational needs of the profession.

Program Evaluation

It has been argued that most program evaluation is really program monitoring and cannot be called research. A majority of the published materials is studies of alumni, employers, and faculty and their perceptions of program effectiveness and appropriateness. Some describe the accreditation process for COA, NCATE, or NASDTEC, while others focus on specific areas of the curriculum.

Ali found that employers want library media personnel with combined library and media background as opposed to a single type of training. Azarmsa studied student perceptions of programs in Colorado; Ball, media specialists in five southeastern states; Bowers, programs in Oklahoma; Hough, programs in Nebraska; and Dabiri, programs in Kansas. Most of these studies conclude that the programs are adequate, but there is room for improvement. Some of this type of research, especially that merely describing programs, may not be necessary if the Statistics Committee of the Association for Library and Information Science Educators expands data collection to school library media education programs not accredited by ALA.

Missing from this area is research comparing programs accredited by ALA with programs accredited by other agencies. The potential exists for shared research to test cooperation among all programs for beginning and continuing education, evaluations of programs related to specific learner characteristics and principles of adult education, non-traditional programs, analysis of teaching styles and delivery systems, and general effectiveness of program organization and administration. Also missing from this area is research related to the special educational needs of part-time students. The role of schools in the education of minority students needs to be researched.

Teacher Education

Fargo, in 1936, pointed out that library education programs should provide "nonprofessional courses in library science devised to equip teachers for the effective use of library resources." There is very little in the literature to suggest that library media educators have gotten beyond the basic "how to use the library" course. The studies cited here suggest that Fargo's admonition is still valid, yet very little of this type of education is going on. While school library media specialists decry the teacher's lack of proper and full use of the library media program and the inappropriate evaluation processes carried on by administrators, little evidence exists to explain why these problems continue. The research undertaken by some indicates that the more education related to school library media programs that other educators have, the more sophisticated their use of the program.

Conclusions

A number of conclusions can be reached:

1. The research base for the education of school library media specialists is meager.

2. Much of the available research in the area describes studies of programs, details professional needs, and presents competencies required for current practice. These studies are based primarily on attitudinal data.

3. When library media services require that a school have an educated library media specialist, the more education the media specialist has, the greater the number and types of programs and services the school library media specialist will provide.

4. Initial preparation programs are perceived by graduates and faculty to be adequate, but there are obviously improvements that need to be made in almost all programs.

Implications for Researchers

Based on the analysis presented above, the following areas need the attention of researchers if a strong knowledge base is to be developed for the practice of educating school library media specialists.

1. Descriptive and experimental studies:

- in adult learning as applied to school library media education programs (SLMEP);

- of courses or approaches to the special needs of special groups such as minorities and part-time students in SLMEP;

- relating to the appropriateness and use of traditional and non-traditional instructional delivery systems, especially those involving existing and emerging technologies (e.g., interactive video, computer based education, telecommunications), in SLMEP;

- in providing for the professional development of library media educators;

- relating to developing optimal relationships between units on a campus responsible for various aspects of a school library media specialist's education;

- relating to inter-institution cooperation among SLMS preparation programs;

- relating to which of the various approaches to the education of school library media specialists has the most direct relationship to positive student learning outcomes of the media specialists themselves, and later for the students in their schools;

- relating to how more effective communication skills and affective educational experiences are or can be taught in SLMEP;

- relating to the role of SLMEP in educating other educators to make more effective use of school library media programs in schools;

- relating to the relative merits of the American Library Association (ALA), Committee on Accreditation (COA); National Association of State Departments of Teacher Education and Certification (NASDTEC); the National Council for the Accreditation of Teacher Education Programs (NCATE); regional accreditation; and other program or institution accreditation processes and procedures for SLMEP;

- relating to the impact and effects of the accreditation and certification processes on SLMEP (which does or should drive which);

- relating to the impact and effects of standardized exams that are required by many state certification units on SLMEP.

2. Theoretically based as opposed to purely philosophical based:

- reasons for determining the appropriate institutional home for SLMEP;

- determinants for the optimal length for SLMEP;

- reasons for a professional vs. academic emphasis in initial preparation programs;

- reasons for the emphasis on the scholar vs. teacher concerns of school library media educators;

- conclusions relating to the extent to which the school library media specialist shares a common core of knowledge with other types of library and information professionals.

Most of the questions and concerns listed above have been voiced by researchers and thinkers throughout the century. While many of those who argue passionately for their positions, regardless of the nature of the position statement, may be correct and very insightful, most stand on a limited knowledge base built on philosophical values more than on the results of carefully devised studies. While these deep thinkers and articulate spokespersons serve to give us direction, their opinions cannot take the place of a firm theoretical base that is just not there.

There are many reasons for the meager research base. One is that fewer people are being attracted to the knowledge-creation doctoral degree and to the holistic field of education generally. It is here that most of the theory building studies are accomplished. Fifth-year and doctoral programs in which more immediately practical studies are encouraged and accepted serve mainly to perpetuate descriptive studies and monitoring. While the latter should not be perceived to be wrong or bad for the individual who is pursuing knowledge at a higher level, the knowledge base is seldom extended as a result.

Related to this is the apparent lack of emphasis that ALA-accredited program schools have been placing on children's and young adult programs, which includes school library media specialists' preparation. With fewer faculty in these programs devoted to attracting students and encouraging preparation at the master's level, it follows that there will be fewer who are devoted to attracting and encouraging scholars at a higher level in the programs. Having fewer faculty also results in a potentially smaller opportunity for research productivity from a group that should be at the forefront of knowledge creation in the field.

The abysmal lack of funding for research in all areas of library and information science research is compounded by an even more abysmal lack of money for research in the area of educating our profession. Compounding the problem further is the fact that there appear to be very limited resources available to study the teaching/learning process in higher education.

The 100th anniversary of library education passes with the same list of questions our historical colleagues had. Some tentative answers may be found in a very small knowledge base, but it appears, that unless a significant change in direction is undertaken, the same list of research needs will be passed on to future generations of library media educators.

Bibliography

Certification

Franklin, Ann York. "School Library Certification Requirements: 1974 Update." School Library Journal 21, 4 (December, 1974): 15-19.

----. "School Library Certification Requirements: 1978 Update." School Library Journal 24, 8 (April, 1978): 38-50.

----. "School Library Media Certification Requirements: 1984 Update." School Library Journal 30, 5 (January, 1984): 21-34.

Kosters, Cleo. "A Critical Analysis of Certification Requirements for School Librarians in the Fifty States from 1950 to 1985." PhD. dissertation, University of South Dakota, 1986.

Perritt, Patsy H. "School Library Media Certification Requirements: 1988 Update—Part I." School Library Journal 35,9 (June-July, 1988): 31-39.

-----. "School Library Media Certification Requirements: 1988 Update—Part II." School Library Journal 34, 11 (August, 1988): 32-40.

Competencies

Barber, Raymond W. "The Media Supervisor as Helper." Drexel Library Quarterly 13, 2 (April, 1977): 14-23.

Canzler, Lillian. "A Program for the Preparation and Certification of School Administrators. Program E--Learning Resource Specialist. In Compliance with Guidelines and Standards for the Development and Approval of Programs of Preparation Leading to Certification of School Professional Personnel." ED 231387 (1983).

Correll, Lou P. "Study of a Library and Information Science Academic Program Accredited by State (TEA), Regional (SACS), and National (NCATE) Accrediting Associations." ED 239624 (December, 1983).

Daniel, Evelyn H., and Ely, Donald P. "Competency-Based Education for School Library Media Specialists." Journal of Education for Librarianship 23, 4 (Spring, 1983): 273-278.

Deer, Elva Mae. "Curriculum Changes, 1973-1982, Affecting the Professional Preparation of School Library Media Personnel." Ph.D. dissertation, East Texas State University, 1983.

Griffiths, Jose-Marie, and King, Donald W. "New Directions in Library and Information Science Education. Final Report." ED 265853 (July, 1985).

Hawley, Catherine Agnes. "An Examination of Management/Communication Perceptions of Library Media Managers." Ph.D. dissertation, University of Colorado-Boulder, 1982.

Intner, Sheila S. "A Giant Step Backward for Technical Services." Library Journal 110, 7 (April 15, 1985): 43-45.

Kulleseid, Eleanor Ranson. "A Study of Survival: Three New York City Elementary School Library Media Centers and Their Support Components." Ph.D. dissertation, Columbia University, 1982.

McNamara, James E. "Competency Based Assessment: An Update." ED 178098 (1978).

Pain, Helen. "Reaching for an Ideal: The Education and Training of School Librarians." Training and Education 2, 1 (1984): 13-21.

Pfister, Fred C. "Competencies Essential for School Media Specialists." Journal of Education for Librarianship 23, 1 (Summer, 1982): 29-42.

Smith, Jane Bandy and Trice, Ronald W. "Competency-Related Bibliography for School Media Specialists." ED 22670 (1981).

Steinfirst, Susan. "Non-Print Media Courses: What Is Needed?" Catholic Library World 54, 5 (December, 1982): 210-213.

Turner, Philip M., and Martin, Nina N. "Environmental & Personal Factors Affecting Instructional Development by the Media Professional at the K-12 Level." ED 172796 (1980).

-----. "Factors Affecting Instructional Development Activities of Selected K-12 Media Professionals." ED 151012 (1978).

Courses

Baskin, Barbara, and Harris, Karen. "Professional Preparation for School Librarians: The Exceptional Child and the Library." ED 079255 (1973).

Christine, Emma R. "Curriculum Design Competencies for School Librarians." International Library Review 12, 4 (October, 1980): 343-357.

----. "Student Contracts As One Method for Individualizing a Course Concerned with the 'Selection of Instructional Materials'." ED 144534 (1977).

Christison, Milton. "Student Contracts as One Method for Individualizing a Course Concerned with the Management of School Media Centers." ED 174254 (1979).

Templeton, Ray. "Training the Librarian for New Technology in the School." Library Micromation News 4 (April, 1984): 2-4.

Distance Learning

Barron, Daniel D. "Alternative Delivery of Library and Information Science Education." Journal of Education for Library and Information Science 27, 4 (Spring, 1987).

Ostrom, Janice Christine. "Continuing Library Education: Practices and Preferences of Kansas School Librarians." (1987).

Wyatt, Roger B. "New Technology and Distance Learning: A Model for Innovation." School Library Media Quarterly 16, 3 (Spring, 1988): 169-172.

Institutes

Baird, Lucille. "Library Media Institute for Paraprofessionals." ED 180489 (1978).

Gorena, Arne A., and Root, Rosemary. "Library Media Inservice Training." ED 184583. (Oklahoma City, Oklahoma State Department of Education, Library and Learning Resources Section, 1978). 637p.

Jackson, Johnny W. "Narrative Evaluation Report on the Institute for Retraining of Classroom Teachers as School Media Specialists at Rust College, Holly Springs, Mississippi, June 21, 1971 to July 30, 1971." ED 056713 (1971).

Johnson, Mary Frances K. "Narrative Evaluation Report on the Institute for Building School Media Collections at the University of North Carolina ... February 20, 1971 to May 1, 1971. Final Report." ED 053760 (1971).

Marbury, Carl H. "Narrative Evaluation Report On: An HEA Institute for Training in Librarianship for Drug Education for Academic and School Library Media Specialists." ED 088431 (1971).

Miller, Gloria. "No One Said It was Easy." School Library Journal 31, 3 (November, 1984): 62-64.

Miller, Marilyn L., and Geppert, Alida L., Eds. "Futurism and School Media Development; Proceedings of a Higher Education Institute (August 10-17, 1974)." ED 114119 (1975).

Ruark, Ardis. "Training Library Media Specialists to Serve the Handicapped Student." ED 179277 (Pierre, South Dakota, State Division of Elementary and Secondary Education, 1979).

Smith, Lotsee. "Narrative Evaluation Report on the Institute for Training Library Aides in Pueblo Indian Schools." ED 136758 (1975).

Knapp School Library Manpower Project

Case, Robert N. "Experimental Models for School Library Media Education." School Library Journal (December 15, 1971): 25-30.

Case, Robert N., and Lowrey, Anna Mary. Curriculum Alternatives: Experiments in School Library Media Education. (Chicago, American Library Association, 1974).

----. "School Library Manpower Project: A Report on Phase I." American Libraries 2, 1 (January, 1971): 98-101.

Case, Robert N., et al. "Evaluation of Alternative Curricula: Approaches to School Library Media Education." ED 104424 (1975).

Lowrey, Anna Mary. "Components of Curriculum Innovation." Journal of Education for Librarianship 12, 4 (Spring, 1972): 247-253.

"Occupational Definitions for School Library Media Personnel. Phase I." ED 047713 (1971).

----. "School Library Manpower Project. Behavioral Requirements Analysis Checklist: A Compilation of Competency-based Job Functions and Task Statements for School Library Media Personnel." (Chicago: American Library Association, 1973).

"School Library Personnel, Task Analysis Survey." American Libraries 1, 2 (February, 1970): 176-177.

Level of Education

Bowie, Melvin McKinney. "The Relationship of Demographic Variables to the Perceived Performance and Importance of Selected Functions of School Media Specialists." Ph.D. dissertation, Iowa State University, 1981.

Coleman, John Gordon, Jr. "Perceptions of the Guiding Principles in Media Programs: District and School." Ph.D. dissertation, University of Virginia, 1982.

Didier, Elaine K. "Research on the Impact of School Library Media Programs on Student Achievement-Implications for School Media Professionals." In School Library Media Annual: 1984 , Eds. Aaron, Shirley L., and Scales, Pat R. Littleton, Colorado, Libraries Unlimited, 1984.

Edwards, Janet Lane. "An Implementation Paradigm Applied to Selection and Utilization of Library Audiovisual Materials." Ph.D. dissertation, Saint Louis University, 1985.

Fleming, Joseph Edward. "Assessment of Media Center Services: An Investigation into the Preferences and Perceptions of Media Staff Members, Principals, and Teachers of Senior High Schools in North Carolina." Ph.D. dissertation, University of Pittsburgh, 1981.

Graff, Diana Tremewan. "An Analysis of the Roles and Responsibilities and the Educational Preparation of the Library/Media Personnel in the Schools of Utah." Ph.D. dissertation, University of Nebraska-Lincoln, 1986.

Hodowanec, George V. "Comparison of Academic Training with Selected Job Responsibilities of Media Specialists." Ph.D. dissertation, Temple University, 1973.

Loertscher, David, and Land, Phyllis. "An Empirical Study of Media Services in Indiana Elementary Schools." School Media Quarterly 10, 4 (Fall, 1975): 8-18.

McGee, Gloria Foreman. "An Analysis of the Perceptions of School Librarians in Tennessee on the Use of Realistic and Pluralistic Literature in Grades K-3." Ph.D. dissertation, George Peabody College for Teachers, 1982.

McMillan, Laura Smith. "Censorship by Librarians in Public Senior High Schools in Virginia." (1987).

Perritt, Patsy H., and Heim, Kathleen M. "ALA-Accredited Master's Degree: Considerations for Youth Services Librarianship." Top of the News 43, 2 (Winter, 1987): 149-159.

Royal, Selvin Wayne. "An Investigation of Relationships Between the Educational Level of School Library Media Personnel and Perceived Competencies Needed to Develop Instructional Activities." Ph.D. dissertation, Florida State University, 1981.

Sitter, Clara Loewen. "The Status of and the Need for the Teaching of Library Media and Information Skills in Public Schools of the State of Colorado." Ph.D. dissertation, University of Colorado-Boulder, 1982.

Skelley, Cornelia Anne. "Library Inservice for K-12 Teachers in Washington State: A Description and Analysis with a Model Workshop for Training School Librarians (K-Twelve)." Ph.D. dissertation, Seattle University, 1984.

Wert, Lucille M. "Library Education and High School Library Services. Final Report." ED 037223 (1969).

Needs

Allen, Melody Lloyd, and Bush, Margaret. "Library Education and Youth Services: A Survey of Faculty, Course Offerings, and Related Activities in Accredited Library Schools." Library Trends 35, 3 (Winter, 1987): 485-508.

"Education for Librarianship on the Grassroots Level. Part 1. Papers." ED 259728 (August, 1984).

"Final Report of the Task Force on Library Manpower and Education to the Council on Library Development." ED 112902 (1975).

Helmer, Donna J., and Mika, Joseph J. "Continuing Education: The Pathway to Professional Development." Journal of Educational Media & Library Sciences 24, 4 (Summer, 1987): 329-336.

Herring, James E. "Future Trends in the Education and Training of School Librarians." Library Review 35, 3 (Autumn, 1986): 176-183.

Hodges, Gerald G. "The Future of Youth Services: Developmental, Demographic, and Educational Concerns." Top of the News 43, 2 (Winter, 1987): 167-175.

Hug, William E. "School Library Media Education and Professional Development." School Library Media Quarterly 16, 2 (Winter, 1988): 115-118.

Kingsbury, Mary E. "Education for School Librarianship: Expectation vs. Reality." Journal of Education for Librarianship 15, 4 (Spring, 1975): 251-257.

"Libraries and the Learning Society. Papers in Response to A Nation at Risk." ED 246920 (1984).

Mancall, Jacqueline C., and Bertland, Linda. "Step One Reported: Analysis of AASL's First Needs Assessment for Continuing Education." School Library Media Quarterly 16, 2 (Winter, 1988): 88-98.

Murray, David R., and Counts, Edward. "Media, Technology and Teacher Education." ED 288488 (1986).

Perritt, Patsy H. and Heim, Kathleen M. "ALA-Accredited Master's Degree: Considerations for Youth Services Librarianship." Top of the News 43, 2 (Winter, 1987): 149-159.

Rogers, A. Robert, and Kim, Mary T. "Alternative Modes for Providing Graduate Education for Librarianship in Ohio. Final Report." ED 207540 (1981).

-----. "Enrollment Projections for Graduate Programs in Library and Information Science and Educational Media in Ohio, 1981-1985+. Alternative Modes for Providing Graduate Education in Librarianship in Ohio. Phase One: Needs Assessment Related Paper Number 3." ED 208832 (1981).

-----. "A Survey of Projected Personnel Needs in Ohio's Academic, Public, Special and School Libraries. Alternative Modes for Providing Graduate Education for Librarianship in Ohio. Phase One: Needs Assessment Related Paper Number 2." ED 208833 (1981).

Rogers, M. Maggie, and Burrell, Peggy. "When Do We Start? Library Continuing Education in Oregon: A Survey and Assessment of Educational Opportunities." ED 158746 (1978).

Schlieve, Paul Lynn. "Perceived Microcomputer Professional Development Needs of Wisconsin Public School Library/Media Specialists." Ph.D. dissertation, Southern Illinois University, 1981.

Speller, Benjamin F., Jr., and Burgin, Robert, Eds. "Microcomputing in North Carolina Libraries: A Special Section." North Carolina Libraries 40, 3-4 (Fall-Winter, 1982): 189-232.

Steinfirst, Susan. "Non-Print Media Courses: What Is Needed?" Catholic Library World 54, 5 (December, 1982): 210-213.

Stone, Sandra Kaye, and Turner, Philip M. "Factors Related to the Requiring and Availability of Instructional Design Competencies and the Programs of Library Schools in the Southeast." ED 191485 (1980).

Turner, Philip M. "Instructional Design Competencies Taught at Library Schools." Journal of Education for Librarianship 22, 4 (Spring, 1982): 275-282.

Wilson, Barbara, and Hubbard, Abigail. "Redefining the Role of School Media Specialists—Bridging the Gap." Online 11, 6 (November, 1987): 50-54.

Program Evaluation

Ali, Abdalla Mahdy. "The Responsiveness of Educational Media and Library Science Graduate Programs to the Demands of Potential Employment Fields." Ph.D. dissertation, Northern Illinois University, 1981.

Azarmsa, Mohammad Reza. "An Evaluative and Comparative Study of the Preparation of School Media Specialists at the University of Northern Colorado." Ph.D. dissertation, University of Northern Colorado, 1983.

Ball, Howard G. "Perceptions of School Media Specialists Toward a Professional Curriculum of Instruction." ED 118077 (1975).

Bowers, Violet Mae. "Nature and Profile of Preparation Programs for School Librarians and Audiovisual Specialists." Ph.D. dissertation, Oklahoma State University, 1981.

Correll, Lou P. "Study of a Library and Information Science Academic Program Accredited by State (TEA), Regional (SACS), and National (NCATE) Accrediting Associations." ED 239624 (December, 1983).

Dabiri, Azar. "An Evaluation of Kansas Preparatory Programs for School Library Media Specialists." Ph.D. dissertation, Kansas State University, 1980.

Daniel, Evelyn H. "Competency-Based Assessment Project. Final Report." ED 191434 (1979).

"Education of School Media Specialists. Master of Library Science Certificate of Eligibility for Permanent Certification." ED 185963 (1978).

Heller, Linda Hall. "A Comparison of Current Curriculum Offerings of School Media Education Programs in Oklahoma, Kansas, Missouri, Texas and Arkansas as Perceived by Media Educators." Ph.D. dissertation, Oklahoma State University, 1983.

Hough, Bruce. "A Survey of Practicing Educational Media Specialists to Determine if Present Media Preparation Programs Adequately Prepare Them for the Professional Roles They Are Expected to Fulfill." Ph.D. dissertation, University of Nebraska-Lincoln, 1983.

Hug, William E. "Project Libra: A Competency-Based, Field-Centered Approach to the Preparation of Library Media Specialists." ED 148734 (1978).

LeMaster, Opal Hunt. "An Assessment of the Graduate School of Library and Information Science Curriculum of the University of Tennessee." Ph.D. dissertation, University of Tennessee, 1981.

MacVean, Donald S. "The Destruction of an Undergraduate Library Science Instructional Program: A Case History." ED 235817 (1983).

Phillips, Rebecca R. "Library Media Technical Assistant Education in the Southwestern and Western United States: A Survey." ED 190166 (1980).

Potts, Rinehart Skeen. "Graduate Education in Librarianship at Glassboro State College, 1967-74: A Description of the Graduates and Their Evaluations of the Program." ED 118076 (1975).

Rosen, Elizabeth McClure. "Educators and Practitioners: A Cooperative Pattern of Curriculum Review." Top of the News 43, 2 (Winter, 1987): 185-188.

Stone, Sandra Kaye, and Turner, Philip M. "Factors Related to the Requiring and Availability of Instructional Design Competencies and the Programs of Library Schools in the Southeast." ED 191485 (1980).

Taylor, Marion W. "The Assessment of a Program for the Preparation of Media Specialists: A Follow Up Study of Graduates of the Master's Degree Program at Chicago State University, 1955-1975." Ph.D. dissertation, Southern Illinois University-Carbondale, 1977.

Tietjen, Mildred C. "A Study, Comparison and Evaluation of Instructional Programs at ALA Accredited Graduate Library Schools in the United States and Canada, with Special Attention Focused on Practical Experience or Field Work Provided Within the Curricula." ED 126892 (1975).

Turner, Philip M. "Instructional Design Competencies Taught at Library Schools." Journal of Education for Librarianship 22, 4 (Spring, 1982): 275-282.

Teacher Education

Barron, Daniel D. "Inclusion of School Library Media Program Concepts in Teacher and Administrator Education Courses as Perceived by the Instructors in These Courses and in Textbooks Required for These Courses." (Unpublished, University of South Carolina, 1986).

Sadler, Virginia B. "Role of the Library in Education: The Library Image as Presented in Selected Teacher Training Textbooks in Use in the State of Kentucky." (University of Kentucky, 1974).

Skelley, Cornelia Anne. "Library Inservice for K-12 Teachers in Washington State: A Description and Analysis with a Model Workshop for Training School Librarians (K-Twelve)." Ph.D. dissertation, Seattle University, 1984.

Urbanix, Mary Kathryn. "Elementary Teachers' Perceptions and Use of the School Library Media Center as a Tool in Curriculum Planning." Ph.D. dissertation, State University of New York at Buffalo, 1984.

Van Orden, Phyllis. "Use of Media and the Media Center, as Reflected in the Professional Journals for Elementary School Teachers." (Wayne State University, 1970).

COLLECTION DEVELOPMENT IN SCHOOL
LIBRARY MEDIA CENTERS

Daniel Callison
Associate Professor, Associate Dean
School of Library and Information Science
Indiana University, Bloomington, Indiana

Introduction

Over 170 studies, articles, government reports, and textbooks were reviewed in the preparation of this paper. Some of this literature dates back to the 1920s, but the vast bulk was written between 1965 and 1988. Of the 81 research-based studies cited, 77 (95 percent) have been written since 1970 and 51 (63 percent) since 1980.

Based on the issues addressed in the literature, this review is organized under eight subtopics. Each of these subtopics could easily represent a life-long research agenda because much work remains to be done. Collection development does seem to be an area that has received a great deal of attention over the past twenty years when compared to the other research topics selected for the Treasure Mountain Retreat.

The subtopic "budgets and collection size" is represented in this review by nine studies, all conducted since 1980. The essential recent documentation in this subtopic comes from the national surveys directed by Marilyn Miller for School Library Journal.

"Evaluation" of collections apparently received more attention in the research arena in the previous decade than it does now. Ten of the 14 studies cited were conducted before 1975. These early studies were concerned with measurement of collections against standards, while more recent studies introduce citation analysis and use studies.

"Networking and collection mapping" studies are, of course, very recent. Twelve of the 14 cited were completed within the past ten years. Only recent studies related to "collection policies and intellectual freedom" are examined, since the main question here is to see if policy development has had any impact on the collection. Censorship issues are addressed in more detail by Dianne Hopkins and Frances McDonald in other reviews written for the Treasure Mountain Retreat.

The "selection process" has been a consistent area of investigation over the past 30 years. Although review of earlier studies for this subtopic is provided, the emphasis is on the selection process studies related to the current dominant formats of the 1980s that seem to require close review before purchase: microcomputer software and video programming. Eight of the 11 studies cited in the "nonprint" area have been written since 1980.

Studies that investigate student preference in materials seem to be rather recent. Four of the five discussed have been written since 1980. The "special collection" subtopic includes studies that evaluate collections and materials for minority groups or students with a handicap. Eight of the ten studies cited were conducted between 1975 and 1985.

An overview of these studies shows that research related to collection development in school libraries has been conducted, although there is "much left to be done." What is of concern is an abundance of studies that seem to be "first-time" and "one-time" efforts? Thirty-four (42 percent) of the cited studies are dissertations. Of these, only four (12 percent) resulted in articles published based on the dissertation and only two of those four researchers published another article related to their dissertation topics.

Are school library media professionals failing to become life-long researchers? Could it be that there are no incentives to encourage dissertation authors to expand on the research agenda resulting from their initial effort. It would be fair to assume that those who complete the doctorate and enter administrative positions in public schools generally fail to continue formal research efforts. Those who enter the teaching profession in higher education may not be required to continue research efforts. Those who take positions in higher education research/teaching positions may actually be expected to change their research focus away from school libraries to "something more substantial."

Of the 34 dissertations cited in this review, 15 (44 percent) were written by graduates from one of four universities: Michigan (five), Illinois (four), Columbia (three), and Pittsburgh (three). Four of the five dissertations from Michigan were written before 1980 and three of the four from Illinois were written before 1980. Seventeen of the cited dissertations written since 1980 were written at 16 different universities. Could it be that, while a large number of schools are represented in the post-1980 pool, the few library science doctoral programs in which the student emphasizing school library media has access to a group of research mentors or a community of research peers have been lost?

These questions and assumptions are based on a surface-level analysis of studies cited in this review, and certainly should not be accepted as conclusive. The basic question, "Are we failing to generate life-long researchers?" remains and should be studied further. Without researchers committed to a life-long agenda, school library media professionals risk losing depth and continuity in the limited amount of inquiry that is to be generated. The literature review includes studies under the three subtopics "budgets and collection size," "evaluation of collections," and "networking and mapping."

Budgets and Collection Size

Several trends in budgets for school library media center collections over the past decade are evident:
- generally, the cost of print materials has doubled;
- the number of quality multi-media and computer-based instructional programs has increased at least four times over;
- although some school library media center budgets have kept pace with the increase in cost for materials, little additional funding has been available for updating the collection;
- federal monies categorically allocated for school library resources have decreased;

- many school library media specialists cannot describe an approach to effectively increase their budget and have become accustomed to accepting whatever dollar figure is given to them by their administration without question.

Most building level school library media specialists do not know how their budget was determined (Taylor, 1981). In most cases, the budget is "given from the central office" and the media specialist is not involved in a budget review process in which specific needs related to specific costs and learner benefits are between the media specialist and the administration.

Media center budgets range from under $3.00 per student to over $80.00 per student. Fewer than ten states have set minimum guidelines for library media center budgets. The highest minimum figure is $6.00 per student. The average per student annual expenditure by a school district for secondary school library books is a little over $5.00 (Miller and Moran, 1985). The average price for one secondary school hardcover book is now over $30.00 (Bowker Annual, 1989). As Miller and Moran concluded in 1985, it is dramatically apparent that high schools are unable to buy one new book per year per student.

Specifically, the increases in the cost for materials over one decade (1975-1985) are as follows, according to the Bowker Annual (see also Van Orden, 1988):

- average price of a hardcover elementary school book: up 88 percent, from $5.82 to $9.89;
- average price of a hardcover secondary school book: up 109 percent, from $16.19 to $31.44;
- average price of an elementary paperback book: up 163 percent, from $81.07 to $2.67;
- average price of a secondary school paperback: up 156 percent, from $81.46 to $3.87;
- average periodical annual subscription for an elementary school title: up 231 percent, from $4.69 to $12.21;
- average periodical annual subscription for a secondary school title: up 106 percent, from $14.36 to $27.90.

The national surveys directed by Marilyn Miller since 1982 provide much of the baseline data for long range comparisons and numbers against which local media specialists can compare their budget and collection figures. One must remember that these figures are taken from a sample of school librarians who subscribe to School Library Journal, and would have to assume that figures for nonsubscribing librarians would be lower on the average. The most recent figures related to collections were reported for fiscal year 1988-1989 (Miller and Shontz, 1989):

> The 1989 average learning materials center, based on median figures, has a collection of 9,982 books -- 16 per pupil. In 1987-88, [each library media specialist responding to the survey] added [an average of] 350 volumes and discarded 133 [on average]. The ... library media specialist spent [on an average of those responding] $3,100 on books, $865.00 on periodicals, $500.00 on microfilm, $428.00 on microfilm, $428.00 on microcomputer software, and $1,250.00 for audiovisual materials.

The average enrollment for the schools analyzed in the 1989 report was around 600 students. The grand total spent on the library media center, excluding salaries for staff, was $8,738 (or $14.47 per pupil); $5.55 of the per pupil amount was spent for books.

Data extracted from the 1989 report and compared to the 1983 report (Miller and Moran, 1983) and data from the Bowker Annual (1989) provide insight into several new areas concerning the funding of collections in school library media centers. In the three major material categories that had comparable figures from 1982 to 1988 (books, periodicals, and audiovisual materials), there was no significant shift in the percentage of the total expenditures for these three categories (see Table 1).

Table 1.
Percentage of Expenditures in Three Material Categories

	1982		1988	
	Average $ Expenditure	Percent of Expenditure	Average $ Expenditure	Percent of Expenditure
Books	$2,725	61	$4,287	58
Periodicals	$ 775	17	$1,217	17
AV Materials	$ 978	22	$1,858	25

Some interesting shifts occurred in the average number of books and audiovisual items reported over this same 1982 to 1988 period. The average number of books per pupil in the elementary schools remained the same, while the 1988 sample showed an increase in titles per student in the middle/junior high schools. The number of audiovisual items per student, on average, dropped by one in elementary schools and remained the same in secondary school collections (see Table 2).

Table 2.
Average Number of Book and AV Items Per Pupil
as reported by Miller and Shontz, 1982-1988

	Level	1982	1988
Books	Elementary	20.4	19.0
	Jr. High/Middle	16.3	21.0
	Senior High	17.0	18.0
AV Items	Elementary	3.7	2.7
	Jr. High/Middle	1.3	1.7
	Senior High	1.4	1.9

Data from the <u>Bowker Annual</u> (1989) provide price increase information for the same time frame as the Miller surveys. The average per pupil expenditures for books have been equal to or slightly greater than the price increase index recorded by Bowker for elementary and secondary school books since fiscal 1982-1983. The price increase for books (hardcover and paperback combined, elementary and secondary combined) has been around 41 percent (see Table 3). The increase in the average per pupil expenditure for library books in the public schools (elementary and secondary combined) has been 51 percent (44 percent if one works from the Miller favored median figure), from $4.59 in 1982-1983 to $6.95 in 1988-1989.

Table 3.
Price Increase Index and Per Pupil Expenditures
for Books, Periodicals and AV
1982-1988

	Bowker Reported Price Increase	Miller Reported Per Pupil Expenditure Increase
Hardcover, Elementary, Books	+37%	
Hardcover, Secondary, Books	+32%	
Total Hardcover Index	+35%	
Paperback, Elementary, Books	+50%	
Paperback, Secondary, Books	+45%	
Total Paperback Index	+48%	
Total Book Index	+41%	+51%
Elementary Periodicals	+68%	
Secondary Periodicals	+25%	
Total Periodical Index	+45%	+54%
Total AV Index	+50%	+80%

Additionally, the per pupil expenditures, on average from the reporting schools in Miller's surveys, have kept pace with the increase in prices for periodicals and audiovisual materials. One must remember that there are easily hundreds of examples of school library media center budgets that have not kept pace with price inflation. More important, while reported expenditures have kept even with inflation, they have <u>not</u> allowed for the necessary additional funds to replace out-of-date and discarded materials nor to meet the opportunity to expand the budget in order to purchase from the ever increasing variety of quality materials on the market.

As Miller and Shontz emphasize in their 1989 report:

> Over a two year period (86-88), library budgets continued to rise slowly: [up] less than $81.00 per pupil for books; $.12 for periodicals; and $.04 for AV materials ... The funds reported for AV include expenditures for supplies, rentals and leasing. The

amount reported for periodicals includes money spent for magazines and journals for both students and professional use.

Loertscher, Ho and Bowie (1987) report in their study of media programs in exemplary elementary schools:

> While many library media specialists are proud of their collections of materials, the majority realize that it is time for a massive effort to renew the collections of the school libraries of the nation. The major spending of the 1960s, coupled with the inflation and declining budgets of the 1970s, has created a problem in supplying materials for budding readers and researchers.

We must remember that the damage inflicted on collections during the 1970s cannot be corrected with budget increases only equal to current price increases. Extensive weeding of materials acquired in the 1960s and 1970s (especially filmstrips and multimedia kits) will lead to the need for extensive additional funding for materials replacement. In addition, schools that are automating their card catalogs find that the expense of such a large project almost requires a thorough weeding of the collection before outdated are put on the system.

Each Miller report has included figures categorized by school enrollment. An examination of these figures highlights the fact that schools with large enrollments (2,000 or more) have reported per pupil expenditures for books and periodicals that have actually declined over the past seven years. In all other enrollment categories, the per pupil expenditures have been generally, on the average, equal to or higher than the price increases for books and periodicals during the 1982-1988 time period. In schools with enrollments of 2,000 or more, the per pupil expenditure for books has declined by 5 percent and has not changed in per pupil expenditure for periodicals over the past seven years.

A final point of interest from the most recent Miller survey (Miller and Shontz, 1989) is that schools that were in a system with a full-time district level supervisor reported, on the average, lower per pupil materials expenditures than schools with either a part-time supervisor or no district level supervisor. Miller has reported a total materials expenditure (TME) figure in each report since 1983. The average TME in schools in a system with a district supervisor rose from $8.80 in 1982 to $17.08 in 1988, an increase of 94 percent. The average TME in schools in systems without district supervisors rose from $10.92 in 1982 to $23.31 in 1988, an increase of 113 percent. Schools with access to a district supervisor, however, reported significantly more frequent services that often lead to greater use of the collection, such as "library media advisory committees," "a selection policy," "plans for automated catalogs," and "online access."

In 1985, the U.S. Department of Education conducted a nationwide survey of the holdings and the budgets of public and private school library media centers. Over 3,500 schools were included in the sample. From this data, 351 public schools were identified as providing high levels of library service (inservice education for teachers in selection and use of media, interlibrary loan services, programs to encourage parents to support reading skills, sequential program of library skills, and more). This subset of high service schools was examined by Howard D. White with advice from Jacqueline Mancall and Roger Tipling to determine the amounts invested in the building level collection (see Table 4). The results of this analysis have been included in the 1988 national guidelines, Information Power, and reflect a substantially greater investment in materials collections by schools providing high levels of instructional service than those school library media programs which provide average or below average instructional services.

Table 4.

Highest Level Library Media Center Collection Holdings and Budget Figures in Public Schools with Enrollment Under 500 Students as of 1985
(All figures represent per one pupil ratio unless otherwise stated.)

	Elementary	Jr. High/Middle	Senior High
Book Titles	38	34	58
Serial Subscriptions (per 100 pupils)	16	24	55
Book Budget	$16.73	$18.74	$31.54
Serial Budget	2.67	5.89	11.36
Software Budget	4.78	4.51	9.68
AV Budget	6.82	6.83	13.65
Total Collection Budget	24.42	33.83	59.65
Total Hardware Budget	16.59	18.43	23.84
Total Library Media Budget	$40.63	$58.26	$92.68

Source: Information Power (1988).

Table 5.

Highest Level Library Media Center Collection Holdings and Budget Figures in Public School with Enrollment Over 500 Students as of 1985.
(All figures represent per one student ratio unless otherwise stated.)

	Elementary	Jr. High/Middle	Senior High	
			500-1,000	Over 1,000
Book Titles	27	23	29	21
Serial Subscriptions (per 100 students)	10	17	26	15
Book Budget	$11.92	$12.08	$17.69	$13.73
Serial Budget	1.70	2.97	7.47	4.95
Software Budget	2.69	3.15	1.84	3.45
AV Budget	5.82	3.88	7.50	5.36
Total Collection Budget	18.34	19.73	25.76	24.16
Total Hardware Budget	15.68	19.73	7.08	8.58
Total Library Media Budget	$34.94	$37.26	$44.52	$39.31

Source: Information Power (1988)

The 1988 guidelines also include suggested formulas for determining budgets for materials and equipment. Testing of these formulas should continue, and an eventual standard will allow for comparisons among schools and over time. The encouraging aspect is that these formulas are based on factors and weights that take the budget calculation beyond dollar amounts strictly based on per pupil enrollment. "Attrition of the collection," and "inflation rate" factors will help to justify some growth in the budget. Added to these factors should be the conclusions drawn from "student use analysis" and "degree of teacher/media specialist collection mapping." The pragmatic allocation formulas tested by William McGrath (Tjoumas and Blake, 1989) should receive more attention in the school library collection and budgeting arena.

Evaluation of Collections

Studies conducted in the 1960s and 1970s that attempted to evaluate the quality of school library collections centered on the use of quantitative measurements. The basic assumption was, "more is better." Keeping in mind the context of the times, this was not an unexpected concept. The need was to grow, to invest, to collect extensively so that the potential of the media center program supported, with a wide variety of materials, could be demonstrated.

In 1977, the National Commission on Libraries and Information Science (Boyd, 1977) reported, "while media centers held over 500 million volumes, this was only 40 percent of the need expressed through national standards." One hundred million nonprint items were owned by the public schools, which reflected only 10 percent of the need. Studies in individual states found similar evidence that collections did not measure up to the high expectations of the national standards (Hutchinson, 1977; Veitch, 1978).

One study in Michigan (Jones, 1965) used a checklist to compare biology titles held to those titles listed by experts in the field. This quality measurement was added to the numerical measurement of proportion of biology books to total number of books in the collection and the number of biology books per student to determine the merit of a given high school's collection. The study did identify some collections as being exceptional, but no attempt was made to tie the collection to excellence in science education or to various curricular activities in biology based on the collection. A second study (Schmitz, 1966) in Michigan a year later concentrated on mathematics and added to the evaluation criteria "proportion of the collection with a recent copyright."

A study published in <u>Business Review</u> (Summers and Wolfe, 1975) reported on the detailed histories of 1,800 students from Philadelphia area schools. One conclusion reported was that above the sixth grade level, additional library books correlated with more achievement for the students. Below the sixth grade, however, no such correlation existed.

A study of a selected sample of elementary schools in Pennsylvania (Sheriff, 1965) identified higher quality collections, based on size and checklist criteria. These collections were usually found under the direction of a <u>professional</u> librarian.

Developing a new library collection in a new school was a frequent occurrence in the early 1970s, and one criterion suggested to determine when the collection had reached a "successful level" was when questions from 90 percent of the inquiring students for a given day could be answered through the resources immediately available in the library (Dean, 1974). Another measurement that involved "use or user" information was a study of librarian and teacher cooperation in book selection (Pool, 1972a). Data from this study did <u>not</u> support the researcher's hypothesis that as selection procedures for elementary school libraries become less centralized and less standardized (based on checklists, recommended reading lists, and other guides provided through the state department of education or professional organizations), the quality of collections improves because librarians and teachers are more actively involved in selection. In the mid-1970s, George Bonn outlined in an article in <u>Library Trends</u> the basic criteria used for evaluation of collections: gross size, volumes added per year, comparisons to other libraries and to standard lists, subject balance, unfilled requests, interlibrary loan requests, expert opinion, circulation, and basic collection expenditures. Bonn also outlined four concepts that have the most far-reaching implications for development and evaluation of collections, in any type of library:

1. The emphasis on library goals and objectives as the foundation for a library's selection and acquisition policy, and as the framework within which the library's collection is to be evaluated.

2. The stress on quality and on user needs rather than on quantity and on basic lists alone are the decisive factors in building a collection and in evaluating it.

3. The realization is coming that no library can ever be completely self-sufficient, and that increased interlibrary cooperation may be the only possible solution to the growing problem of providing library collections adequate to meet the needs of library users, wherever they may be.

4. Having competent professional librarians in such strategic spots as selection and public service, is necessary to insure proper development and use of the library's collection.

Until recently, school library media center literature did not reflect much activity in the area of planning, goal setting, community analysis, use, and user studies related to collection development decisions. Researchers such as DeProspo and Zweizig have set the stage for extensive work in these areas for public librarians. Questions such as the following have been raised in their work and should be considered in the school library media center research agenda for collection development:

- How do the existing library users compare with the overall demographic profile of the community (school)? Are there community (school) information needs not being met by the library?
- What do people (students) get from libraries (school media centers) that they can't get elsewhere?
- What uses are made of the (school) library collection? What uses could be made with changes in the collection and cooperation with other libraries?

What materials students use has been studied to some degree over the past ten years. These use studies have been based on bibliometric methods or citation analysis of the references found in the students' completed term papers. Drott and Mancall (1980) have documented the use of such methods extensively. Their findings include:

- heavy use of book materials by students;
- little use of nonprint, pamphlet, encyclopedia, or government document materials;
- little discretion used by students concerning dated materials;
- extensive use of common news or general science periodicals;
- although most materials students used were located at a local school library, many students investigate materials at other libraries.

Such information, however, does not translate directly into collection development decisions, as might be expected in the academic or research library setting where users are assumed to know what they want and need. Thus the record of what the researcher uses becomes a map for what should be purchased in the future. Collection development decisions in the elementary and secondary school setting, based on citation analysis, require the educated and professional expertise of the media specialist who understands the need for information education of young people, and the need to expand information opportunities for students. Bibliometric studies must be analyzed carefully in any environment. False conclusions can easily lead to misguided adjustments in collection patterns (Wallace, 1987).

Citation analysis will confirm what is popular among young adult patrons, but does not tell us if their information needs have been met. Thus, much of the citation analysis work of Drott and Mancall may tell more about what library media specialists should be teaching students in the selection and use of information than about what should be purchased for them.

Providing a wide variety of resources also means teaching the student how to use a wide variety of resources and the value of knowing the merits of each information format. Callison (1988) used citation analysis to identify specific titles students located through online databases, acquired from collections outside their local school, and used extensively in order to complete a term paper. Information from such analysis, leading to key or essential sources, provides a guide to specific titles for purchase, even though many of those titles may be out of print.

As automated circulation systems evolve, the potential for gathering data that will support collection decisions increases. Bertland (1988) has documented some methods for analysis by determining the "use factor" for general areas of the collection. As with citation analysis, use factors based on circulation must be examined with an open and educated mind. Relatively low use of one area of the collection that is a relatively high portion of the collection should not lead to the immediate conclusion that one should greatly reduce the amount of money and attention given to that area. Evidence provided from use factor reports helps to identify collection areas that may need weeding and updating along with promotion of that area of the collection. It has been shown that weeding the collection in small public libraries results in more circulation (Slote, 1975; Roy, 1987).

High circulation for a small portion of the collection may not necessarily mean there is a need to accelerate the investment for new materials in that area. Paperback cartoon books, for example, have always proven to have high circulation figures, but there is a limit to the amount one should invest in these books, no matter how popular they might be.

Callison (1988) maintained a record of student use rates for materials identified through various computerized databases. Such data must be maintained for several user groups on a variety of projects and over several semesters in order to be meaningful.

The fact that such use studies have been conducted and can be easily replicated in practice means that more should be done to see what the true disadvantages and merits are in citation and circulation analysis. There is a great deal of work to be done in applying the recommendations resulting from use studies for school library collections. Researchers should work with practicing school library media specialists to implement promotional and user education projects, weeding plans, or budget adjustments and to document results of changes made based on use studies. It may be that the most valuable aspect of documenting use of the collection and recording adjustments that are recommended from such analysis will be the potential for greater communication between media specialist and administrator about future collection needs and additional funding required. The tools for gathering circulation data are increasingly available, the number of schools that have automated circulation systems doubled between 1986 and 1988 (Miller and Shontz, 1989).

Networking and Mapping

The collections found in library media centers will evolve dramatically as more and more schools join resource sharing networks. Although Weeks (1982) found that cooperative purchasing arrangements between school and public libraries have been ranked as a low need, such cooperation will be almost essential over the coming decade (Rogers, 1984). Do school libraries have materials that are not held by their local public libraries? Several recent overlap studies (Altman, 1972; Jacob, 1974; Aceto, 1984; Doll, 1984) have indicated that not only do schools have unique titles to share with public library patrons, but also that there seems to be little overlap in title holdings among schools in the same district.

Just as a conspectus of academic library systems provides a "road map" of areas of specialization and concentration among the research collections of our nation, so will such mapping allow for local resource communication among public libraries, other schools, and local curriculum planning committees. Ho and Loertscher (1985) and Murray et al. (1985) have listed the advantages to mapping the contents of the collection:

- increased focus on the reference and periodical collections;
- encouragement for a complete review and weeding of the collection;
- identifying the vast variety in the contents of the collections among schools;
- increased appeal in some depths (numbers and variety) in selected areas of the curriculum beyond just literature, science, and social studies;

- setting collection goals that match the curriculum and encourage teachers to be a part of a long-range acquisitions plan (Eisenberg and Berkowitz, 1988; Turner and Naumer, 1983);
- improving collections supporting the professional development of teachers, and establishing connections to other professional collections.

Do students benefit from interlibrary loan? Greenberg (1981) found that there is a high relationship between amount of material available and the quality of other services provided in school libraries. Those who tended to supply a great many materials in-house also tended to extend beyond their collection by borrowing from others. Walker (1982, 1983) reported that interlibrary loan, when provided and promoted, is used extensively by high school students, teachers of all grade levels, and school administrators. The service was used to provide access to materials for assignments and professional presentations. A majority of the requests, 78 percent, were filled within a 12-day period.

Studies of student use of online systems also provide evidence of student acquisition of materials. Some reported that a low percentage of the borrowed materials was actually used by the students (Wozny, 1982; Mancall and Deskins, 1984). Others have reported that items identified through online searching and borrowed from other libraries were essential to the completion of several student assignments (Pruitt and Dowling, 1985; Callison, 1988).

Collection Policies and Intellectual Freedom

Most recent surveys of school librarians (Woodworth, 1976; Kamhi, 1981; Hopkins, 1984; Kemp, 1986) report that up to half of the nation's school collections have been "developed" without a written policy in place. It is very likely that most of the school building level collections have been gathered without written policy guidelines similar to those described by Helen Adams in Writing Policy Statements (Libraries Unlimited, 1986). A majority of school librarians can pull from a file a "written selection policy." However, a very small percentage can provide a plan for "collection development" that has been written through a committee effort to describe specifically the philosophy, direction, selection, and evaluation process of the local collection and those who make the final collection development decisions. Written long-range plans seldom exist. The collection development policy is the written document through which the school library media specialist can clearly express direction for a gathering of quality instructional materials and how extensive the selection process is in involving teachers, administrators, and even members of the community.

It is known that the presence of a well-constructed and board-approved policy will not decrease the likelihood of a challenge to specific controversial titles in the media center collection. Presence of such a policy will, however, increase the likelihood that challenged materials will be fairly reviewed and retained (Kamhi, 1981; Bracy, 1982).

Several studies have indicated that selection decisions made by media specialists will be influenced by their perceived narrow standards of the community or their self-imposed narrow standards (Bump, 1980). "Warnings" contained in book reviews "overly" influence the acquisition practices of many school library media specialists (Watson, 1981). Written policies may help not only to counter the vocal biases found in many communities, but also to broaden the selection criteria of some media specialists. Written policies can prove to be the difference between an unwillingness to "take a risk" and the willingness to "innovate with a progressive collection" in support of the information needs faced by our youth today.

The brief attention given by researchers to policy development has focused mainly on written policy and intellectual freedom issues. More attention needs to be given to the impact of written policy on the development of a quality collection in support of the educational goals and objectives of the local school system.

Selection Process

Several studies in the 1970s (Blazek, 1971; Beilke, 1974; Baker, 1978; Belland, 1978;) identified the strong influence teachers play in the selection process. During this period, social studies, English, and science teachers tended to take the most active role in use of instructional materials. Blazek demonstrated the tendency of students to emulate teachers in extensive use of a variety of resources when teachers provided a model of those who critically selected and used many resources for their own teaching presentations. A high degree of teacher influence was reported as a major factor in acquisitions of new materials, although school library media specialists also reported in a majority of cases no systematic process for involving teachers in the selection process. At "best" teachers were involved through individual contacts and were seldom involved in collection planning.

Belland reported that the factor that seemed to influence the media specialist in making a final selection for purchase was "a favorable review." Evaluation of review sources (Galloway, 1965; Haith, 1972; Missavage, 1977) has consistently raised questions about their value in terms of being critical and providing enough information to make selections that support the local curriculum. Vandergrift (1978) reacted to the conclusion that reviews hold such a high degree of influence: "This would tend to imply that school personnel have neither the time nor the commitment to analyze materials in terms of a particular curricular need. They defer judgment to those persons who are professionally involved in reviewing a wide variety of materials." By not engaging in the preview, teacher committee review, and student feedback processes the media specialist forfeits a major communication for influencing curriculum through development of the collection and vice versa.

Brodeur (1980) reported that catalogs, mail advertisements, and sales representatives seem to have as much influence as opinions from teachers on the purchase of nonprint materials. A majority of the surveyed media directors reported that they included teachers in the preview of films. Media directors with library science education backgrounds did not perceive training of teachers in a systematic selection process to be one of their important duties, while those with a curriculum design background did perceive teaching teachers how to evaluate nonprint media as a major part of their job.

Billeter (1979) found that a larger percentage of books on a recommended checklist were selected when the books were available for "hands-on" examination rather than simply described in a review. She also reported that a larger percentage of non-recommended books were selected when "hands-on" evaluation was possible. Pool (1972b) found that librarians and teachers, using local dealers, compiled resources in the sciences that were slightly more up-to-date and closer to the reading lists from textbooks more frequently than did those free to use review sources.

Crow (1986) concluded that the School Library Journal would be the "best source" when one is looking for broad coverage of titles, prompt reviewing, and thorough discussions of controversial elements in books. She noted that smaller portions of the reviews in Booklist and Bulletin of the Center for Children's Books are devoted to discussions about controversial elements, and that Horn Book is less helpful on this topic.

Blazek (1985-1986) has provided the most conclusive evidence that more attention should be given to specialized selection guides and teacher committee review and less to the general selection journals. He found that two specialized journals, Arithmetic Teacher and Mathematics Teacher, provided over 80 percent of the relevant reviews pertaining to the subject area of mathematics. Under 5 percent of relevant reviews were found in Booklist, School Library Journal, Media and Methods, and VOYA. A total of 75 percent of the most relevant materials could be located only through the specialized journals.

Ho and Loertscher (1986) have also documented the need for media specialists to search a wider spectrum of selection guides and to involve teachers more in the collection planning process, and for publishers of major school library materials selection guides to give more attention to curricular areas beyond literature, social studies, and science:

> Perhaps the best advice to library media specialists that research offers is to build collections in topical segments rather than just buying things. Nationally-published core lists may be useful in building a few basic materials in a topical area, but building strength and depth into a collection requires a different approach.

Nonprint Collections

Each document written for the purpose of describing national guidelines for collections in school libraries and school library media specialists published since 1918 has included a specific section promoting the use of nonprint materials. The justification has always been that in order to introduce a wide variety of learning experiences that will meet the many ability levels found in public education, much more than just the printed word should be available to students. Thus the evolution over the past seven decades from stereopticon slide collections, to 16mm educational films, to videotaped programs, to microcomputer software has resulted.

School library media centers have become true centers for multi-media supported education. Teachers and students can access materials based on sound or visual expression, and often can produce their own instructional products if the local collection does not house the needed slide, overhead transparency, or video program. The collection includes a wide array of equipment or technology as well as the information programming or software. Research in the nonprint collection area has centered on the learner-verification or field-testing of nonprint materials.

In the late 1970s, media specialists ranked information on grade level and source of reviews for nonprint materials as being more important to them than results of learner-verification. This was the case at a time when only one in four librarians had access to "hands-on" examination of audiovisual materials through centralized preview centers. Few actually used the preview services available because of lack of time for such activity (Belland, 1978).

Daly-Lewis (1982) identified several selection and evaluation practices among building level library media specialists in New York. This statewide survey concluded that:

- media specialists often did not investigate the claims of the audiovisual software producer;
- media specialists usually selected from the first few items noted in catalogs, seemingly unaware of the many options;
- media specialists were often not aware of the educational context in which the material would be used;
- media specialists seldom considered the possible need for teacher training in order to establish effective use of the software;
- in only a few cases, media specialists shared their evaluative data of the merits of the software purchased so that others could use such information in decisions for purchase of audiovisual materials.

While a majority of the librarians (66 percent) responding to the New York survey indicated that they "involve" students in the preview of nonprint materials, only 7 percent attempted to gain some student feedback following the preview. None reported field-testing audiovisual materials to determine "what students learn" from the software.

Most previewing practices seem to involve teacher "screening" of materials sent from the distributor to the school building for a 30- to 60-day loan. In the 1982 New York survey, schools with higher budgets for audiovisual materials tended to preview nearly all potential audiovisual material purchases. Schools with the lowest range of money (per pupil) allotted for audiovisual materials tended not to preview.

"Opinion of the teacher," "curriculum applicability," and "age appropriateness" tend to be the key evaluation factors for audiovisual materials. Collections tend to be built strictly to meet the instructional needs of the classroom teacher. Often material will be purchased to meet only the "curricular demand." This means that some items are purchased in order to have "something in the collection" on a particular new topic regardless of the quality of the material. Additional studies in New York (Masters, 1977) and Pennsylvania (Miller, 1977) have found the audiovisual selection process to be "loose and disjointed," and a need for a more systematic approach. Kahler (1985) found that when elementary school library media specialists engaged teachers in "giving and seeking feedback" on selection of audiovisual materials and involved teachers through inservice training for selection and use of audiovisual materials, that there was substantial increase in use of such materials in the classroom.

Over the past decade, thousands of computerized software programs have been placed on the market. Often, especially in the first few years of the "computer revolution," these programs were not field-tested in their intended educational environment (Truett, 1984). Studies that investigated teacher evaluation of computer software (Gonce-Winder, 1985; Callison 1987-1988, 1989) have agreed that teachers with more experience and exposure to computers tend to rate computer software higher than those without such experience. Studies have also shown that:

- when a teacher has experience in use of a variety of software on a similar topic from which to compare and evaluate, the conclusion concerning acquisitions of the proposed software will be more specific and direct than the general and often nonconclusive evaluations from teachers who have not examined similar programs prior to the evaluation of the software proposed for acquisition;
- teachers will give more time to an evaluation of the software if they can tell within the first few minutes that the content has relevance to their class objectives;
- teachers and students tend to agree on software they do not like, but disagree on software they favor;
- students tend to favor simulation formatted programs while teachers tend to favor tutorials which match established lesson plans.

The 16mm film format has become the dinosaur of the instructional and educational media world. Over 60 percent of homes with school-aged children now own VCR players. The growth in the video formatted educational media field has been astronomical during the past four years, while 16mm film production has become stagnant. As more and more public library collections (over 50 percent) now offer video programming, local school media specialists may see the need for more cooperation in planning video collections (Dewing, 1988; Scholtz, 1989). The trend may be toward larger building level video collections with less emphasis on regional film centers.

Student Preference

Research studies have shown that among elementary school children, boys prefer biographies, books on science, social studies, and sports, while girls prefer adventure, fantasy, humor, and poetry (Chiu, 1975). Children's preferences often differ from adults on what they would select to read. Caldecott winners are seldom the child's first choice (Oksas, 1986). Bard and Leide (1985) report the following conclusions about library books selected by elementary school children:

- girls seem to read more than boys (at least they charge out more books);
- girls prefer fiction while boys prefer information books;
- older children choose fewer books categorized as imagination literature and more realistic fiction, mysteries, and information books;
- a few authors are extremely popular with children, and the child tends to ask for books by such authors;
- children do not choose poetry books for independent reading;

- children charge out fewer books from the school library in grades five and six than in grade four (This does not mean they read less. They may be more frequent patrons of the public library, and read more books, magazines, and newspapers available at home. They may also purchase more paperbacks than when [they were] younger);
- children do not tend to charge out books concerning local history or ethnic history unless assigned to do so.

Mancall and Drott (1983) have summarized the following findings from examination of sources used by high school students:

- the typical student will use materials from other libraries, and often use materials from "home library" extensively;
- the typical student will tend to use materials [no matter how dated] unless otherwise required or instructed;
- the typical student will favor books as an information source over journals, newspapers, pamphlets or documents.

Special Collections

Although there has been a great deal written about "how we provide good materials for the low achiever," or "special reading collections for individuals whose second language is English," very little appears in the school library research concerning methods for development of collections to meet the special information needs of various minority groups. Schon, Hopkins, and Davis (1982) reported that Hispanic students display increased enthusiasm and improved attitudes when provided with a wide selection of books in Spanish. High school students who immigrate to the United States tend to display more desire to read books in Spanish than United States born Hispanic students. Schon and Glass (1988) later reported that librarians' positive attitudes and increased acquisition of Spanish language materials seem not to have changed by the new "English-only" law, Proposition 63, in California. Clarke (1973) found the reading tastes of Indian, black, and white high school students to be widely varied and that ethnic origin does have a major influence on the students' interest in materials selected for reading.

Stevens (1977) reported that the reading choices of gifted students in elementary school resulted in the students giving highest ratings to Newbery Award books, while classics received lowest ratings. There was a close correlation between books chosen by the students and those chosen by adults for students. More recent studies (Carter and Harris, 1981; Swisher et al., 1984) have reported that there is a great deal of difference of opinion between student review groups and adult review groups, especially in the area of contemporary fiction.

Finally, one has to raise questions concerning the development of collections for handicapped students, both in areas of access and collection content. Public Law 93-112 of 1973 and Public Law 94-142 of 1975 have certainly had an impact on general school facilities and curriculum. Yet no documentation has been collected on the impact of these public laws on school media center collections.

Vinson (1983) has reviewed the history of school library media service for handicapped students from 1950 to 1980. She has noted that library services and special education programs developed quite separately over those three decades, and it is only in the past decade, because of the equal rights and equal access legislation, that services and collections for the handicapped student are being seriously considered. Opocensky (1975) surveyed 50 schools listed as public residential schools from the <u>American Annals of the Deaf: Directory of Programs and Services</u>. She found that the schools failed to meet the minimum collection requirements for deaf students as stated in the 1967 <u>Standards for Library-Media Centers in Schools for the Deaf</u>:

> Collections of professional materials were minimal in spite of the fact that most of the schools also had teachers-in-training. Print collections for students were generally considered adequate even though they fell short of the numbers recommended. Captioned films and filmstrips were plentiful in the nonprint collections and transparencies were reported in large numbers. Selection guides specifically developed and published for use with the deaf are needed. Fewer than one-fifth of the schools [specifically serving the deaf student] met or exceeded the minimum recommendations of the standards.

Buckley (1978) surveyed selected Southern states to determine the status of library media services for exceptional students enrolled in public schools. She reported that "media specialists perceived the collections of resources to be 'moderately adequate'." School library media specialists perceived a need for more knowledge and training on their part in access to materials for exceptional students and general knowledge about special education programs. Buckley recommended future study of model programs that have more fully developed services and collections to support "mainstreamed" environments.

Davie (1978) conducted a descriptive survey of school library resources and services to exceptional students in Florida. She found that investment in library media materials seemed to take place to a greater degree among those media specialists who had access to an above average budget. Thus, investment in special materials was more likely if funding remained in the budget after the ["necessary expenditures"] were made. Davie concluded that "appropriate materials and equipment are generally available to meet the needs of exceptional students but additional amounts and more variety are needed to enable the needs to be met more adequately." She also concluded that "few media centers have the materials and equipment in their own collections to meet adequately many of the special needs of exceptional students, thus they utilize other sources [special and public library collections]." Implications from the study indicate that heightened awareness of resources and their potential use for exceptional students can be implemented through communication between media personnel and those persons who are more directly involved with exceptional students.

Implications for Practitioners

Budgets

1. School library media specialists should establish a record of the per pupil expenditures in categories such as books, periodicals, audiovisual software, microcomputer software, microforms, and use of online or CD-ROM services. Such information will allow the media specialist to determine budget variations over time, compare budget allocations to similar libraries (statewide and nationally), and monitor changes in market prices compared to local budget allocations. Having access to such baseline data will be useful for those media specialists who want to play a more vocal role in the budget planning process of the local school district. All school library media specialists should become aware of how local budget allocations are determined.

2. Budgets for school library media collections over the past decade have had "zero-growth" (on average) when inflation is taken into account. The media specialist will need to demonstrate the need for more funding above the regular budget in order to update the collection and to acquire a higher percentage of the quality materials placed on the market. Budgets should be developed by building level school library media specialists to reflect long-range plans for three to five years. Budgets should be based on formulas that reflect both quantitative and qualitative factors. Teachers should be directly involved in both the collection mapping and budget justifications for such planning. Administrators should be made aware that the presence of a professional district media supervisor will allow for more coordinated and progressive efforts in promotion of effective use of collections through inservice training, networking, electronic databases, policy development, and local online catalogs.

Evaluation and Planning

3. Media specialists in larger schools should pursue dramatic increases in per pupil allotments for purchase of books and periodicals. Budgets in schools with a population of 2,000 or more have not increased over the past seven years, while the cost and number of instructional materials available have increased dramatically.

4. Collections need to be evaluated and weeded of out-of-date and unused materials. Systematic methods such as the CREW method (Segal, 1980) should be considered (Buckingham, 1984).

5. Collection development decisions should be based on a long-range plan, resulting from a community analysis and a written collection development policy that has been established through clear input and debate among representatives of all local parties who have a role in the educational process (Callison and Kittleson, 1985). Greater involvement in the collection development process may lead to greater support of the media center program.

6. Citation analysis and circulation analysis can tell us what students use or "like to read." Additional information, especially from teachers through cooperative curriculum planning and collection mapping processes, is necessary in order to make

intelligent acquisition decisions. The media specialists cannot gain the necessary local collection development information by limiting their selection procedures to simply reading review sources and recommended purchase lists. One major objective of use and user analysis should be "what specific sources are essential for advancing student communication and thinking skills." The collection should have breadth and depth in selective areas that match specific local curricular objectives.

7. School library media center collections are varied to a great degree and resource sharing should be established among local school, public, and academic libraries. Schools should strive to lend their fair share of materials as well as to borrow materials. Collection policies should describe local holdings in relationship to other library collections within the same community.

8. Content of a local professional collection to support educators should be considered and access to such materials should be supported by the school library media specialist.

Policy Development and Selection

9. Collection development policies should result from an educational communication process that will increase the probability that an informed administration will support both "innovative" and "controversial" areas of the school's library collection.

10. School library media specialists should seek methods for field-testing instructional media with the students of the local schools (Callison and Haycock, 1988). Impressions and results of such field-testing should be shared with teachers, administrators, and other media specialists as widely as possible. Library media specialists should take a stronger role in leading and coordinating the preview, selection, and evaluation process for instructional materials. Lack of time and lack of understanding of the preview or field-testing process seem to be the major barriers to greater teacher/media specialist cooperation in the selection process. Close professional planning and communication must replace quick purchase decisions based only on reviews or limited preview of materials. School library media specialists need to explore the video programming revolution and prepare for the shift from the 16mm film format to the video format, because there seems to be a dramatic change in the market toward extensive growth in the VHS formatted educational and training tapes.

11. Evidence of student reading preferences should be gathered and considered. Student reading habits and their most common information sources should also be identified. With knowledge of such behaviors, school library media specialists should strive to continue to widen the information base available to their students. As children become aware of and seek to use different information modes and information gathering institutions, media specialists should advocate greater information access through their own local collections and through all local information collections as well.

12. Collections for special youth patron groups should be considered after a thorough analysis of the community. "Special" materials targeted for the minority student or for the student who has a handicap should be integrated with the regular

collection whenever possible. School library media specialists must give more time to becoming knowledgeable about materials, equipment, and information services for the physically and mentally disadvantaged.

Implications for Researchers

Budgets

1. Researchers should work with media specialists to establish a method for effective documentation and presentation of media center budget allocations so that the media specialist will have greater understanding of the budget process and can communicate budget needs for collection development to administrators.

2. Budget formulas need to be introduced and tested for the purpose of moving the average allocation for materials beyond the level of only financing "zero-growth." Budget requests should include justification to encourage extensive weeding and updating of collections. Evidence should be gathered to determine if the presence of a professional district level supervisor leads to services that encourage effective use of collections. It seems that less money per student is invested in collections that employ a district supervisor; however, if full-time professional media specialists are employed at both building and district levels, the resulting increase in patron collection use, greater access to more materials, and increase in user education services may offset lower collection budgets. District media supervisors may also develop acquisition systems that allow for greater quantity and quality in materials purchased for fewer dollars invested. Researchers should explore the value that administrators and teachers place on media collections compared to the value they place on media specialists. If there is strong evidence that full-time professionals are being replaced by clerks so that school district funds can be shifted from the personnel line to the materials line, then this field must increase efforts to educate administrators, teachers, and even media specialists about the merits of the professional library media specialist who selects quality materials and promotes their effective use.

3. Researchers should examine the budget allocations per pupil within their own state to determine areas of strength and weakness. Information from such studies should be shared with state legislatures.

Evaluation and Planning

4. Systematic collection evaluation methods should be tested in school library media centers, such as the CREW method for weeding. Limitations of citation analysis should be expressed clearly to practicing library media specialists. Media specialists should be made aware of a variety of evaluation techniques, and educated in the advantages and disadvantages of each method. Methods in the use of automated circulation systems to support circulation analysis should be tested and implemented.

5. Methods for community analysis of the school and potential community user groups should be developed. Such methods should address not only current use, but potential use and potential users.

6. Methods for cooperative efforts between teacher and media specialists for the purpose of collection policy and collection mapping development and implementation should be documented. Methods that increase the emphasis on such planning and decrease emphasis on review literature should be tested.

7. Resource sharing networks should be described and the degree of success and failure documented. Evidence should be gathered to determine how extensively public schools "can" and "should" share their collections.

8. Methods for development and techniques for effective use of professional collections should be documented.

Policy Development and Selection

9. The difference between a "selection process policy" and a "collection development plan or policy" in the media center arena should be defined. The advantages and disadvantages of extensive involvement by representatives of parents, teachers, administrators, and board members under the direction of the media specialist should be documented. Field studies may show the potential for school library media specialist leadership in curriculum planning as the media specialist establishes the guiding role in collection planning.

10. Methods for local field-testing, learner-verification, or previewing of materials (especially nonprint and microcomputer software) should be presented through local workshops and conferences. Case studies in which adequate time is allowed for such media evaluation activity should be documented. The growth (explosion) in the video software area for educational and training materials should be examined in relationship to the curricular needs of public schools. Building level video program collections may grow as district or regional level film collections become smaller and dated. Methods for duplication rights and access to video programming through cable should be explored and documented.

11. More direction needs to be given about the value of student (or user) preferences. Researchers should explore the impact of user behavior on collection decisions.

12. Researchers need to document the extent of school library media center collections that have been established to serve such groups as "minority students" and "handicapped students." Documentation should be made of the content of the local collection in relationship to local user groups. It is not known if school library media specialists are fully aware of the materials now available for handicapped children and young adults.

References

Aceto, Vincent J. "Library Film Collections: Can a Review Committee List Make a Difference?" Top of the News, 40 (Spring 1984), 343-51.

Altman, Ellen. "Implications of Title Diversity and Collection Overlap for Interlibrary Loan Among Secondary Schools." Library Quarterly, 42 (April 1972), 177-94.

American Association of School Librarians and Association for Educational Communications and Technology. Information Power: Guidelines for School Library Media Programs. Chicago: ALA, 1988.

Baker, D. Philip, and David R. Bender. "Marketing, Selection, and Acquisition of Materials for School Media Programs." School Media Quarterly, 6 (Winter 1978), 97-102.

Bard, Therese Bissen, and John E. Leide. "Library Books Selected by Elementary School Students in Hawaii as Indicated by School Library Circulation Records." Library & Information Science Research, 7 (April-June 1985), 115-43.

Beilke, Patricia F. "A Study of Acquisition and Usage of Instructional Media by Teachers in Selected Michigan Public High Schools." Ed.D. dissertation, Western Michigan University, 1974.

Belland, John. "Factors Influencing Selection of Materials." School Media Quarterly, 6 (Winter 1978), 112-19.

Bertland, Linda H. "Usage Patterns in a Middle School Library: A Circulation Analysis." School Library Media Quarterly, 16 (Spring 1988), 200-203.

Billeter, Anne M. "Selections of Children's Books for Public and School Libraries: Examination of the Books by the Local Librarian as a Method of Selection." Ph.D. dissertation, University of Illinois, 1979.

Blazek, Ron. "Reviewing Journals in Mathematics for School Librarians and Teachers." Collection Management, 7 (Fall 1985 / Winter 1985-1986), 219-38.

Blazek, Ronald D. "Teacher Utilization of Nonrequired Library Materials in Mathematics and the Effect on Pupil Use." Ph.D. dissertation, University of Illinois, 1971.

Bonn, George S. "Evaluation of the Collection." Library Trends, 22 (January 1974), 265-304.

Bowker Annual: Library and Book Trade Almanac, 1989-90. New York: R. R. Bowker, 1989.

Boyd, Ladd. National Inventory of Library Needs, 1975: Resources Needed for Public and Academic Libraries and Public School Library Media Centers. Washington, D. C.: National Commission on Libraries and Information Science, 1977.

Bracy, Pauletta B. "Censorship and Selection Policies in Public Senior High School Library Media Centers in Michigan." Ph.D. dissertation, University of Michigan, 1982.

Brodeur, Doris Rita. "The Organizational Buyer Behavior of District and Regional Media Directors in the Selection of Nonprint Educational Media." Ph.D. dissertation, Indiana University, 1980.

Buckingham, Betty Jo. "Weeding the Library Media Collection." Iowa Department of Public Instruction, 1984. ERIC Document 242 324.

Buckley, Cozetta White. "Media Services for Exceptional Students: An Exploratory Study of the Practices and Perceptions of Library Media Specialists in Selected Southern States." Ph.D. dissertation, University of Michigan, 1978.

Bump, Myrna M. "Censorship Practices by High School Librarians Prior to Actual Book Selection." Ph.D. dissertation, Kansas State University, 1980.

Callison, Daniel. "Experience and Time Investment Factors in Public School Teacher Evaluation of Educational Microcomputer Software." Journal of Educational Technology Systems, 16 (1987-1988), 129-49.

Callison, Daniel. "Methods for Measuring Student Use of Databases and Interlibrary Loan Materials." School Library Media Quarterly, 16 (Winter 1988), 138-42.

Callison, Daniel, and Gloria Haycock. "A Methodology for Student Evaluation of Educational Microcomputer Software." Educational Technology, 28 (January 1988), 25-32.

Callison, Daniel, and Cynthia Kittleson. "Due Process Principles Applied to the Reconsideration Process." Collection Building, 6 (Winter 1985), 3-9.

Carter, Betty, and Karen Harris. "The Children and the Critics: How Do Their Book Selections Compare?" School Library Media Quarterly, 10 (Fall 1981), 54-58.

Chiu, L. H. "Reading Preferences of Fourth Grade Children Related to Sex and Reading Ability." Journal of Educational Research, 66 (1975), 369-73.

Center for Educational Statistics, Office of Educational Research and Improvement, U.S. Department of Education. Statistics of Public and Private School Library Media Centers, 1985-1986. Washington, D.C.: GPO, 1987.

Clarke, Polly S. "Reading Interests and Preferences of Indian, Black, and White High School Students." Ed.D. dissertation, North Texas State University, 1973.

Crow, Sherry R. "The Reviewing of Controversial Juvenile Books: A Study." School Library Media Quarterly, 14 (Winter 1986), 83-86.

Daly-Lewis, Joan. "Selection and Evaluation of Nonprint Media Materials as Perceived by Building Level Library Media Specialists: A Survey of Practice in New York." Ed.D. dissertation, Columbia University Teachers College, 1982.

Davie, Judith Fields. "A Survey of School Library Media Resources for Exceptional Students in Florida Public Schools." Ph.D. dissertation, University of Michigan, 1978.

Dean, Frances. "Design of Initial Media Collection for New Facilities." School Media Quarterly, 2 (1974), 234-6.

DeProspo, Ernest R. "The Use of Community Analysis in the Measurement Process." Library Trends, 24 (January 1976), 557-67.

Dewing, Martha, (ed.). Home Video in Libraries. White Plains: Knowledge Industry Publications, 1988.

Doll, Carol A. "A Study of Overlap and Duplication among Children's Collections in Selected Public and Elementary School Libraries." Library Quarterly, 54 (Winter 1984), 277-89.

Drott, M. Carl. "Budgeting for School Media Centers." Drexel Library Quarterly, 14 (July 1978), 78-94.

Drott, M. Carl, and Jacqueline C. Mancall. "Magazines as Information Sources: Patterns of Student Use." School Media Quarterly, 8 (Summer 1980), 240-50.

Eisenberg, Michael B., and Robert E. Berkowitz. Curriculum Initiative. Norwood: Ablex, 1988.

Galloway, Mabel Louise. "An Analytical Study of the Extent and Nature of the Reviewing of Juvenile Books in Eight Journals and Newspapers with Special Regard to Their

Usefulness as Selection Aids for School Libraries." Ph.D. dissertation, Columbia University, 1965.

Gonce-Winder, Cheryl. "Evaluating Software: Factors Influencing Secondary English Teachers' Evaluations of Instructional Software." Ph.D. dissertation, University of Maryland, 1985.

Greenberg, Marilyn W. "Availability of Library Materials in Thirteen Secondary Schools." Ph.D. dissertation, University of Chicago, 1981.

Haith, Dorothy M. "A Content Analysis of Information about Educational Filmstrips in Selected Periodicals." Ph.D. dissertation, Indiana University, 1972.

Ho, May Lein, and David V. Loertscher. "Collection Mapping: The Research." Drexel Library Quarterly, 21 (Spring 1985), 22-39.

Ho, May Lein, and David V. Loertscher. "Collection Mapping in School Library Media Centers." 1986 Annual Conference of the Association for Educational Communications and Technology, Las Vegas, 1986. ERIC Document 267 775.

Hopkins, Dianne McAfee. "Censorship of School Library Media Materials and Its Implications, 1982-83." In School Library Media Annual 1984 Volume Two, 9-22. Edited by Shirley L. Aaron and Pat R. Scales. Littleton: Libraries Unlimited, 1984.

Hutchinson, Ola Mae. "A Study of Secondary School Library Media Programs in the Public Schools of Alabama as Compared to National Standards of Media Resources for the Period 1967 Through 1972." Ph.D. dissertation, University of Alabama, 1977.

Jacob, Gale Sypher. "The High School Library Collection: An Introductory Study of Six High School Libraries." Williamsport: Bro-Dart Inc., 1974.

Jones, Norma Louise. "A Study of the Library Book Collections in the Biological Sciences in Fifty-four Michigan High Schools Accredited by the North Central Association of College and Secondary Schools." Ph.D. dissertation, University of Michigan, 1965.

Kahler, Carol. "An Implementation Paradigm Applied to Selection and Utilization of Library Audiovisual Materials." Ph.D. dissertation, Saint Louis University, 1985.

Kamhi, Michelle. Limiting What Students Shall Read: Books and Other Learning Materials in Our Public Schools. Washington, D.C.: The Association of American Publishers, 1981.

Kemp, Betty. School Library and Media Center Acquisitions Policies and Procedures. Phoenix: Oryx, 1986.

Loertscher, David V., May Lein Ho, and Melvin M. Bowie. "Exemplary Elementary Schools and Their Library Media Centers: A Research Report." School Library Media Quarterly, 15 (Spring 1987), 147-53.

Mancall, Jacqueline C., and Dreama Deskins. "High School Students, Libraries, and the Search Process." 1984. ERIC Document 262 823.

Mancall, Jacqueline C., and M. Carl Drott. Measuring Student Information Use. Littleton: Libraries Unlimited, 1983.

Masters, Judith H. "Film Evaluation and Selection: A Study of Practices in the New York State BOCES." D.L.S. dissertation, Columbia University, 1977.

Miller, Marilyn L., and Barbara B. Moran. "Expenditures for Resources in School Library Media Centers FY '82-'83." School Library Journal, 30 (October 1983), 105-14.

Miller, Marilyn L., and Barbara B. Moran. "Expenditures for Resources in School Library Media Centers FY '83-'84." School Library Journal, 31 (May 1985), 19-31.

Miller, Marilyn L., and Marilyn L. Shontz. "Expenditures for Resources in School Library Media Centers, FY '88-'89." School Library Journal, 35 (June 1989), 31-40.

Miller, Rudolph P. "A Study of the Selection and Evaluation Practices of the Instructional Media Service Centers of the Pennsylvania Intermediate Units." Ed.D. dissertation, University of Pittsburgh, 1977.

Missavage, Leonard R. "A Study of Selected Characteristics of Reviews and Indexes of Audiovisual Materials from 1969 through 1972." Ph.D. dissertation, Florida State University, 1977.

Murray, William, et al. "Collection Mapping and Collection Development." Drexel Library Quarterly, 21 (Spring 1985), 40-51.

Oksas, Joan K. "First-, Second-, and Third-Grade Children's Picture Preference of Caldecott Award Winners and Runners-Up, 1972-1984 in Selected Schools." Ed.D. dissertation, Loyola University of Chicago, 1986.

Opocensky, Virginia Belle Larson. "A Comparison of Library-Media Centers in Public Residential Schools for the Deaf with Standards for Library-Media Centers in Schools for the Deaf." Ph.D. dissertation, University of Nebraska at Lincoln, 1975.

Pool, Jane. "An Analysis of Book Selection Processes for Elementary School Libraries." Project No. 9-G 076, Grant No. OEG-7-9-530076-0136-(095). Washington, D.C.: Office of Education, 1972a.

Pool, Jane. "Selection of Science Books for Elementary School Libraries: An Analysis of Selection from National Selection Sources and a Local Buying List." Ph.D. dissertation, University of Illinois, 1972b.

Pruitt, Ellen, and Karen Dowling. "Searching for Current Information Online." Online, 9 (March 1985), 47-60.

Rogers, Joann V. "Progress in Access to Nonprint Materials." School Library Media Quarterly, 12 (Winter 1984), 127-35.

Roy, Loriene. "An Investigation of the Use of Weeding and Displays as Methods to Increase the Stock Turnover Rate in Small Public Libraries." Ph.D. dissertation, University of Illinois, 1987.

Schmitz, Eugenia Evangeline. "A Study of Library Book Collections in Mathematics and the Physical Sciences in Fifty-four Michigan High Schools Accredited by the North Central Association of Colleges and Secondary Schools." Ph.D. dissertation, University of Michigan, 1966.

Scholtz, James C. Developing and Maintaining Video Collections in Libraries. Santa Barbara: ABC-CLIO, 1989.

Schon, Isabel, and Gene V. Glass. "Effects of an English-Only Law on Public Library Acquisition Policies, Practices, and Librarians' Attitudes Toward Books in Spanish for Children and Young Adults." Library & Information Science Research, 10 (October-December 1988), 411-24.

Schon, Isabel, Kenneth D. Hopkins, and W. Alan Davis. "The Effects of Books in Spanish and Free Reading Time on Hispanic Students' Reading Abilities and Attitudes." NABE Journal, 7 (Fall 1982), 13-20.

Segal, Joseph P. Evaluating and Weeding Collections in Small and Medium-sized Public Libraries: The CREW Method. Chicago: ALA, 1980.

Sheriff, Ralph William. "A Study of the Level of Quality Used in Selecting Library Books in Elementary Schools in Pennsylvania." Ph.D. dissertation, Pennsylvania State University, 1965.

Slote, Stanley J. Weeding Library Collections. Littleton: Libraries Unlimited, 1975.

Stevens, Mary E. "The Recreational Reading Book Choices of Gifted Children in Grades Four, Five, and Six in Dade County, Florida Public Schools." Ed.D. dissertation, University of Miami, 1977.

Summers, Anita A., and Barbara L. Wolfe. "Which School Resources Help Learning? Efficiency and Equity in Philadelphia Public Schools." Business Review (February 975), 1-29.

Swisher, Robert, et al. "Involving Young Adults in Fiction Selection." Top of the News, 40 (1984), 163-70.

Taylor, Mary M. School Library and Media Center Acquisitions Policies and Procedures. Phoenix: Oryx, 1981.

Tjoumas, Renee, and Virgil L. P. Blake. "Calculating Budget Allocations for Secondary School Library Media Centers: New Perceptions Based Upon a Perusal of the Past." Collection Management, ll, nos. 1/2 (1989), 107-35.

Truett, Carol. "Field Testing Educational Software: Are Publishers Making the Effort?" Educational Technology, 24 (1984), 7-12.

Turner, Philip M., and Janet N. Naumer. "Mapping the Way Toward Instructional Design Consultation by the School Library Media Specialist." School Library Media Quarterly, 12 (Fall 1983), 29-37.

Van Orden, Phyllis J. The Collection Program in Schools. Englewood: Libraries Unlimited, 1988.

Vandergrift, Kay E. "Selection: Reexamination and Reassessment." School Media Quarterly, 6 (Winter 1978), 103-11.

Veitch, Carol Jean. "An Analysis of School Library Media Resources in Kentucky as Compared with State and National Standards." Ph.D. dissertation, University of Pittsburgh, 1978.

Vinson, Rhonda J. "School Library Media Center Service for Handicapped Students." Ph.D. dissertation, Southern Illinois University at Carbondale, 1983.

Walker, H. Thomas. "Networking and School Library Media Centers: A Report of a Pilot Project of the Howard County (Maryland) Public School System and the Maryland Interlibrary Organization." School Library Media Quarterly, 12 (Fall 1983), 20-28.

Walker, H. Thomas. "A Study of the Participation of a Public School System in a Large Public and Academic Library Consortium." Ed.D. dissertation, University of Maryland, 1982.

Wallace, Danny P. "A Solution in Search of a Problem: Bibliometrics & Libraries." Library Journal, 112 (May 1, 1987), 43-47.

Watson, Jerry J., and Bill C. Snider. "Book Selection Pressure on School Library Media Specialists and Teachers." School Media Quarterly, 9 (Winter 1981), 95-10l.

Weeks, Ann Carlson. "A Study of the Attitudes of New York State School Library Media Specialists Concerning Library Networking and Technology." Ph.D. dissertation, University of Pittsburgh, 1982.

Woodworth, Mary L. "Intellectual Freedom, the Young Adult, and Schools: A Wisconsin Study." Ph.D. dissertation, University of Wisconsin-Madison, 1976.

Wozny, Lucy Anne. "Online Bibliographic Searching and Student Use of Information: An Innovative Teaching Approach." School Library Media Quarterly, 11 (Fall 1982), 35-42.

Zweizig, Douglas, and Brenda Dervin. "Public Library Use, Users, Uses: Advances in Knowledge of the Characteristics and Needs of the Adult Clientele of American Public Libraries." In Advances in Librarianship Volume 7, 231-55. Edited by Melvin J. Voigt and Michael H. Harris. New York: Academic Press, 1977.

FACILITIES

Blanche Woolls
Professor
School of Library and Information Science
University of Pittsburgh

Introduction

When school library media centers are practical applications of theory, they exist in a building, in spaces of varying shapes and sizes, with different applications for spaces. The uniform element is that they exist as a facility for use by students and teachers in a school. Although Information Power[1] highlights facilities with a full chapter and several pages of "library media center space recommendations," research on this topic is very limited.

Facilities have seldom been the single focus of study. Facilities are included as one of a much longer list of variables, including such items as "growth of school library media centers; staff and volunteers; expenditures; collections; and services, usage, technology, and facilities,"[2] or ninth in a series of twelve topics:

Findings are organized according to 12 basic topics addressed by the study: (1) responsibilities of the district media director; (2) district level media program staff; (3) policies (planning and selection); (4) services; (5) resource sharing; (6) union catalogs; (7) membership in professional associations; (8) audiovisual equipment; (9) facilities; (10) budget maintenance; (11) staff changes; and (12) district media director profile.[3]

It would seem that facilities are given very little importance in relationship to library media center staff, programs, resources, and services. With such lack of interest in facilities, one might wonder if the space housing the collection and staff does make any difference. School library media specialists attract students to facilities with ever-changing programming and activities. A variety of services are offered to interest teachers in integrating the media center into their curriculum planning, and students can be urged to use the center for reading and research within limited space. When the suggestion is made that more exciting activities could reach more students more often with more space, some media specialists seem content to keep the existing square footage. As long as the program is exciting, neither teachers nor parents appear to think that their children have been in any way "deprived."

One reason for conducting research in the area of facilities would be to determine if more space would provide for more exciting activities and better services, and what the optimum space for a student population served by one or more school library media specialists would be.

The School Environment

It is difficult to locate studies of school library media facilities as a part of an educational plant or as a single focal point. Studies of school buildings seldom include the library media center. Several studies were reviewed. The first, a study of spatial, curricular, and financial characteristics, mentions the library media center with six short references cited below. The first four characteristics are taken from information presented in tables rather than in the text.

- Building Characteristics: Individual study carrels
- Interior Building Characteristics: Carpeting -- Office; Library
- Individual or group listening stations in materials center
- Instructional materials centrally located for easy access
        88% included12% not included[4]

A fifth characteristic is described thus: "The instructional materials centers in the majority, or eighty-eight percent of the schools were centrally located for easy pupil and staff access. . . . The libraries were carpeted in fifty percent of the new buildings.[5] The final characteristic is given as a recommendation: "The increased development of pupil resource centers as an extension of the instructional materials center into each area of the building should be encouraged.[6]

Lack of attention to the school library media center was evident in other studies reviewed. Keenan, in her review of two open-space schools, was more interested in how to institute successful change in an educational plant. None of the twenty-two teachers interviewed and seventeen observations conducted included the media specialist.[7]

Duncan studied the longitudinal effects of diverse school organizational patterns on the cognitive and affective achievement of secondary students, and the comparative effectiveness of the open-space school concept and the traditional self-contained school. She found that the level of ability of students had more effect on the predictability of adult success than the type of school organizational pattern.[8] Therefore, what might have appeared to be a comparative study of two types of facilities, was actually a study of student achievement.

Selected attitudes of students and teachers were measured by Hoy (12) to determine if spatial design could modify attitudes and behavior. His emphasis was on comparison of newly built, both open-space and traditional schools. Visits were made to twelve schools, six open and six traditional. While architectural design did not appear to contribute significantly to differences in attitudes of students and teachers, a positive trend was found in the attitudes of students attending the traditional school. Hoy concluded that students in the open school performed significantly better in the seven cognitive areas of the Pennsylvania Educational Quality Assessment Attitude. Positive teacher attitudes showed in the open school, and the researcher pointed out that control of one's environment was a significant outcome of the open school design.[9] The media center was not included in this study.

Murdock's case study of an innovative school tested the extent to which implementation of the planned program took place. The program was judged as open because there was a high degree of individualization of instruction, cross-grading of fifth and sixth grade students, student self-scheduling, and choice within subject areas. Extensive use was made of mini-courses as a means of meeting student interests. No reference was made to the impact of the library media center. The programs became less open over time, and there was a decrease in individualized instruction. This was attributed to excessive staff turnover, lack of continuity in team leadership, lack of clarity among staff members about goals and objectives, growing teacher frustration over continuing unresolved obstacles, lack of needed resocialization of new team members, lack of a changed reward structure for team members, increasing formulation of rules, and organizational incompatibilities.[10]

Smith also reviewed teacher attitudes about open-space and traditional elementary schools.[11] Again, no mention was made of the media center. Winter reviewed the reasons that open-space facilities were altered. Of the fifty-five schools identified, thirty-one had been modified. Fourteen were chosen randomly to be a part of the final research. The strongest factor leading to modification of open-space schools appeared to be changing educational concepts.[12] Again, no mention was made of the media center.

Media Centers and Children's Rooms in Public Libraries

Bush visited thirteen school library media centers in Boston and children's departments in ten public libraries in eastern Massachusetts and New Hampshire. She concluded:

Planning, some reasonable amount of space, and an enthusiasm for people, materials and ideas, along with some appreciation for aesthetic harmony, are all major ingredients in establishing facilities which are attractive, comfortable and dynamic. Librarians do not know what the future will bring in the way of new materials, services or needs. They do know that they have not begun to live up to their current potential. In some cases, clutter and faddishness have obscured their sense of purpose, and we, as children's librarians, cannot afford this at a time when it is necessary to defend our need for funds. Imagination and courage are needed to try new ideas, evaluate efforts and admit mistakes. Foresight to keep open the opportunity to try again is essential.[13]

While a few people did like their libraries very much, the reason most often given was the attractiveness and "plenty of space." School library media respondents were pleased because they had had to "fight enormous obstacles" to create their media centers. Dissatisfaction came from "lack of space," "the feeling that staff had had no say in planning new or expanded buildings," and the "fixed nature of unattractive wall graphics or inconvenient structural features which the staff could not change."[14]

Facilities: One of Many Variables

Research concerning school library media programs regularly includes facilities but only as a minor aspect. Greater emphasis is placed on other variables. Because facilities house the collection and furnishings and provide for the in-house use of the contents, national and state standards and evaluative criteria of regional accrediting agencies offer some guidelines for the amount of space and types of rooms needed within the school for a library media center. Such space allocations are given in square foot allocations for suites of rooms and in seating in terms of the percent of the total student body that may be accommodated in the media center at any given moment. These statistics have seldom been developed based on the results of any research studies, and, as pointed out above, little research exists concerning the influence of the media center facility as an entity on any other aspect of the media center program. In most instances, statistics on size have been collected and evaluated by applying the size of centers to appropriate guidelines or standards.

Survey forms from the federal government have collected national statistics about school library media centers. In 1974 and 1978, projects of the Library General Information Survey (LIBGIS) collected statistics from state departments of education concerning their school library media centers. Included in these forms were staffing, physical *facilities*, collections, interlibrary loan, and expenditure. The latest survey, <u>Statistics of Public and Private School Library Media Centers, 1985-1986</u>, included staff and volunteers, certified staff, expenditures, collections, services, participation in library skills instruction, circulation and attendance, technology, and *facilities*.[15]

A recent dissertation found that: "state school library supervisors from thirty-five states indicated that an agency in their states collects public school library statistics on a regular basis. Fourteen types are being collected: personnel, expenditures, clientele served, budget/income, collections, technology, equipment, instructional television, facilities, services, hours, selection, interlibrary loan, and circulation."[16]

Staff in Iowa's State Department of Public Instruction conducted a second survey of media services in Iowa in 1980 to "measure trends." The range of standards met for materials, equipment, staff and budget, support staff, expenditures, and facilities was with a 1976 survey. "Facilities" here were evaluated for size. These measurements have been a part of an overall matching process for all phases of the media program.[17]

Some states have decided not to gather information on facilities. In the most recent survey conducted in Pennsylvania, statistics that related directly to curriculum implementation and qualifications of media personnel were gathered rather than information about size of facilities or furnishings. The questions under the section "Facilities and Resources" related to resource sharing, size of collection, cataloging and classification systems used, and total budget for resources.[18]

Mancall and Deskins, in their study of high school students, libraries, and the search process, included the use of facilities. However, this contained the students' going to the facility rather than an analysis of the ambience or other factors that might be related to a facilities study.[19] In her dissertation, McAfee included the facility among her "observable conditions of positive self-concept." Students found a positive atmosphere in the media center and the library media center was considered to be a challenging area.[20]

Facilities: Major Focus

Two studies conducted twenty or more years ago discussed the facility itself. Herald matched facilities to the sizes required in the 1946 standards.[21] While the study is old, the methodology might be useful to researchers designing a study to match facilities to standards. Porter reviewed related research and queried a panel of experts to determine desirable components for a media center facility in a secondary school. He then visited twenty-six Indiana schools to see if they contained these components.[22] Although the Porter study is also over twenty years old, some of his components might be used as a preliminary measuring tool for planning a new facility.

Three studies have measured the media center in an open school. Hayes and Leeper compared open media centers to the more traditional, self-contained center. Hayes looked at reference skills of sixth graders on a wide variety of variables as well as openness of the media center. While students in the traditional program exhibited better performance than students in the open program, students in the open program more often used the media center.[23] Implications for the center appeared to be more for scheduling than for arrangement of the facilities.

Leeper studied the effects of the facility on use, expenditures, services, collections, staff, and attitudes of school personnel: teachers, students, administrators, and media personnel. Using twenty-four school districts in north central Colorado, he found more services offered, more instruction given, more positive attitudes, more clerical help, larger facilities, and larger budgets in open schools, while traditional schools had larger collections and more certified staff.[24] While it was not so specified, open facilities more often were found in newer schools, which may have explained the smaller collections and the larger facilities.

In her national study, Marxsen analyzed the background of open-space schools and the status of library media centers in open-space schools at the present time. While media specialists were seldom involved in the primary decision to build an open school, they did not originally hold negative attitudes toward this type of building. However, book loss, traffic control, student behavior, visual distractions, and vandalism were reasons for enclosure of open-space media centers, and only 15 of the 215 media specialists participating in the study would recommend open-space. Several of these fifteen had reservations.[25]

District Level Facilities

In an effort to establish criteria for the design of district instructional materials centers, one dissertation study made a questionnaire survey of 143 California school systems. A more in-depth review was made of 15 of these systems. The absence or presence of a district center was determined, and spacial statistics, types of parking facilities, and other similar information was gathered. The study reviewed the procedures followed in planning centers, and described sizes and shapes of areas. The desirable and undesirable features of the facilities studied were then reported.[26]

Furnishings and Equipment

The advent of the computer expanded the use of the term "ergonomics." According to Novak, this is an "overworked and misused concept."[27] Placement of microcomputers in library media centers has been accomplished most often in existing facilities not designed for such use. Research needs to be done by practitioners to confirm that students and teachers are able to use this and other technologies comfortably and in a manner that is not damaging to their health.

Implications for Practitioners

Finding out about the past is often helpful in planning for the future. Matching needs to arrangement of facilities has changed as new technologies have been developed; yet there is much to be learned from the thinking of librarians from the past.

Measuring instruments have been found in the literature. One historical measuring instrument for elementary school facilities is in "Essential Standards for Basic Plans in the Elementary Libraries."[28] These were developed by the Long Beach, California Public Schools and published November 23, 1948. The author stressed the need for "telephones in house and outside" that are not necessarily standard equipment in all school media centers today. The presence or absence of a communication link from the media center facility to the outside world may be a component of the media center program that will show limited student gains when compared with students attending schools that have school media programs with telecommunications capabilities for electronic mail, interlibrary loan, and online database searching. Confirming the increase in students' research skills and the quality of reporting would help media specialists convince their principals, superintendents, and school boards of the necessity for online database searching and interlibrary loan.

Information Power discusses the need to provide access to all users. Research could demonstrate the various activities of practitioners who meet the needs of the handicapped. Rapid changes in information delivery demand "built-in flexibility." The methods media specialists use to design flexibility into their programs would be helpful to others. Certainly few would argue with the need for facilities that are "aesthetically pleasing in appearance, convenient and comfortable to use."[29] Again, one or two studies of the factors that encourage media specialists to develop aesthetically pleasing environments would be more helpful than fifty "how we did it good" testimonies. Results of research carry importance beyond an individual's opinion of what might have worked. Collecting information on what has worked and comparing several types will better establish a model.

Willett has designed a rating scale for public library children's services that may have some implications for the school library media specialist. This is a seven point Likert scale with the terms "inadequate, minimal, good, and excellent" superimposed above the seven numbers and four descriptive sentences listed below. The section "furnishings" includes climate control, materials and space for activities, room arrangement, and child-related display.[30]

Implications for Researchers

Research needs to be done to help the library media specialist when facilities are planned. Research has shown that administrators seldom consult with library media specialists when facilities are being designed in new or remodeled buildings. Research showing the number of students who should be able to use a media center at any given time and the types of activities in which they would engage would help architects to better plan spaces. Such research must be ongoing as media center services and technologies change.

Architects often propose aesthetically pleasing drawings that are functional nightmares. Balconies in media centers are a perfect example of this. If research could show what has been done with balconies when their presence was not positive, library media specialists might better be able to convince their administrators to request that the architect design a different arrangement.

Perhaps case studies of situations in which library media specialists were able to influence architects, administrators, and school boards would help other library media specialists contribute to the planning process in their school districts. The changes in the plans and their outcomes would provide both information and, in a sense, support for the library media specialist working in a district with no director of media programs, who feels less adequate in the construction or remodeling situation.

Information is further needed to confirm some of the guidelines from Information Power. How necessary is it to have a separate outside entrance? How many school library media centers have been open in the evening? How long did this practice continue? How was this service evaluated? When guidelines suggest "adequate space," what is "adequate?" It is difficult for library media specialists to demonstrate the need for larger spaces if most library media specialists are satisfied with what they currently have. Research is needed to show what occurs in larger spaces.

Information Power stresses the need for climate control for the preservation of materials and equipment. Preservation is an extremely worthwhile topic with special application to the historical collections in major research libraries and the rare books and manuscripts in some libraries. How essential is the preservation of Charlotte's Web? What argument can be made to administrators who are approving building or remodeling plans when they say the material should be destroyed through wear, that school library media centers are not rare book depositories? How much space is needed for the library media specialist to carry out administrative, technical, and consultant services? Is it possible to justify any closed space?

This author has always wondered at the reluctance of some library media specialists to rearrange spaces. Very few media centers have any furnishings that cannot be moved to another location. Any study of the attitudes of media specialists toward change should include their views on moving furniture.

A developmental study could be used as a basis for an evaluation tool of function within a facility. If such an instrument, perhaps a checklist, were constructed using a variety of settings, it would be useful for the media specialist who would like to explain things to an architect.

In spite of the lack of research on facilities, this is an area that warrants attention. Only when the results of carefully designed research studies are available to practitioners will they have the information they need when it is time to justify changes in the media center. With the results of research, the appropriate changes will be made to a facility and the best of all possible planning will go into the construction of new media centers.

Notes

1. American Association of School Librarians and Association for Educational Communications and Technology. Information Power. Chicago: American Library Association, 1988.

2. Williams, Jeffrey W., et al. Statistics of Public and Private School Library Media Centers, 1985-86 (with Historical Comparisons from 1958-1985). Rockville, Md.: Westat, Inc., 1987. ED 284545.

3. District Level Instructional Media Programs in Wisconsin Public Schools, 1982. A Status Report. Bulletin No. 2416. Madison, Wis.: Wisconsin State Department of Public Instruction, Division of Library Services, 1982. ED 233689.

4. Dolence, Glenn Dale. "Spatial, Curricular, and Financial Characteristics of Secondary School Facilities in Arkansas, 1966-1969." Ed.D. dissertation, University of Arkansas, 1970, pp. 54, 65, 70, 71.

5. Ibid., p. 80.

6. Ibid., p. 90.

7. Keenan, Michele Ann. "After the Change: A Comparative Case Study of Two Open Space Schools." Ed.D. dissertation, Columbia University Teachers College, 1984.

8. Duncan, Margaret Elizabeth. "A Comparative Longitudinal Study of the Cognitive and Affective Achievement of Secondary Students with a Traditional and Open-space Elementary Experience and Predictability of Adult Success." Ph.D. dissertation, George Peabody College for Teachers of Vanderbilt University, 1980.

9. Hoy, James Michael. "A Survey of Secondary and Teacher Attitudes in Selected Schools in the Commonwealth of Pennsylvania Differing in Architectural Design." Ed.D. dissertation, The Pennsylvania State University, 1980.

10. Murdock, Elaine Marie. "A Case Study and Analysis of an Innovative Elementary School." Ph.D. dissertation, New York University, 1980.

11. Smith, Mary Lynne. "Experience in Open-Space and Traditionally-Constructed Elementary Schools and Teacher Attitudes Toward Open Education." Ed.D. dissertation, North Texas State University, 1981.

12. Winter, Warren Julian. "A Study of the Modification of Selected Open Space Elementary Schools Constructed in Virginia from 1969-1970 to 1975-1976." Ed.D. dissertation, University of Virginia, 1981.

13. Bush, Margaret. "Library Facilities for Children or the Candy-Colored Polyurethane 10-Speed Learning Environment." In Richardson, Selma K. Children's Services of Public Libraries. Urbana-Champaign, Ill.: University of Illinois Graduate School of Library Science, 1977, p. 116.

14. Ibid., pp. 109-110.

15. U.S. Department of Education, Office of Educational Research and Improvement, Center for Education Statistics. Statistics of Public and Private School Library Media Centers, 1985-1986. Washington, D.C.: Government Printing Office, 1987; reprinted by Hi Willow Research and Publishing, 1990.

16. Williams, Frank E. "A National Study of the Public School Library Statistics Collected by State Agencies." Ph.D. dissertation, University of Pittsburgh, 1989.

17. McGrew, Mary Low and Buckingham, Betty Jo. Survey of the Status of Media Service in Iowa Public Schools. Des Moines, Iowa: Iowa State Department of Public Instruction, 1982.

18. Pennsylvania School Libraries: A Status Report on Curriculum, Staff, Resources and Policies. Harrisburg, Pa.: State Library of Pennsylvania, August, 1986.

19. Mancall, Jacqueline C., and Deskins, Dreama. "High School Students and Facilities Usage Patterns in Delaware Following Introduction of Online Bibliographic Database Searching." 1984. ED 262 823

20. McAfee, Dianne T. "A Study to Determine the Presence of Observable Conditions of Positive Self-Concept in Elementary School Media Centers." Ph.D. dissertation, University of Wisconsin, Madison, 1981.

21. Herald, Homer Wayne. "Planning Library Facilities for the Secondary Schools." Ed.D. dissertation, Stanford University, 1957.

22. Porter, Hugh Calvert. "A Determination of the Physical Components, Spatial Relationships of a Secondary School Instructional Materials Center and Their Application to Selected Secondary Schools in the State of Indiana." Ed.D. dissertation, Indiana University, 1968.

23. Hayes, Linda Manning. "A Comparative Study of Traditional and Open Media Centers: Sixth Grade Students' Reference Skills Achievement, Attitudes and Utilization." Ph.D. dissertation, University of South Carolina, 1977.

24. Leeper, Dennis Patterson. "A Comparative Study of Open Space and Self-Contained Elementary School Library-Media Centers." Ph.D. dissertation, University of Colorado, 1975.

25. Marxsen, Sarah Lewis. "Open Space Library Media Centers in Senior High Schools in the United States: A Historical View." Ph.D. dissertation, Florida State University, 1986.

26. Kittinger, Frank William. "School District Instructional Materials Center Buildings." Ed.D. dissertation, University of Southern California, 1967.

27. Novak, Gloria. "Working Within the Systems," American Libraries 19 (April, 1988): 271.

28. [Fannin, Lois]. "Here are Specifications for an Elementary School Library," Library Journal 74 (December 15, 1949): 1887-1888.

29. Information Power, p. 99.

30. Willett, Holly G. "Environment Rating Scale for Public Library Children's Services." Unpublished paper.